UNDERSTANDING HISTORY

UNDERSTANDING History

MARXIST ESSAYS
by George Novack

PATHFINDER

NEW YORK   LONDON   MONTREAL   SYDNEY

ISBN 0-87348-605-6 paper; ISBN 0-87348-219-0 cloth
Library of Congress Catalog Card No. 75-186684
Manufactured in the United States of America

First edition, 1972
Second edition, 1974
Third edition, 1980
Second printing, 1992

Cover design by Toni Gorton

Cover illustrations (clockwise from top right): 1848 revolution in
Paris; Fidel Castro and Rebel Army fighters from the Cuban
revolution; Spanish attack on Aztec people in what is now Mexico;
blacksmith at work in ancient Rome.

Pathfinder

410 West Street, New York, NY 10014, U.S.A.

Pathfinder distributors around the world:
Australia (and Asia and the Pacific):
    Pathfinder, 19 Terry St., Surry Hills, Sydney, N.S.W. 2010
Britain (and Europe, Africa except South Africa, and Middle East):
    Pathfinder, 47 The Cut, London, SE1 8LL
Canada:
    Pathfinder, 6566, boul. St-Laurent, Montreal, Quebec, H2S 3C6
Iceland:
    Pathfinder, Klapparstíg 26, 2d floor, 121 Reykjavík
New Zealand:
    Pathfinder, La Gonda Arcade, 203 Karangahape Road, Auckland
    Postal address: P.O. Box 8730, Auckland
Sweden:
    Pathfinder, Vikingagatan 10, S-113 42, Stockholm
United States (and Caribbean, Latin America, and South Africa):
    Pathfinder, 410 West Street, New York, NY 10014

Contents

George Novack

George Novack joined the communist movement in 1933 at the age of twenty-eight. For six decades he has been a member and leader of the Socialist Workers Party.

As national secretary of the American Committee for the Defense of Leon Trotsky, Novack helped organize the 1937 International Commission of Inquiry, headed by John Dewey, which investigated the Moscow frame-up trials. In the 1940s Novack was national secretary of the Civil Rights Defense Committee, which gathered support for leaders of the Socialist Workers Party and of the Midwest Teamsters strikes and organizing drives who were framed up and jailed during World War II under the witch-hunting Smith Act. He played a prominent role in numerous other civil liberties battles over subsequent decades.

He has lectured widely on Marxism at universities and public forums across the United States, Europe, Latin America, and the Pacific. Among the works he has authored or edited:

An Introduction to the Logic of Marxism • *Genocide against the Indians* • *The Origins of Materialism* • *Existentialism versus Marxism* • *Empiricism and Its Evolution* • *How Can the Jews Survive? A Socialist Answer to Zionism* • *The Marxist Theory of Alienation* • *Democracy and Revolution* • *Understanding History* • *Humanism and Socialism* • *Their Morals and Ours* • *The Revolutionary Potential of the Working Class* • *Pragmatism versus Marxism* • *America's Revolutionary Heritage* • *Polemics in Marxist Philosophy*

Introduction

The articles in this collection were written at various times over the past fifteen years in response to theoretical and political questions posed in the socialist movement. They cover a broad range of topics, from an interpretation of the totality of history to the identity of the social forces capable of redirecting its course. All of them attempt to apply the Marxist method of analysis to some of the most perplexing problems of the historical process.

The opening essay, "Major Theories of History from the Greeks to Marxism," is a discussion of pre-Marxist theories of history that traces the efforts of the keenest minds for 2,500 years to throw light on the procession of human events and render them intelligible. This is likewise the principal aim of the Marxist method of sociology. Historical materialism seeks to discover and formulate the laws that have governed the activities and achievements of humanity from the emergence of the hominids to the present day.

Is this span of events, covering more than a million years, too colossal and complex to be understood, at least in its main lines of evolution? There are plenty of skeptics who, on one basis or another, aver that the progress of humankind from the most primitive social organization to the nuclear age is beyond the reach of scientific investigation and must forever remain impenetrable to human knowledge. Historical materialism rejects all variants of skepticism and irrationalism from existentialism to positivism, which in principle and in advance bar the possibility — or deny the necessity or advisability — of acquiring insight into the historical process.

Like Vico, historical materialists believe that since history embodies and records what humans have done, we can through successive approximations eventually find out what our species has accomplished — and why.

The review of the major schools of historical theory since the ancient Greeks indicates that they sought to ferret out the motive forces of history and delineate the pattern of their development. Although these contributions to the science of history have not had such far-reaching effects upon our lives as the discoveries of the natural scientists, they have had cumulative and enduring results. Their valid findings on the philosophy of history over the past 2,500 years have been critically evaluated and integrated into the structure of historical materialism, the most probing and comprehensive instrument for analyzing and summarizing the works of the human race.

"The Long View of History" offers a popularized account of evolution from the fish to humankind, from savagery to civilization, and from Indian life to contemporary capitalism in the United States. This is an extremely simplified outline of that immense and intricate evolutionary process. The facts set forth are well known — but their interpretation in these pages differs from that taught in the schools and universities of capitalist America.

This introduction to a study of the march of humanity from the standpoint of scientific socialism is especially directed toward newly awakened minds among the younger generation, who are concerned about the fundamental problems of life and who are seeking enlightenment on the principal issues of the social and political struggle.

Its arguments are aimed at the two prevailing notions that tend to reinforce antisocialist prejudices and uphold belief in the sanctity and eternity of the existing system. One is the idea that it is impossible, undesirable, and somehow unscientific to seek out the central course of development in history, above all the history of civilization; to link together its successive stages and place them in proper sequence; to distinguish the lower from the higher; and to indicate the nature of the next step forward.

The second prejudice, although supported by the first, is more specific: the assumption that the capitalist regime in the United States embodies an unsurpassable type of social organization.

These propositions are wrong in theory and thoroughly reactionary in their practical consequences. Socialism has the merit of explaining how and why the growing discontent among the oppressed and the exploited and their striving for a better way of life are reasonable and founded on scientific premises. The drive of the working masses toward a fundamental reorganization of the capitalist social and political structure harmonizes with the thrust of human progress.

"From Lenin to Castro" deals with the perennial and fascinating problem of the place and weight of the individual in history.

The answers given to this problem have ranged from omnitude to nullity. The earliest and most superficial impression of history elevated the individual in the person of the sacred monarch to an almighty dictator of human life and destiny. Later, those under the spell of mechanical determinism during the eighteenth and nineteenth centuries deprived the individual of any power to shape the course of events.

Historical materialism rejects both extremes. It takes a dialectical view of the interplay between the objective and subjective elements of historical development. It gives priority in the multiplex processes of historical determination to supra-individual forces and holds that the strictly personal is subordinate.

Within the context of objectively given, historically created conditions, an individual is capable of making a mark on the pace and pattern of events. The degree of that influence can vary from a bare minimum through the average exerted by any other members of the same era or class to a maximum impetus. The masses are the principal makers of history. But an individual can be of crucial importance at exceptional points in a historical process where intervention or inertia proves decisive in propelling the movement of the masses along one path or another.

The experience of the Stalin regime in the Soviet Union, and later of Communist China under "the thought of Mao Tse-tung," has given great political relevance to the question of the individual's function in history. In revulsion against Stalin's one-man rule and the personality cult associated with it, current Soviet ideologists have returned to the idea that people are the decisive force in historical development and insist that Marxism is incompatible with "the blind worship of a great man allegedly endowed with superhuman ability to make history at his own will."

This is a step forward from the aberrations of the Stalin era. Nonetheless, Soviet scholars have yet to present an objective materialist explanation of their country's relapse into the ideology of Oriental despotism. Professor Lewis Feuer describes his interviews with upwards of 150 sociologists and philosophers during an eighteen week visit to the Soviet Union in 1963. When he asked if they were in any way concerned with the sociological and philosophical problems arising from the cult phenomenon, he reports, "the most frequent answer I got [was] that is not my problem." Despite this uncandid disavowal, it does remain the most burning issue for most Soviet citizens.

Unfortunately, the Communist intellectuals have been unable to apply historical materialism freely and fully to its solution. They have been driven to attributing the personality cult to Stalin's mistakes or pathological traits. This circular procedure of explaining the cult of the individual by the acts of a single individual leaves unanswered the basic question: How could such a superstition have arisen and fastened itself upon an enlightened nation that had succeeded in overthrowing capitalism, had adopted Marxism, and was progressing toward socialism?

Those Soviet scholars who want to be faithful to Marxism have not taken this untenable posture by choice. It has been imposed upon them by Stalin's successors, who fear the consequences of permitting uninhibited examination of such a sensitive subject. If critical minds were to think through its implications, they would be led to agree with the theoretical and political conclusions of the Marxist opponents of bureaucratic domination in the Communist countries.

Foremost among them was Leon Trotsky, who was preoccupied with this problem after Lenin's death and who devoted to it many pages during his last exile. He followed the growth of the Stalin cult step by step, setting forth the reasons for its prevalence while fighting it all the way.

He traced its genesis to potent objective historical factors. Its roots were to be found in the defeats of the world working class since 1918, the postponement of the proletarian revolution in the highly industrialized countries, the prolonged isolation of the first workers' republic in the vise of imperialist encirclement, the inherited economic and cultural backwardness of Russia, which came into conflict with its extremely advanced political structure, the overwhelming preponderance of the peasantry over the proletariat, the weariness of the Soviet masses and their loss of faith in the immediate prospects for world revolution.

The social and political manifestations of these setbacks appeared in the bureaucratization of the Soviet state and the conservatizing of the Communist Party at its head. Profound changes occurred in their function, leadership and orientation: the destruction of Soviet and party democracy, the crushing of the Leninist wing of the party, and the replacement of internationalism with strictly Russian considerations. These provided the preconditions for the entrenchment of a new aristocracy and its despotic rule.

Stalin's tyranny was rooted in special economic as well as

historical circumstances. Soviet productive capacities fell far below the requirements of socialist equality and abundance, even below the levels of the richer capitalist countries. The system could supply enough consumer goods to give privileges to the few but not enough to raise the living standards of the many. Given these conditions of scarcity, a supreme power had to decide who was to get what and how much. Once the institutions of democratic control by the masses had been extirpated, the overlords of the monolithic party, merged with the state administration, monopolized all the powers of decision and the means of coercion to enforce them.

But this caste of upstarts themselves needed a master, an arbiter as unchallengeable as they, but one who could settle internal disputes while guaranteeing their sovereign sway. The bureaucracy created in its own image that omnipotent, omniscient promotor of its interests. Stalin, the individual, was lifted to the top and kept there for almost three decades because he satisfied the collective demands of the new elite.

Thus, Trotsky explained the cult of the individual fostered by Stalinism, which was antithetical to the spirit and principles of scientific socialism, by applying the teachings and methods of scientific socialism. The aberration in the progress of the Russian Revolution had not come about because of original sin (lust for power) nor from the inherent vices of Bolshevism (its alleged totalitarian tendencies). It was the outgrowth of a specific set of historical circumstances that marred the first steps in the transition from class society to socialism.

The Marxist interpretation of this political development in Soviet life had a logical corollary. When the international and internal conditions that had generated and sustained the Stalinist autocracy and its attendant ideology were changed, the cult would be weakened and abandoned.

That has been the significance of the dethronement of Stalin and the reforms that his successors have introduced under pressure from the masses. Up to now, they have been limited to those concessions compatible with the preservation of the bureaucracy's privileges and monopoly of political power. However, the process of de-Stalinization cannot be arbitrarily and indefinitely curtailed to suit the needs of the ruling caste. They tend irresistibly toward direct confrontation between the regime and the people — to decide whether the Soviet Union shall be thoroughly de-bureaucratized and made democratic.

The practical usefulness of historical materialism is illustrated by its capacity to explain both the predominance of the personality cult and the reasons for its undoing. The insight offered by Marxism into the sources of bureaucratism in post-capitalist societies — and the centralization of sovereign power in an individual that can result from its strangulation of workers' democracy — is indispensable for combatting those tendencies, which are so harmful to the advance of socialism.

The next brace of essays, "Uneven and Combined Development in History," present variations on a single theme: the law of uneven and combined development, first formulated by Leon Trotsky. They constitute the most extended discussion of these fundamental and universal aspects of human history in Marxist or any other literature.

Although acquaintance with this law is still extremely limited within historical, sociological and political circles, it is one of the most versatile tools for deciphering otherwise puzzling problems in these fields. Consider, for example, this cameo description of the Indian scene taken from the first chapter of the late Professor D. D. Kosambi's authoritative *Ancient India.*

Cultural differences between Indians even in the same province, district, or city are as wide as the physical differences between the various parts of the country. Modern India produced an outstanding figure of world literature in Tagore. Within easy reach of Tagore's final residence may be found Santals and other illiterate primitive peoples still unaware of Tagore's existence. Some of them are hardly out of the food-gathering stage. An imposing modern city building such as a bank, government office, factory, or scientific institute may have been designed by some European architect or by his Indian pupil. The wretched workmen who actually built it generally used the crudest tools. Their payment might be made in a lump sum to a foreman who happens to be the chief of their small guild and the head of their clan at the same time. Certainly these workmen can rarely grasp the nature of the work done by the people for whom the structures were erected. Finance, bureaucratic administration, complicated machine production in a factory, and the very idea of science are beyond the mental reach of human beings who have lived in misery on the margin of overcultivated lands or in the forest. Most of them have been driven by famine conditions in the jungle to become the cheapest form of drudge labour in the city" (p. 2).

In one area, there is a gamut of historical types, ranging from the food-gatherer, the most rudimentary stage of social activity, to scientists, representing the high point of human development. This immense diversity has come together in the construction of an institute through methods that combine the most modern architecture and facilities with the use of the crudest tools, a welding of capitalist control with feudal and tribal survivals in the production process. Here is a vivid image of the relevance of uneven and combined development in understanding highly heterogeneous social forms and historical phenomena.

These essays explain the elements of this twofold law and show how it is evidenced in world history, the successive eras of the bourgeois-democratic revolutions and the socialist revolutions of the twentieth century.

1

Major Theories of History
From the Greeks to Marxism

Historical materialists would be untrue to their own principles if they failed to regard their method of interpreting history as the result of a prolonged, complex and contradictory process. Mankind has been making history for a million years or more as it advanced from the primate condition to the atomic age. But a science of history capable of ascertaining the laws governing our collective activities over the ages is a relatively recent acquisition.

The first attempts to survey the long march of human history, study its causes, and set forth its successive stages along scientific lines were made only about twenty-five hundred years ago. This task, like so many others in the domain of theory, was originally undertaken by the Greeks.

The sense of history is a precondition for a science of history. This is not an inborn but a cultivated, historically generated capacity. The discrimination of the passage of time into a well-defined past, present and future is rooted in the evolution of the organization of labor. Man's awareness of life as made up of consecutive and changing events has acquired breadth and depth with the development and diversification of social production. The calendar first appears, not among food-gatherers, but in agricultural communities.

Primitive peoples, from savagery to the upper stages of barbarism, have as little concern for the past as for the future. What they experience and do forms part of an objective universal history. But they remain unaware of the particular place they occupy or the part they play in the progression of mankind.

The very idea of historical advancement from one stage to the next is unknown. They have no need to inquire into the motive forces of history or to mark off the phases of social development. Their collective consciousness has not reached the point of a historical outlook or a sociological insight.

The low level of their productive powers, the immaturity of

their economic forms, the narrowness of their activities and
the meagerness of their culture and connections are evidenced
in their extremely restricted views of the course of events.

The amount of historical knowledge possessed by primitive
minds may be gauged from the following observations made
by the Jesuit priest Jacob Baegert in his *Account of the Aboriginal Inhabitants of the California Peninsula* written two
hundred years ago. "No Californian is acquainted with the
events that occurred in the country prior to his birth, nor
does he even know who his parents were if he should happen
to have lost them during his infancy. . . . The Californians . . .
believed that California constituted the whole world, and they
themselves its sole inhabitants; for they went to nobody, and
nobody came to see them, each little people remaining within
the limits of its small district."

In pre-Spanish times, they marked only one repetitive event,
the pitahaya fruit harvest. Thus, a space of three years is
called three pitahayas. "Yet they seldom make use of such
phrases, because they hardly ever speak among themselves of
years, but merely say, 'long ago,' or 'not long ago,' being
utterly indifferent whether two or twenty years have elapsed
since the occurrence of a certain event."

Until several thousand years ago, peoples took their own
particular organization of social relations for granted. It appeared to them as fixed as the heavens and earth and as natural as their eyes and ears. The earliest peoples did not even
distinguish themselves from the rest of nature or draw a sharp
line of demarcation between themselves and other living creatures in their habitat. It took a far longer time for them to
learn to distinguish between what belonged to nature and what
belonged to society.

So long as social relations remain simple and stable, changing extremely slowly and almost imperceptibly over vast
stretches of time, society melts into the background of nature.
The experiences of one generation do not differ much from
another. If the familiar organization with its traditional rou-
tine is disrupted, it either vanishes or is rebuilt on the old
pattern. Moreover, surrounding communities, so far as they
are known (and acquaintance does not extend very far either
in space or time), are much the same. Before the arrival of
the Europeans, the North American Indian could travel from
the Atlantic to the Pacific, or the Australian native thousands
of miles, without encountering radically different types of human society.

Under such circumstances, neither society in general nor

one's own special mode of living is looked upon as a peculiar object worth special attention and study. The need for theorizing about history or the nature of society does not arise until civilization is well advanced, and sudden, violent and far-reaching upheavals in social relations take place during the lifetime of individuals or within the memories of their elders.

When swift strides are taken from one form of social structure to another, the old ways stand out in marked contrast, even conflict, with the new. Through trade, travel and war, the representatives of the expanding social system undergoing construction or reconstruction come into contact with peoples of quite different customs on lower levels of cultural development.

More immediately, glaring differences in the conditions of life within their own communities and bitter conflicts between antagonistic classes induce thoughtful men who have the means for such pursuits to speculate on the origins of these conflicts, to compare the various kinds of societies and governments, and to try to arrange them in an order of succession or worth.

The English historian M. I. Finley makes a similar point in reviewing three recent books on the ancient East in the August 20, 1965, *New Statesman:* "The presence or absence of a 'historical sense' is nothing less than an intellectual reflection of the very wide differences in the historical process itself."

He cites the Marxist scholar, Professor D. D. Kosambi, who attributes "the total lack of historical sense" in ancient India to the narrow outlook of village life bound up with its mode of agricultural production. "The succession of seasons is all-important, while there is little cumulative change to be noted in the village from year to year. This gives the general feeling of 'the Timeless East' to foreign observers."

The other civilized peoples of the ancient Near and Middle East likewise lacked a sense of history. There is nothing, notes Professor Leo Oppenheim, "that would attest the awareness of the scribes of the existence of a historical continuum in the Mesopotamian civilization." This is confirmed by the fact that "the longest and most explicit Assyrian royal inscriptions . . . were imbedded in the substructure of a temple or a palace, safe from human eyes and only to be read by the deity to whom they were addressed."

The preconditions for a historical outlook in the West were brought into being from about 1100 to 700 B.C. by the transition from the Bronze to the Iron Age in the Middle East and Aegean civilizations. The comparatively self-sufficient agricultural kingdoms and settlements were supplemented or supplanted by bustling commercial centers, especially in the Phoenician and Ionian ports of Asia Minor. There, new classes — merchants, shipowners, manufacturers, artisans, seafarers — came to the fore and challenged the institutions, ideas and power of the old landed gentry. Patriarchal slavery became transformed into chattel slavery. Commodity relations, metal money, mortgage debt corroded the archaic social structures. The first democratic revolutions and oligarchic counterrevolutions were hatched in the city-states.

The Ionian Greeks, who set down the first true written histories, were associates of traders, engineers, craftsmen and voyagers. The pioneer of Western historians, Hecaeteus, lived in the same commercial city of Miletus as the first philosophers and scientists; and he adhered to the same materialist trend of thought.

The writing of history soon engendered interest in the science of history. Once the habit of viewing events in sequence was established, the questions arose: How did history unfold? Was there any discernible pattern in its flux? If so, what was it? And what were its causes?

The first rational explanation of the historical process was given by the outstanding Greek historians from Herodotus to Polybius. This was the cyclical conception of historical movement. According to this view, society, like nature, passed through identical patterns of development in periodically repeated rounds.

Thucydides, the preeminent Greek historian, declared that he had written his record of the Peloponnesian wars to teach its lessons because identical events were bound to happen again. Plato taught the doctrine of the Great Year at the end of which the planets would occupy the same positions as before and all sublunary events would be repeated. This conception was expressed as a popular axiom in *Ecclesiastes:* "There is no new thing under the sun."

The notion of a cyclical character of human affairs was closely affiliated with the conception of an all-powerful, inscrutable, inflexible Destiny which came to replace the gods as sovereign of history. Destiny was mythologized in the persons of the Three Fates and further rationalized by learned men as the ultimate law of life. The notion of cosmic tragic fate from which human appeal or escape is impossible became the major theme of classic Greek drama and of the historical work of Herodotus, as well.

Comparisons with other peoples, or between Greek states in different stages of social, economic and political development, produced, along with the first inklings of historical progression, a comparative history. As early as the eighth century B. C., the poet Hesiod talked about the copper age that had preceded iron. Several centuries later, Herodotus, the first anthropologist as well as the father of history, gathered valuable information on the customs of the Mediterranean peoples living in savagery, barbarism or civilization. Thucydides pointed out that the Greeks had once lived as the barbarians did in his own time. Plato, in his *Republic, Laws* and other writings, and Aristotle, in *Politics,* collected specimens of different forms of state rule. They named, classified and criticized them. They sought to ascertain not only the best mode of government for the city-state, but also the order of their forms of development and the causes of political variation and revolution.

Polybius, the Greek historian of the rise of the Roman empire, viewed it as the prize example of the natural laws which regulated the cyclical transformation of one governmental form into another. He believed, as did Plato, that all states inevitably passed through the phases of kingship, aristocracy and democracy, which degenerated into their allied forms of despotism, oligarchy and mob rule. The generation and degeneration of these successive stages of rulership was due to natural causes. "This is the regular cycle of constitutional revolutions, and the natural order in which institutions change, are transformed, and return to their original stage," he wrote.

Just as they knew and named the major kinds of political organization from monarchy to democracy, so did the Greek thinkers of both the idealist and materialist schools originate the basic types of historical interpretation which have endured to the present day.

They were the first to try to explain the evolution of society along materialist lines, however crude and awkward were their initial efforts. The Atomists, the Sophists and the Hippocratic school of medicine put forward the idea that the natural environment was the decisive factor in the molding of mankind. In its extreme expressions, this trend of thought reduced social-historical changes to the effects of the geographical theater and its climatic conditioning. Polybius wrote: "We mortals have an irresistible tendency to yield to climatic influences; and to this cause, and no other, may be traced the great distinctions which prevail among us in character, physical formation and complexion, as well as in most of our habits, varying with nationality and wide local separation."

These early sociologists taught that mankind had climbed from savagery to civilization by imitating nature and improving upon her operations. The finest exponent of this materialist view in Graeco-Roman culture was Lucretius who gave a brilliant sketch of the development of society in his poem *On The Nature of Things*.

Predominant among the Greek thinkers, however, were the sorts of theory that have ever since been the stock-in-trade of historical idealists:

1. *The Great God Theory*. The most primitive attempts to explain the origin and development of the world and humanity are the creation myths of preliterate peoples. We are best acquainted with the one in *Genesis* which ascribes the making of heaven and earth to a Lord God who worked on a six-day schedule. These fanciful stories do not have any scientific validity.

The raw materials for genuine history-writing were first collected in the chronicles of kings in the river valley civilizations of the Near East, India and China. The first synthetic conception of history arose from the fusion of elements taken over from the old creation myths with a review of these records. This was the Great God version of history, which asserted that divine beings directed human and cosmic affairs.

Just as the royal despots dominated the city-states and their empires, so the will, passions, plans and needs of the gods were the ultimate causes of events. The king is the agent who maintains the world in being by means of an annual contest with the powers of chaos. This theological theory was elaborated by the Sumerians, Babylonians and Egyptians before it came down to the Greeks and Romans. It was expounded in the Israelite Scriptures whence it was taken over and reshaped by the Christian and Mohammedan religions and their states.

Under the theocratic monarchies of the East, the divine guidance of human affairs was wrapped up with the godlike nature of the priest-king. In Babylon, Egypt, the Alexandrian Empire and Rome, the supreme ruling force of the universe and the forceful ruler of the realm were regarded as equally divine. The Great God and the Great Man were one and the same.

2. *The Great Man Theory*. The straightforward theological view of history is too crude and naive, too close to primitive animism, too much in conflict with civilized enlightenment to persist without criticism or change except among the most

ignorant and devout. It has been supplanted by more refined versions.

The Great Man theory emerged from a dissociation of the dual components of the Great God theory. The immense powers attributed to the gods became concentrated in some figure at the head of the state, the church or another key institution or movement. This exceptionally placed personage was supposedly endowed with the capacity for molding events as he willed. This is the source of the tenacious belief that unusually influential and able individuals determine the direction of history.

Fetishistic worship of the Great Man has come down through the ages from the god-kings of Mesopotamia to the adoration of a Hitler. It has had numerous incarnations according to the values attached at different times by different people to the various domains of social activity. In antiquity these ranged from the divine monarch, the tyrant, the lawgiver (Solon), the military conqueror (Alexander), the dictator (Caesar), the hero-emancipator (David), and the religious leader (Christ, Buddha, Mohammed). All these males — women were given no such preeminence in patriarchal societies — were put in the place of the Almighty as prime movers of history.

The most celebrated latter-day exponent of this viewpoint was Thomas Carlyle who wrote: "Universal History, the history of what man has accomplished in this world, is at bottom the History of the Great Men who have worked here."

3. *The Great Mind Theory.* A more sophisticated philosophical variant of the Great God-Man line of thought is the notion that history is drawn forward or driven ahead by an ideal force in order to realize its preconceived ends. The Greek Anaxagoras said: "Reason (*Nous*) governs the world." Aristotle held that the prime mover of the universe, and thereby the ultimate animator of everything within it, was God, who was defined as pure mind engaged in thinking about itself.

Hegel was the foremost modern exponent of the theory that the progress of mankind consisted in the working out and consummation of an idea. He wrote: "Spirit, or Mind, is the only motive principle of history." The goal of the World Spirit, the outcome of its laborious development, was the realization of the idea of freedom.

The Great Mind Theory easily slides into the notion that a set of brilliant intellects, or even one genius, constitutes the mainspring of human advancement. Plato taught that there are "some natures who ought to study philosophy and to be leaders in the State; and others who are not born to be philosophers, and are meant to be followers rather than leaders."

Thus, some eighteenth-century rationalists who believed that "opinion governs mankind" looked toward an enlightened monarch to introduce the necessary progressive reconstruction of the state and society. A more widespread manifestation of this approach contrasts to the unthinking mob an upper stratum of the population as the exemplar of reason which alone can be entrusted with political leadership and power.

4. *The Best People Theory.* All such interpretations contain infusions of the prejudice that some elite, the Best Race, the favored nation, the ruling class, alone make history. The Old Testament assumed that the Israelites were God's chosen people. The Greeks regarded themselves as the acme of culture, better in all respects than the barbarians. Plato and Aristotle looked upon the slave-holding aristocracy as naturally superior to the lower orders.

5. *The Human Nature Theory.* Most persistent is the view that history has been determined by the qualities of human nature, good or bad. Human nature, like nature itself, was regarded as rigid and unchanging from one generation to another. The historian's task was to demonstrate what the invariant traits of the human character were, how the course of history exemplified them, and how the social structure was molded or had to be remodeled in accordance with them. Such a definition of human nature was the starting point for the social theorizing of Socrates, Plato and Aristotle and other great idealists.

But it will also be found in the social and political philosophy of the most diverse schools. Thus, the empiricist David Hume flatly asserts in *An Enquiry Concerning Human Understanding:* "Mankind are so much the same, in all times and places, that history informs us of nothing new or strange in this particular. Its chief use is only to discover the constant and universal principles of human nature."

Many of the nineteenth-century pathfinders in the social sciences clung to this old standby of "the constant and universal principles of human nature." For example, E. B. Tylor, the founder of British anthropology, wrote in 1889: "Human institutions, like stratified rocks, succeed each other in series substantially uniform over the Globe, independent of what seems the comparatively superficial differences of race and language, but shaped by similar human nature."

Although they may have held different opinions of what the

essential qualities of humanity were, idealist and materialist thinkers alike have appealed to permanent principles of human nature to explain social and historical phenomena. Thus, as M. I. Finley tells us in his introduction to *The Greek Historians,* the materialist-minded Thucydides believed that "human nature and human behavior were . . . essentially fixed qualities, the same in one century as another."

For many centuries after the Greeks, scientific insight into the workings of history made little progress. Under Christianity and feudalism, the theological conception that history was the manifestation of God's plan monopolized social philosophy. In contrast to the stagnation of science in Western Europe, the Moslems and Jews carried forward the social as well as the natural sciences. The most original student of social processes between the ancients and moderns was the fourteenth-century thinker of the Maghreb, Ibn Khaldun, who analyzed the development of the Mohammedan cultures and the origins of their typical institutions in the most materialist manner of his epoch. This eminent Moslem statesman was very likely the first scholar to formulate a clear conception of sociology, the science of social development. He did so in the name of the study of culture.

He wrote: "History is the record of human society, or world civilization; of the changes that take place in the nature of that society, such as savagery, sociability, and group solidarity; of revolutions and uprisings by one set of people against another with the resulting kingdoms and states, with their various ranks; of the different activities and occupations of men, whether for gaining their livelihood or in the various sciences and crafts; and, in general, of all the transformations that society undergoes by its very nature."

The next big advance in scientific understanding of history came with the rise of bourgeois society and the discovery of other regions of the globe associated with its commercial and naval expansion. In their conflicts with the ruling feudal hierarchy and the Church, the intellectual spokesmen for progressive bourgeois forces rediscovered and reasserted the ideas of class struggle first noted by the Greeks, and they instituted historical comparisons with antiquity to bolster their claims. Their new revolutionary views demanded not only a wider outlook upon the world but a deeper probe into the mechanism of social change.

Such bold representatives of bourgeois thought as Machiavelli and Vico in Italy; Hobbes, Harrington, Locke and the classical economists in England; Adam Ferguson in Scotland; and Voltaire, Rousseau, Montesquieu, D'Holbach and others in France helped to prepare a more realistic picture of society and a more rigorous understanding of its modes and stages of development.

On a much higher level of social and scientific development, historical thought from the seventeenth to the nineteenth centuries tended to become polarized, as in Greece, between idealist and materialist schools. Both schools of thought were animated by a common aim. They believed that history had an intelligible character and that the nature and sources of its laws could be ascertained.

Theological interpreters, such as Bishop Bossuet, continued to see God as the director of the historical procession. Although most other thinkers did not dispute that divine providence ultimately shaped the course of events, they were far more concerned with the mundane operation of history.

Giambattista Vico of Naples was the great pioneer among these thinkers. He asserted at the beginning of the eighteenth century that because history, or "the world of nations," had been created by men, it could be understood by its makers. He emphasized that social and cultural phenomena passed through a regular sequence of stages which was cyclical in character.

He insisted that "the order of ideas must follow the order of things" and that the "order of human things" was "first the forests, after that the huts, thence the village, next the cities and finally the academies." His "New Science" of history sought to discover and apply "the universal and eternal principles . . . on which all nations were founded, and still preserve themselves." Vico brought forward the class struggle in his interpretation of history, especially in the heroic age represented by the conflict between the plebeians and patricians of ancient Rome.

The materialists who came after Vico in Western Europe looked in very different quarters for the "universal and eternal principles" that determined history. But neither school doubted that history, like nature, was subject to general laws which the philosopher of history was obligated to find.

The key thought of the English and French materialists of the seventeenth and eighteenth centuries was that men were the products of their natural and social environments. As Charles Brockden Brown, an American novelist of the early nineteenth century, put it: "Human beings are molded by the circumstances in which they are placed." In accord with this principle, they turned to the objective realities of nature and society to explain the historical process.

Montesquieu, for example, regarded geography and government as the twin determinants of history and society. The physical factor was most influential in the earlier and more primitive stages of human existence, although its operation never ceased; the political factor became more dominant as civilization advanced.

He and his fellow materialists of that time ignored the economic conditions that stood between nature and political institutions. The economic basis of political systems and the struggles of contending classes that issued from economic contradictions were beyond their field of vision.

The French historians of the early nineteenth century acquired a deeper insight into the economic conditioning of the historical process through their studies of the English and French revolutions. They had watched the French revolution go through a complete cycle which had started with the overthrow of the absolute monarchy, passed through the revolutionary regime of Robespierre and the bourgeois-military dictatorship of Napoleon, and ended with the Bourbon Restoration. In the light of these vicissitudes, they learned the crucial role of class struggles in pushing history forward, and they pointed to sweeping shifts in property ownership as the prime cause of social overturns. However, they remained unable to uncover the determinants of a reconstruction and replacement of property relations as well as political forms.

Many leading philosophers of the bourgeois era had a materialist view of nature and man's relations with the world around him. But none of them succeeded in working out a consistent or comprehensive conception of society and history along materialist lines. At a certain point in their analyses, they departed from materialist premises and procedures, attributing the ultimate causal agencies of human affairs to human nature, a far-seeing human reason, or a great individual.

What was responsible for their deviation into nonmaterialist types of explanation in the areas of historical and social determination? As bourgeois thinkers, they were confined by the capitalist horizon. So long as the ascending bourgeoisie was on its way to supremacy, its most enlightened ideologists had a passionate and persistent interest in boring deeply into economic, social and political realities. After the bourgeoisie had consolidated its position as the ruling class, its ideologists shrank from probing to the bottom of social and political processes. They became more and more sluggish and shortsighted in the fields of sociology and history because discov-

ery of the causes of change in these fields could only threaten
the continuance of capitalist domination.

One barrier to a serious study of social science was their
tacit assumption that bourgeois society and its institutions
embodied the highest attainable form of social organization.
All previous societies led up to that point and stopped there.
There was apparently no progressive exit from the capitalist
system. That is why the ideologists of the English bourgeoisie
from Locke to Ricardo and Spencer tried to fit their concep-
tions of the meaning of all social phenomena into the categories
and relations of that transitory order. This narrowness made
it equally difficult for them to decipher the past, get to the
bottom of their present, and foresee the future.

Idealistic interpretations of history were promoted by a number of theorists from Leibnitz to Fichte. Their work was consummated by Hegel. In the early decades of the nineteenth century, Hegel revolutionized the understanding of world history;
his was the broadest historical perspective of the bourgeois era.
His contributions may be summed up as follows:

1. Hegel approached all historical phenomena from the standpoint of their evolution, seeing them as moments, elements,
phases in a single creative, cumulative, progressive and ceaseless process of becoming.

2. Because the world about him, which he called "Objective
Mind," was the work of man, he, like Vico, was convinced
that it could be explicated by the inquiring mind.

3. He conceived of history as a *universal* process in which
all social formations, nations and persons had their appropriate
but subordinate place. No single state or people dominated
world history; each was to be judged by its role in the development of the totality.

4. He asserted that the historical process was essentially
rational. It had an internal logic that unfolded in a
law-governed manner defined by the dialectical process. Each
stage of the whole was a necessary product of the circumstances of its time and place.

5. Every essential element of each stage hung together as
components of a unified whole which expressed the dominant
principle of its age. Each stage made its own unique contribution to the advancement of mankind.

6. The truth about history is concrete. As the Russian thinker
Chernyshevsky wrote: "Every object, every phenomenon has
its own significance, and it must be judged according to the
circumstances, the environment, in which it exists. . . . A definite judgement can be pronounced only about a definite fact,

after examining all the circumstances on which it depends."

7. History changes in a dialectical manner. Each stage of social development has had sufficient reasons for coming into existence. It has a contradictory constitution, arising from three different elements. These are the durable achievements inherited from its predecessors, the special conditions required for its own maintenance, and the opposing forces at work within itself. The development of internal antagonisms supplies its dynamism and generates its growth. The sharpening of contradictions leads to its disintegration and eventual dispossession by a higher and antithetical form which grows out of it by way of a revolutionary leap.

8. Thus, all grades of social organization are linked in a dialectically determined series from lower to higher.

9. Hegel brought forward the profound truth later developed by historical materialism that labor is imposed upon man as the consequence of his needs and that man is the historical product of his own labor.

10. History is full of irony. It has an overall objective logic that confounds its most powerful participants and organizations. Although the heads of states apply definite policies, and peoples and individuals consciously pursue their own aims, historical actuality does not accord with their plans. The course and outcome of history is determined by internal necessities independent of the will and consciousness of any of its institutional or personal agencies. Man proposes . . . the historical necessity of the Idea disposes.

11. The outcome of history is the growth of rational freedom. Man's freedom comes not from arbitrary, willful intervention in events, but from growing insight into the necessities of the objective, universal contradictory processes of becoming.

12. The necessities of history are not always the same; they change into their opposites as one stage succeeds another. In fact, the conflict of lower and higher necessities is the generator of progress. A greater and growing necessity is at work within the existing order, negating the conditions that sustain it. This necessity keeps depriving the present necessity of its reasons for existence, expands at its expense, renders it obsolete and eventually displaces it.

13. Not only do social formations and their specific dominant principles change from one stage to the next, but so do the specific laws of development.

This method of interpreting history was far more correct, all-encompassing and profound than any of its predecessors. Yet it suffered from two ineradicable flaws. First, it was incurably idealistic. Hegel pictured history as the product of abstract principles which represented differing degrees of the ceaseless contest between servitude and freedom. Man's freedom was gradually realized through the dialectical development of the Absolute Idea.

Such a logic of history was an intellectualized version of the notion that God directs the universe and history is the fulfillment of His design, which in this case is the freedom of humanity. As envisaged by Hegel, freedom was not realized through the emancipation of mankind from oppressive social conditions but from the defeat of false, inadequate ideas.

Second, Hegel closed the gates on the further development of history by having it culminate with the German kingdom and the bourgeois society of his own era. The exponent of a universal and never-ending history concluded that its ultimate agent was the national state, a characteristic product of its bourgeois phase. And in its monarchical form, modified by a constitution! He mistook a transient creation of history for its final and perfected embodiment. By thus setting limits upon the process of becoming, he violated the fundamental tenet of his own dialectic.

These defects prevented Hegel from arriving at the true nature of social relations and the principal causes of social change. However, his epoch-making insights have influenced all subsequent thought and writing about history. With indispensable revisions, they have all been incorporated into the structure of historical materialism.

Hegel, the idealist dialectician, was the foremost theorist of the evolutionary process. The French social thinkers and historians carried the materialist understanding of history and society as far as it could go in their day. But even within their own provinces both fell short. Hegel could not provide a satisfactory theory of social evolution and the materialists did not penetrate to the basic moving forces of history.

Not until the valid elements of these two contrary lines of thought converged in the minds of Marx and Engels in the middle of the nineteenth century was a conception of history produced that was anchored in the dialectical development of the material conditions of social existence from the emergence of early man to contemporary life.

All the different types of historical explanation cast up in the evolution of man's thought survive today. Not one has been permanently buried, no matter how outmoded, inadequate or scientifically incorrect. The oldest interpretations can be revived and reappear in modern dress to serve some social need or stratum.

What bourgeois nation has not proclaimed in time of war that "God is on our side"? The Great Man theory strutted about under the swastika. Spengler in Germany and Toynbee in England offer their versions of the cyclical round of history. The school of geopolitics makes geographical conditions into the paramount determinant of modern history.

Nazi Germany, Verwoerd's South Africa and the Southern white supremacists exalt the master race as the dictator of history. The conception that human nature must be the basis of social structure is the last-ditch defense of the opponents of socialism as well as the point of departure for the utopian socialism of the American psychoanalyst Erich Fromm and others.

Finally, the notion that reason is the motive force in history is shared by all sorts of savants. The American anthropologist Alexander Goldenweiser stated in *Early Civilization:* "Thus the whole of civilization, if followed backward step by step, would ultimately be found resolvable, without residue, into bits of ideas in the minds of individuals." Here ideas and individuals are the creative factors of history.

In describing his philosophy, the Italian thinker Croce wrote: "History is the record of the creations of the human spirit in every field, theoretical as well as practical. And these spiritual creations are always born in the hearts and minds of men of genius, artists, thinkers, men of action, moral and religious reformers." This position combines idealism with elitism, the spirit using geniuses, or the creative minority, as the agency which redeems the masses.

These diverse elements of historical interpretation can appear in the most incongruous combinations in a given country, school of thought or individual mind. Stalinism has provided the most striking example of such an illogical synthesis. The votaries of "the personality cult" sought to fuse the traditions and views of Marxism, the most modern and scientific philosophy, with the archaic Great Man version of the contemporary historical process.

Except in Maoist China, this odd and untenable amalgam of ideas has already crumbled. Yet it demonstrates how generalized thought about the historical process can retrogress after making an immense leap forward. The history of historical science proves in its own way that progress is not even or persistent throughout history. Thucydides, the narrator of the Peloponnesian Wars in the fourth century B. C., had a far more realistic view of history than did St. Augustine, the celebrator of the City of God, in the fourth century A. D.

Marxism has incorporated into its theory of social development the verified findings of modern scientific research as well as the insights of its philosophical predecessors — whether materialist, idealist or eclectic — that have proved valid. To do otherwise would flout the mandate of its own method, which teaches that every school of thought, every stage of scientific knowledge, is an outgrowth of past study, modified and sometimes revolutionized by the prevailing conditions. Scientific inquiry into history and society, like the process of history itself, has given positive, permanent and progressive results.

At the same time, Marxism rejects all versions of antiquated theories that have failed to provide an adequate or correct explanation of the origins and evolution of society. It does not deny that historical idealism contains significant ingredients of truth and has at times been historically progressive. Their progression since the Greeks has been from heaven to earth, from God to man, from the imaginary to the real. Individuals, influential or insignificant, and ideas, innovative or traditional, are essential to society; their roles in the making of history have to be taken into account.

The idealists rightly pay attention to these factors. Where they go wrong is in claiming decisive importance for them in the total process of historical determination. Their method confines their analyses to the outer layers of the social structure so that they remain on the surface of events. Science has to delve into the nuclear core of society where the real forces that determine the direction of history are at work.

Historical materialism turns away from the Divine Director, the Great Man, the Universal Mind, the Intellectual Genius, the Elite, and an unchanging Human Nature for its explanation of history. The formation, reformation and transformation of social structures over the past million years cannot be understood by recourse to any supernatural beings, ideal agencies, petty personal or invariant causes.

God did not create the world and has not superintended the development of mankind. On the contrary, man created the idea of the gods as a fantasy to compensate for lack of real control over the forces of nature and of society. Man made himself by acting upon nature and changing its elements to satisfy his needs through the labor process. Man has worked his way up in the world. The further development and diversification of the labor process from savagery to our present civilization has continued to transform his capacities and characteristics.

History is not the achievement of outstanding individuals, no matter how powerful, gifted or strategically placed. As early as the French Revolution, Condorcet protested against this narrow elitist view, which disregarded both what moves the mass of the human race and how the masses rather than the masters make history. He wrote, "Up to now, the history of politics, like that of philosophy or of science, has been the history of only a few individuals: That which really constitutes the human race, the vast mass of families living for the most part on the fruits of their labor, has been forgotten, and even of those who follow public professions, and work not for themselves but for society, who are engaged in teaching, ruling, protecting or healing others, it is only the leaders who have held the eye of the historian."

Marxism builds on this insight that history is the result of the collective actions of multitudes, of mass effort extending over prolonged periods within the framework of the powers of production they have received and extended and the modes of production they have created, built up and revolutionized. It is not elites but the many-membered body of the people who have sustained history, switched it in new directions at critical turning points, and lifted humanity upward step by step.

History has not been generated, nor has its course been guided, by preconceived ideas. Social systems have not been constructed by architects with blueprints in hand. History has not proceeded in accord with any plan. Socioeconomic formations have grown out of the productive forces at hand; its members have fashioned their relations, customs, institutions and ideas in accordance with their organization of labor.

Human nature cannot explain the course of events or the characteristics of social life. Changes in the conditions of life and labor underlie the making and remaking of human nature.

In the introduction to the English edition of *Socialism: Utopian and Scientific,* Engels defined historical materialism as "that view of the course of history which seeks the ultimate cause and the great moving power of all historic events in the economic development of society, in the changes in the modes of production and exchange, in the consequent division of society into distinct classes, and in the struggles of these classes against one another."

These are the principles from which the Marxist theory of the historical process is derived. They have come from two and a half millenia of inquiry into the laws of human activity and social development. They represent its most valid conclusions. Historical materialism is itself the synthetic product of historically elaborated facts and ideas that are rooted in the economy and come to fruition in the science of society.

2

The Long View of History

How Humanity Climbed to Civilization

I propose first to trace the main line of human development from our remote animal ancestors to the present when humanity has become lord of the earth but not yet master of its own creations, not to mention its own social system. After that, I will deal with the central course of evolution in that specific segment of society which occupies the bulk of North America and represents the most developed form of capitalist society.

I will try to show not only how our national history is related to world development, but also how we, collectively and individually, fit into the picture. This is a broad and bold undertaking, a sort of jet-propelled journey through the stratosphere of world history. It is forced upon us by the urge to grasp the whole vast spread of events and to understand our specific place within them, as well as by the very dynamic of scientific theory in sociology, which has its highest expression in Marxism. The movement based upon scientific socialism, which prepares most energetically for the future, likewise must probe most deeply into the past.

I shall start from the political case history of an individual. In January 1935, a book appeared which set the style for a series of reflective reports on the trends of our times. It had considerable influence upon radicalized intellectuals here until the outbreak of the second world war. That book *Personal History,* was written by Vincent Sheean. This autobiography was a serious effort to find out what the history of his generation was leading to and what his attitude should be toward its mainstream and its cross currents.

Sheean told how he started as an ignorant student at the University of Chicago at the close of the first world war. He knew as little about the fundamental forces at work in the world then as millions like him today who are encased in a similar provincialism. As he remarked:

31

The bourgeois system insulated all its children as much as possible from a knowledge of the processes of human development, and in my case succeeded admirably in its purpose. Few Hottentots or South Sea Islanders could have been less prepared for life in the great world than I was at twenty-one.

This innocent American went abroad as a newspaperman and learned from the great events of the twenties. He observed the effects of the first world war and the Russian Revolution; he witnessed the stirrings in the Near East, in Morocco and Palestine — precursors of the vaster colonial disturbances after the second world war. He was also a spectator and played an incidental role in the defeated second Chinese revolution of 1926. His experiences were topped by the economic collapse of capitalism after 1929 and the spread of fascism in Europe.

These upheavals jolted Sheean from his doze, opened his eyes, and propelled him toward Marxism and the revolutionary socialist movement. He was swept along in the swirling torrent of that first stage in the crack-up of capitalist civilization — and began to recognize it as such. Great social, economic and political events exposed the bankruptcy of the ideas about the world he had acquired through his middle-class education in the Midwest and impelled him to cast them off.

Sheean found in Marxism the most convincing explanation of the processes of social development and the causes of the decisive events of his own age. He was inspired by its ability to answer the question that besets every thinking person: What relation does my own life have to those who have preceded me on this earth, all my contemporaries, and the incalculable generations who will come later?

Scientific, political and moral considerations combined to attract him to the science of the socialist movement. Sheean admired Marxism, he emphasized, because it took "the long view." This is not a phrase he coined, but one he borrowed from a participant in the struggle. Marxists, he noted, were or should be guided, not by partial views and episodic considerations, but by the most comprehensive outlook over the expanse of biological evolution and human achievement.

The all-embracing synthesis of history offered by Marxism contrasted sharply with the worm's-eye view he had had in the Midwest. The interior of the United States had the most up-to-date gadgets, but it was dominated by extremely old-fashioned ideas about social evolution.

Sheean had caught on to one of the outstanding features of that system of thought which bears the name of its creator, Karl Marx. Scientific socialism does provide the most consistent, many-sided and far-reaching of all the doctrines of evolution — and revolution. "The long view" it presents is the march of mankind seen in its full scope, its current reality and its ultimate consequences, so far as that is possible under present limitations.

What was this long view that attracted Vincent Sheean and so many millions before him and since? What can a review of the process of evolution, analyzed by Marxist methods, teach us about the way things change in this world?

We can single out four critical turning points in the timetable of evolution. The first was the origin of our planet about three or four billion years ago. The second was the emergence of life in the form of simple one-celled sea organisms about two and a half billion years ago. (These are only approximate but commonly accepted dates at the present time.) Third was the appearance of the first back-boned animals about four- to five-hundred million years ago. Last was the creation of mankind within the past million years or so.

Let us examine the third great chapter in this historical panorama — the first fish species. The American Museum of Natural History has prepared a chart which portrays the principal stages in organic evolution from the first fish up to ourselves, the highest form of mammalian creatures. The backbone introduced by the fish was one of the basic structures for subsequent higher evolution.

Astraspis, as one of the first vertebrate specimens is called, lived in the Paleozoic era near Canon City, Colorado, where its plates were found in delta deposits. This native American of four- to five-hundred million years ago was very revolutionary for its day. Here is what a popular authority, Bryan Curtis, says about this development in "The Life Story of the Fish."

An animal with a backbone does not seem strange to us today. But at the time that the first fish appeared upon earth, which we know from geological records to have been roughly five hundred million years ago, he must have seemed a miraculous thing. He was the very latest model in animal design, a radical, one might almost say a reckless experiment of that force which we find it convenient to personify as Mother Nature.

What did its "radicalism" consist of?

> For up to that time no creature had ever been made
> with the hard parts inside instead of outside. . . . Nature
> might be said to have had a brainstorm, abandoned all
> the earlier methods and turned out overnight something
> absolutely new and unheard of.

Although the fish retained some of the old external armor,
what was decisive from the standpoint of evolution was its
acquisition of the backbone. This converted the fish into a
creature basically different from anything living before. Thus,
the new backboned type both *grew out of* the old and *out-
grew* it. But that is not all. It then went on to conquer new
realms of existence and activity. The most revolutionary feature of the fish was the fact that it became the starting point
for the entire hierarchy of backboned creatures which has
culminated in ourselves.

These first vertebrates subsequently advanced from the fish
through the amphibians (which lived both in water and on
land) through the reptiles, and finally branched off into the
warm-blooded creatures: birds and mammals. Mankind is the
culminating point of mammalian development. This much of
animal evolution is accepted by all scientific authorities.

But these ideas and facts, so commonplace today, were the
subversive thoughts of yesterday. We readily adopt this scientific view of organic evolution without realizing that this
very act of acceptance is part of a reversal in human thinking about the world and the creatures in it which has taken
place on a mass scale only during the past century. Recall,
for example, the prevalence of the Biblical myth of creation
in the Western world up to a few generations ago.

Two aspects of the facts about the vertebrates deserve special
discussion. First, the transfer of the bony parts of the fish
from the outside to the inside embodied a qualitatively new
form of organic structure, a break in the continuity of development up to that time, a jump onto a higher level of life.
Every biologist acknowledges this fact. But this fact has a
more profound significance, which tells us much about the
methods of evolutionary change in general. It demonstrates
how, at the critical point in the accumulation of changes outside and inside an organism, the conflicting elements which
compose it break up the old form of its existence and the progressive formation passes over, by way of a leap, to a qualitatively new and historically higher state of development. This
is true not only of organic species but of social formations
and systems of thought as well.

This radical overturn is undeniable in the case of the birth and evolution of the fish and its ultimate surpassing by higher species. But it is much harder for many people to accept such a conclusion when it comes to the transformation of a lower social organization into a higher social organization. This reluctance to apply the teachings of evolution consistently to all things, and above all to the social system in which we live, is rooted in the determination to defend powerful but obsolete and narrow class interests against opposing forces and rival ideas that aim to create a genuinely new order of things.

The second point to be stressed is the fact that the fish, as the first vertebrate, occupies a specific place in the sequence of the evolution of organisms. It is one link in a chain of the manifestations of life extending from one-celled protozoa to the most complex organisms. This first creature with a backbone came out of and after a host of creatures which never had such a skeletal structure and in turn gave rise to superior orders which had that and much more.

Contradictory as it is, many scholars and scientists who take the order of evolution of organic species for granted, stubbornly resist the extension of the same lawfulness to the changing species of social organizations. They will not admit that there has been, or can be, any definite and discernible sequence in the social development of mankind analogous to the steps in the progress from the invertebrates to the fish, through the reptile and mammalian creatures, up to the advent of mankind.

This skepticism in sociology is especially pronounced in the present century, and in our own country and its colleges. Thinkers of this type, of course, know that there have been many changes in history, that many diverse formations are found in the fields of anthropology, archaeology, history, sociology and politics.

What they deny is that these typical manifestations of social life can — or even should — be arranged in any determinate order of historical development in which each has its given place from the beginning to the end, from the lower to the higher. They teach that all the various forms of culture and ways of life are merely dissimilar to one another and that it is impossible or unnecessary to try to discover any regular sequence or lawful affiliation in their emergence into social reality.

This view and method is thoroughly anti-evolutionary, anti-scientific and essentially reactionary. But it is explainable. The denial of the possibility of finding out the order of advancement in social structures springs — if you will permit the analogy — from the resistance by today's invertebrates to the oncoming vertebrates who represent a superior form of organization and are destined to supplant them in the struggle for social survival.

The evolutionary record itself, starting with the upward climb of the fish, most effectively refutes this tenacious conservatism. The first vertebrate was followed by six further progressive types of fish in the next hundred million years. The most advanced was a freshwater, medium-sized carnivorous species whose fossils have been found in Canada. Although this specimen spent much of its life in the water, it had acquired many of the functions required for living on land. Fish, as you know, are customarily at home in water, breathe through gills and have fins. It was unbecoming to established fish-nature for the first amphibians to get up out of the water and crawl onto land, breathe through lungs, and move about on legs.

Let us imagine a fish (if you will go along with the fancy) who looked backward rather than forward, as some fish do. This backward-looking fish could exclaim to the forward-moving amphibians: "We fish, the oldest inhabitants, have never before done such things; they can't be done; they shouldn't be done!" And, when the amphibians persisted, shrieking: "These things mustn't be done; it's subversive of the good old order to do them!" However, the resistance of inertia did not prevent some water-dwellers from turning into land animals.

Animal life continued to move forward as species were modified and transmuted in response to decisive changes in their genetic constitutions and natural habitats. Amphibians turned into reptiles which had better developed brains, were rib-breathing, egg-laying, had limbs for locomotion and well-developed eyes. The reptile kingdom evolved gradually toward the mammal, with transitional types that had features belonging to both, until once again a full-fledged new order stepped into the world.

About 135 million years ago, the animal prototype which gave rise to our own tree-living ancestor emerged. This was a rodent-like creature who took another big leap in evolutionary adaptation and activity by quitting the land for the trees. Arboreal existence over six hundred thousand years so altered our animal ancestors from head to toes, from grasping functions to teeth-changes, that they elevated themselves to monkey and ape forms. The kinship of the latter with our own kind is so close that it is difficult to distinguish an embryo of the highest apes from that of a human.

The natural conditions had at last been created for the emergence of mankind. It seems likely that changes in climate and geographical conditions connected with the first Ice Age drove certain species of primates down from the trees, out of the forests and onto the plains. A series of important anatomical developments paved the way for the making of the human race. The shortening of the pelvic bone made it possible for the primate to stand erect, to differentiate forelimbs from hindlimbs and emancipate the hands. The brain became enlarged. Binocular vision and vocal organs made human sight and speech possible.

The central biological organ for the making of mankind was the hand. The hands became opposed to the legs and the thumb became opposed to the four fingers. This opposition between the thumb and the other fingers has been one of the most fruitful and dynamic of all the unions of opposites in the evolution of humanity. The thumb's ability to counterpose itself to each of the other fingers gave the hand exceptional powers of grasping and manipulating objects and endowed it with extreme flexibility and sensitivity. This acquisition made possible the biological combination of hand-eye-brain. Combined with the prolonged period of care by the mother for her offspring, the natural prerequisites for social life were at hand.

At this point something should be said about the most common argument against socialism: "You can't change human nature!" How much substance is there to this contention?

Once the record of organic evolution is accepted, one proposition, at least, inevitably flows from it: *Fish nature can be changed!* It has been changed into amphibian, reptile, bird, mammalian and ultimately into human natures. The salt in our bodies is one reminder, among many, of our descent from great-grandfather fish in the oceans of ages ago.

This poses the following pertinent questions to the resisters to social change: If fish can change, or be changed so much, on what grounds can narrow restrictions be imposed upon the changeability of mankind? Did our species lose its plasticity, its potentialities for radical alteration somewhere along the line from the transition of the primate to the human?

The contrary is the case. In the passage to humanity, our species not only retained all the capacities for progressive change inherent in animality but multiplied them to an infinitely higher degree, lifting them onto an entirely new dimension by creating previously unknown ways and means of evolutionary progress.

It required four- to five-hundred million years to create the biological conditions necessary for the generation of the first subhumans. This was not brought about through anyone's forethought or foresight, or in accord with any plan, or with the aim of realizing some preconceived goal. It happened, we may say, as the lawful outcome of a series of blind and accidental developments in the forms of natural life, spurred forward in the struggle for survival, which eventually culminated in the production of a special kind of primate equipped with the capacities for acquiring more than animal powers.

At this juncture, about a million or so years ago, the most radical of all the transmutations of life on this planet took place. The emergence of mankind embodied something totally different which became the root of a unique line of development. What was this? It was the passage from animal separatism to human collectivism, from purely biological modes of behavior to the use of acquired social powers.

Where did these added artificial powers come from that have marked off emerging mankind from all other animal species, elevated our species above the other primates, and made mankind into the dominant order of life? Our dominance is indisputable because we command the power to destroy ourselves and all other forms of life, not to speak of changing them.

The fundamentally new powers mankind acquired were the powers of production, of securing the means of sustenance through the use of tools and joint labor, and sharing the results with one another. I can do no more than single out four of the most important factors in this process.

The first was associated activities in getting food and dividing it. The second was the use, and later the manufacture, of implements for that purpose. The third was the development of speech and of reasoning, which arose from and was promoted by living and working together. The fourth was the use, the domestication and the production of fire. Fire was the first natural force, the first chemical process, put to socially productive use by ascending humanity.

Thanks to these new powers, emerging mankind enormously speeded up the changes in our own species and later in the world around us. The record of history for the past million years is essentially one of the formation of humanity and its continual transformation. This in turn has promoted the transformation of the world around us.

What has enabled mankind to effect such colossal changes in himself and his environment? All the biological changes in our stock over the past million years, taken together, have not been a prominent factor in the advancement of the human species. Yet during that time humanity has taken the raw materical inherited from our animal past, socialized it, humanized it, and partially, though not completely, civilized it. The axis of human development, contrasted to animality, revolves around these social rather than biological processes.

The mainspring of this progress comes from the improvement of the powers of production, acquired along the way and expanded in accordance with man's growing needs. By discovering and utilizing the diverse properties and resources of the world around him, man has gradually added to his abilities of producing the means of life. As these have developed, all his other social powers, the power of speech, of thought, of art and of science, etc., have been enhanced.

The decisive difference between the highest animals and ourselves is to be found in our development of the means and forces of production and destruction (two aspects of one and the same phenomenon). This accounts not only for the qualitative difference between man and the animals but also for the specific differences between one level of human development and another. What demarcates the peoples of the Stone Age from those of the Iron Age, and savage life from civilized societies, is the difference in the total powers of production at their disposal.

What happens when two different levels of productive and destructive power measure strength was dramatically illustrated when the Spanish conquerors invaded the Western Hemisphere. The Indians were armed with bows and arrows and slings; the newcomers had muskets and gun powder. The Indians had canoes and paddles; the Spaniards had big sailing ships. The Indians wore leather or padded jackets for protection in warfare; the Spaniards had steel armor. The Indians had no domesticated draught animals but went on foot; the Spaniards rode horses. Their superior equipment inspired terror and enabled the Conquistadors to defeat their antagonists with inferior manpower.

This basic proposition of historical materialism should be easier for us to grasp because we are privileged to witness the first stage of a technological revolution comparable in importance to the taming of fire a half million years ago. That is the acquisition of control over the processes of nuclear fission and fusion. This new source of power has already revolutionized the relations among governments and the art of warfare; it is about to transform industry, agriculture, medicine and many other departments of social activity.

What brought this technological revolution about? Mankind underwent no biological changes in the preceding period. Nor were there any sudden alterations in human modes of thinking, in their sentiments or their moral ideas. This incalculably powerful force of production and destruction issued from the entire previous development of society's productive forces and all the scientific knowledge and instruments connected with them. Atomic power is the latest link in the chain of acquired powers that can be traced back to the earliest elements of social production: associated labor in securing the necessities of life, tool-using and -making, speech, thought and fire. Atomic energy is the latest fruit of the seeds planted back in ancient society which have been cultivated and improved by humanity in its upward climb.

Let us come back to that remarkable organ of ours, the hand. The hand, which among the primates originally conveyed food to the mouth, was converted by humanity into an organ for grasping and guiding the materials used and then shaped for tools. The hand is the biological prototype of the tool and the handle; it is the prerequisite and parent of laboring activity. The passage from the hand to the tool coincides with the creation of society and the progressive development of mankind and its latent powers.

The connection between the most rudimentary tools and the complex material instruments of production in today's industrial system has been graphically illustrated in a chart prepared for the Do-All Corporation, of Des Plaines, Illinois, sponsor of a traveling exhibit on "How Basic Tools Created Civilization." This exhibit, which claims to be "the first attempt ever made to assemble the complete history of man's tools," documents the stages in the progress of technology.

The first known tools formed by man, called eoliths, date back, some scientists say, to one and a half million years ago. These were sections of broken stone with edges useful for cutting meat, scraping hides or digging for roots. They were little more than simple extensions of the hand. They were not designed for specific functions but were adaptable for pounding, throwing, scraping, drilling, cutting, etc.

In the next stage, tools underwent improvement along two main lines: their cutting edges were made more efficient; and they became fashioned for special purposes. Men learned to chip stone to a predetermined shape, thereby producing a sharper cutting edge. A wider variety of working tools, such as axes, sharp-pointed drills, thin-edged blades, chisels and other forerunners of today's hand tools, came into existence.

These tools reduced the time needed to produce sustenance and shelter, thereby raising the social level of production and improving living conditions. Moreover, these new productive activities enhanced man's mental capacities. The complexity of special-purpose tools indicates the development of a mentality capable of understanding the necessity of producing the *means* before the *end* could be attained. Mental concepts of specific use preceded both the design and construction of these special-purpose tools.

Each of the subsequent steps in the improvement of tool-using and toolmaking likewise resulted in the economizing of labor time, an increased productivity of labor, better living conditions and the growth of man's intellectual abilities. The motive force of human history comes from the greater productivity of labor made possible by decisive advances in the techniques and tools of production.

This can be seen in the development of hunting. At first, mankind could as a rule capture only small and slow animals. Regular consumption of big game was made possible by the invention of such hunting weapons as the thrusting spear, the throwing spear, the spear-thrower and the bow and arrow. The latter was the first device capable of storing energy for release when desired. These implements increased the range and striking force of primitive hunters and enabled them to slaughter the largest and fleetest animals.

All the basic hand tools in use today, the ax, adze, knife, drill, scraper, chisel, saw, were invented during the Stone Age. The first metal, bronze, did not replace stone as the preferred material for toolmaking until about 3,500 years ago. Metal not only imparted a far more efficient and durable cutting edge to tools but enabled them to be resharpened instead of thrown away after becoming dulled.

During the period when bronze tools were the chief implements of production, means and standards of measurements were devised; mathematics and surveying were developed; a calendar was calculated; and great advances were made in sculpturing. Such basic inventions as the potter's wheel, the balance scale, the keystone arch, sailing vessels and glass bottles were created.

About 2,500 years ago, iron, the most durable, plentiful

and cheap metal, began to displace bronze in toolmaking. The introduction of iron tools tremendously advanced productivity and skills in agriculture and craftsmanship. They enabled more food to be grown and better clothing and shelter to be made with less expenditure of time and energy; they gave rise to many comforts and conveniences. Iron tools made possible many of the achievements of Greece and Rome from the Acropolis of Athens to the tunnels, bridges, sewers and buildings of Rome.

The energy for all these earlier means and modes of production was supplied exclusively by human muscles which, after the domestication of herds, was supplemented to some extent by animal muscle power. The Industrial Revolution of the eighteenth century was based upon the utilization of energy from other sources, from fossil fuels such as coal. The combination of mechanical power generated by steam engines, machine tools, improved implements and production machinery, plus the increased use of iron and steel, have multiplied society's powers of production to their present point. Nowadays, machines and tools operated by mechanical and electrical power are the principal material organs of our industry and agriculture alike.

The most up-to-date machine tools have been developed out of simple hand tools. While using hand tools, men began to understand and employ the advantages of the lever, the pulley, the inclined plane, the wheel and axle, and the screw to multiply their strength. These physical principles were later combined and applied in the making of machine tools.

This entire development of technology is organically associated with and primarily responsible for the development of mankind's intellectual abilities. This is pointed out in the following explanatory paragraph from the Do-All Corporation exhibit:

> Machine tools perform in complicated ways the same basic functions and operations as hand tools. These basic functions were established by hand-held stone tools shaped by primitive man. It was through devising and using hand-wrought stone tools that mankind developed powers of mental and bodily coordination . . . and this in turn accelerated the increase in men's mental capabilities.

Such ideas about the influence of technology upon thought, taken from the publication of a respectable capitalist corporation, resemble those to be found in the writings of Marx and

Engels. The thought-controllers may try to drive historical materialism out of the socialist door but here it sneaks back in through a capitalist window.

The Do-All exhibit demonstrates that the evolution of tools can be arranged in a chronological series and ascending order from wood and stone hand tools through metal hand tools to power-driven machine tools. Is it likewise possible to mark off corresponding successive stages in social organization?

Historical materialism answers this question affirmatively. On the broadest basis — and every big division of history can be broken down for special purposes into lesser ones — three main stages can be distinguished in man's rise from animality to the atomic age: savagery, barbarism and civilization.

Napoleon said that an army marches on its stomach. This has been true of the forward march of the army of humanity. The acquisition of food has been the overriding aim of social production at all times, for men cannot survive, let alone progress, without regularly satisfying their hunger.

The principal epochs in the advancement of humanity can therefore be divided according to the decisive improvements effected in securing food supplies. Savagery, the infancy of humanity, constitutes that period when people depend for food upon what nature provides ready-made. Their food may come from plants, such as fruit or roots, from insects, birds or animals, or from seashore or sea life. At this stage, men forage for their food much like beasts of prey or grub for it like other animals — with these all-important differences: they cooperate with one another, and they employ crude tools along with other means and powers of production to assist them in "appropriating" the means of subsistence for their collective use.

The chief economic activities at this stage are foraging for food, hunting and fishing; and they were developed in that sequence. The club and spear enable the savage to capture the raw materials for his meals, clothing and shelter — all of which are embodied in animals on the hoof. The net catches fish and the fire prepares it for consumption. The Indians of southern California were at this stage when the first white settlers arrived two centuries ago.

Barbarism is the second stage of social organization. It was based upon the domestication of animals and the cultivation of plants. Food is now not merely *collected* but *produced*. The domestication of cattle, sheep, pigs, and other animals provided reserves of meat as well as food in the form of milk from goats and cows. The planting and growing of crops made regular and plentiful food supplies available.

This food-producing revolution, which started in Asia from six to ten thousand years ago, relieved mankind from subjection to external nature for the first time. Up to that point humanity had had to rely upon what the natural environment contained to take care of its needs and had been dependent for survival upon completely external and uncontrollable natural conditions. Entire stocks and cultures of people arose, flourished, and then succumbed, like plant or animal species, in response to the beneficence or hostility of nature around them.

For example, about twenty to thirty thousand years ago, there arose a society centered around southern France called the Reindeer Culture. These people thrived by hunting huge reindeer and other herds which browsed upon the lush vegetation there. The drawings they made, which have been discovered in caves over the past seventy-five years, testify to the keenness of their eyes and minds and the trained sensitivity of their hands and place them among the most superb artists that have ever appeared on earth. However, when changed climatic and botanic conditions caused the reindeer herds to vanish, their entire culture, and very likely the people as well, died out.

The early hunters had no assured control over their mobile sources of food. The insecurity of savage life was largely overcome, or at least considerably reduced, with the advent of stockbreeding, and especially with the development of agricultural techniques. For the first time, methods were instituted for obtaining extensive and expanding supplies of food products and fibers by systematic and sustained activities of working groups. These branches of economic activity made much larger and more compact populations possible.

These activities and their increased output provided the elements for the higher culture of barbarism. Farming and stockraising led to the development of such handicrafts as smelting metals and pottery-making, as accumulated food supplies generated the need to store and transport articles for the first time. Men became more stationary; denser populations aggregated; permanent dwellings were built; and village life sprang into existence.

In their further and final development, the economic activities under barbarism created the prerequisites for the coming of civilization. The material foundation for civilization was the capacity acquired by the most advanced peoples for the regular production of far more food and goods than were required for the physical maintenance of their members. These surpluses had two results. They permitted specific sections of the communities to engage in diversified activities other than the direct acquisition and production of the basic means of life. Such specialists as priests, nobles, kings, officials, smiths, potters, traders, builders and other craftsmen made their appearance.

With the growth of specialization and the extension of trade, the top layers of these groups moved into strategic positions which enabled the more fortunate and powerful to appropriate large personal shares of the surplus of wealth. The drive to increase personal wealth flowing from the growing social division of labor and exchange of goods, led in time to the development of private property, the family, slavery, class divisions, commodity production on a large scale, trade, money, the city and the territorial state with its army, police, courts and other relations and institutions characteristic of civilization.

In its evolution to our own century, civilized society can be divided into three main epochs: slavery, feudalism and capitalism. Each of these is marked off by the special way in which the ruling propertied class at the head of the social setup manages to extract the surplus wealth upon which it lives from the laboring mass who directly create it. This entire period covers little more than the past five to six thousand years.

Civilization was ushered in and raised upon direct slavery. The very economic factors that broke up barbarism and made civilized life possible likewise provided the material preconditions for the use of slave labor. The division of labor based upon tending herds, raising crops, mining metals, and fashioning goods for sale enabled the most advanced societies to produce more than the actual laborers required for their maintenance. This made slavery both possible and profitable for the first time. It gave the most powerful stimulus to the predatory appetites of individual possessors of the means of production who strove to acquire and increase their surpluses of wealth. Slave production and ownership became the economic foundation of a new type of social organization, the source of supreme power, prestige and privileges. And it eventually reshaped the whole structure of civilized life.

Chattel slavery was an extremely significant human contrivance — and it is distinctively human. Animals may feed upon carcasses of other animals, but they do not live upon the surpluses they create. Although we rightly recoil against any manifestations of servitude today and burn to abolish its last vestiges, it should be recognized that in its heyday slavery had imperative reasons for existence and persistence.

Science demands that every phenomenon be approached, analyzed and appraised with objectivity, setting aside personal reactions of admiration or abhorrence. Historical materialism has to explain why slavery came to be adopted by the most advanced contingents of mankind. The principal reason was that, along with the private ownership of the means of production and the widening exchange of its products, slave labor increased the forces of production, multiplied wealth, comforts and culture—although only for the lucky few—and on the whole spurred mankind forward for an entire historical period. Without the extension of slave labor, there would not have been incentives unremitting enough to pile up wealth on a sizeable scale which could then be applied to further the productive processes.

The historical necessity for slavery can be illustrated along two lines. The peoples who failed to adopt slave labor likewise did not proceed to civilization, however excellent their other qualities and deeds. They remained below that level because their economy lacked the inner drive of the force of greed and the dynamic propulsion arising from the slaveholder's need to exploit the slave to augment his wealth. That is a negative demonstration.

But there is more positive proof. Those states based on some form of servitude, such as the most brilliant cultures of antiquity from Babylon and Egypt to Greece and Rome, also contributed the most to the civilizing processes from wheeled carts and the plow to writing and philosophy. These societies stood in the main line of social progress.

But if slavery had sufficient reasons for becoming the beginning and basis of ancient civilization, in turn and in time, it generated the conditions and forces which would undermine and overthrow it. Once slavery became the predominant form of production either in industry, as in Greece, or in agriculture, as in Rome, it no longer furthered the development of agricultural techniques, craftsmanship, trade or navigation. The slave empires of antiquity stagnated and disintegrated until after a lapse of centuries they were replaced by two main types of feudal organization: Asiatic, as in India, China and Japan, and West European.

Both of these new forms of production and social organization were superior to slavery, but the West European turned out to be far more productive and dynamic. Under feudalism, the laborers got more of their produce than did the slaves; they even had access to the land and other means of production. Serfs and peasants had greater freedom of activity and could acquire more culture.

As the result of a long list of technological and other social advances, merging with a sequence of exceptional historical circumstances, feudalized Europe became the nursery for the next great stage of class society, capitalism. How and why did capitalism originate?

Once money had arisen from the extension of trading several thousand years ago, its use as capital became possible. Merchants could add to their wealth by buying goods cheap and selling them dear; moneylenders and mortgage-holders could gain interest on sums advanced on the security of land or other collateral. These practices were common in both slave and feudal societies.

But if money could be used in precapitalist times to return more than the original investment, other conditions had to be fulfilled before capitalism could become established as a separate and definite world economic system. The central condition was a special kind of transaction regularly repeated on a growing scale. Large numbers of propertyless workers had to hire themselves to the possessors of money and the other means of production in order to earn a livelihood.

Hiring and firing seem to us a normal way of carrying on production. But such peoples as the Indians never knew it. Before the Europeans came, no Indian ever worked for a boss (the word itself was imported by the Dutch) because they possessed their own means of livelihood. The slave may have been purchased, but he belonged to and worked for the master his whole life long. The feudal serf or tenant was likewise bound for life to the lord and his land.

The epoch-making innovation upon which capitalism rested was the institution of working for wages as the dominant relation of production. Most of you have gone into the labor market, to an employment agency or personnel office, to get a buyer for your labor power. The employer buys this power at prevailing wage rates by the hour, day or week and then applies it under his supervision to produce commodities which his company subsequently sells at a profit. That profit is derived from the fact that wage workers produce more value than the capitalist pays for their labor.

Up to the twentieth century, this mechanism for pumping surplus labor out of the working masses and transferring the surpluses of wealth they create to the personal credit of the capitalist was the mightiest accelerator of the productive forces and the expansion of civilization. As a distinct economic system, capitalism is only about 450 years old; it has conquered the world and journeyed from dawn to twilight in that time. This is a short lifespan compared to savagery, which stretched over a million years or more, or to barbarism, which prevailed for four thousand to five thousand years. Obviously, the processes of social transformation have been considerably speeded up in modern times.

This speeding up in social progress is due in large measure to the very nature of capitalism, which continually revolutionizes its techniques of production and the entire range of social relations issuing from them. Since its birth, world capitalism has passed through three such phases of internal transformation. In its formative period, the merchants were the dominant class of capitalists because trade was the main source of wealth accumulation. Under commercial capitalism, industry and agriculture, the pillars of production, were not usually carried on by wage labor but by means of small handicrafts, peasant farming, slave or serf labor.

The industrial age was launched around the beginning of the nineteenth century with the application of steam power to the first mechanized processes, concentrating large numbers of wage workers into factories. The capitalist captains of this large-scale industry became masters of the field of production and later of entire countries and continents as their riches, their legions of wage laborers, social and political power swelled to majestic proportions.

This vigorous, expanding, progressive, confident, competitive stage of industrial capitalism dominated the nineteenth century. It passed over into the monopoly-ridden capitalism of the twentieth century which has carried all the basic tendencies of capitalism, and especially its most reactionary features, to extremes in economic, political, cultural and international relations. While the processes of production have become more centralized, more rationalized, more socialized, the means of production and the wealth of the world have become concentrated in giant financial and industrial combines. So far as the capitalist sectors of society are involved, this process has been brought to the point where the capitalist monopolies of a single country, the USA, dictate to all the rest.

The most important question to be asked at this point is: What is the destiny of the development of civilization in its capitalist form? Disregarding in-between views, which at bottom evade the answer, two irreconcilable viewpoints assert themselves, corresponding to the world outlooks of two opposing classes. The spokesmen for capitalism say that nothing more remains to be done except to perfect their system as it stands, and it can roll on and on and on. The Do-All Corporation, for example, which published so instructive a chart on the evolution of tools, declares that more and better machine tools, which they hope will be bought at substantial profit from their company, will guarantee continued progress and prosperity for capitalist America — without the least change in existing class relations.

Socialists give a completely different answer based upon an incomparably more penetrating, correct and comprehensive analysis of the movement of history, the structure of capitalism and the struggles presently agitating the world around us. The historical function of capitalism is not to perpetuate itself indefinitely but to create the conditions and prepare the forces that will bring about its own replacement by a more efficient form of material production and a higher type of social organization. Just as capitalism supplanted feudalism and slavery, and civilization swept aside savagery and barbarism, so the time has come for capitalism itself to be superseded. How and by whom is this revolutionary transformation to be effected?

In the last century, Marx made a scientific analysis of the workings of the capitalist system which explained how its inner contradictions would bring about its downfall. The revolutions of our own century since 1917 are demonstrating in real life that capitalism is due to be relegated to the museum of antiquities. It is worthwhile to understand the inexorable underlying causes of these developments, which appear so inexplicable and abhorrent to the upholders of the capitalist system.

Capitalism produces many things, good and bad, in the course of its evolution. But the most vital and valuable of all the social forces it creates is the industrial working class. The capitalist class has brought into existence a vast army of wage laborers, centralized and disciplined, and set it into motion for its own purposes, to make and operate the machines, factories and all the other production and transportation facilities from which its profits emanate.

The exploitation and abuses, inherent and inescapable in the capitalist organization of economic life, provoke the workers time and again to organize themselves and undertake militant action to defend their elementary interests. The struggle between these conflicting social classes is today the dominant and driving force of world and American history, just as the conflict between the bourgeois-led forces against the precapitalist elements was the motivating force of history in the immediately preceding centuries.

The current struggle, which has been gathering momentum and expanding its scope for a hundred years, has entered its decisive phase on a world scale. Except for Cuba, the preliminary battles between the procapitalist and the anticapitalist forces have so far been waged to a conclusion in countries outside the Western Hemisphere. Sooner or later, however, they are bound to break out and be fought to a finish within this country, which is not only the stronghold of capitalist power but also the home of the best-organized and technically most proficient working class.

The main line of development in America, no less than the course of world history, points to such a conclusion. Why is this so?

The Main Course of American History And Its Next Stage

We have reviewed the course by which humanity climbed out of the animal state and marked the successive steps in that climb. Mankind had to crawl through savagery for a million years or more, walk through barbarism and then, with shoulders hunched and head bowed, enter the iron gates of class society. There, for thousands of years, mankind endured a harsh schooling under the rod and rule of private property, which began with slavery and reached its highest form in capitalist civilization. Now our own age stands, or rather struggles, at the entrance to socialism.

Let us now pass from the historical progress of mankind, viewed as a whole, to inspect one of its parts, the United States of North America. Because U. S. imperialism is the mainstay of the international capitalist system, the role of the American people is crucial in deciding how quickly and how well humanity crosses the great divide between the class society of the past and the reorganization and reinvigoration of the world along socialist lines.

I shall try to give brief answers to the following four questions: What has been the course of American history in its essentials? What are its connections with the march of the rest of humankind? What has been the outcome to date? Finally, where do we fit into the picture?

American history breaks sharply into two fundamentally

different epochs. One belongs to the aboriginal inhabitants, the Indians; the other starts with the coming of white Europeans to America at the end of the fifteenth century. The beginnings of human activity in the Western Hemisphere are still obscure. But it is surmised that from twenty to thirty thousand years ago, early Stone Age Asiatics, thanks to favorable climatic conditions which united that part of Alaska with Siberia, crossed over the Bering Strait and slowly made their way throughout North, Central, and South America. Later streams of migration may have brought the practices of gardening with them. It is upon these bequests that the Indians fashioned their type of existence.

Whoever regards the Indians as insignificant or incompetent has defective historical judgment. Humanity has been raised to its present estate by four branches of productive activity. The first is food-gathering, which includes grubbing for roots and berries as well as hunting and fishing. The second is stock-raising. The third is agriculture. The fourth is craftsmanship, graduating into large-scale industry.

The Indians were extremely adept at hunting, fishing and other ways of food-gathering. They were ingenious craftsmen whose work in some fields has never been excelled. The Incas, for example, made textiles which were extremely fine in texture, coloring and design. They invented and used more different techniques of weaving on their hand looms than any other people in history.

However, the Indians showed the greatest talent in their development of agriculture. They may even have independently invented soil cultivation. In any case they brought it to diversified perfection. We are indebted to the Indians for most of the vegetables that today come from the fields and through the kitchens onto our tables. Most important are corn, potatoes and beans, but there is in addition a considerable list including tomatoes, chili, pineapples, peanuts, avocados, and for after-dinner purposes, tobacco. They knew and used the properties of 400 separate species of plants. No plant cultivated by the American Indians was known to Asia, Europe or Africa prior to the white invasion of America.

Much is heard about all that white men brought over to the Indians, but little about what the Indians gave the European whites. The introduction of the food plants taken from the Indians more than doubled the available food supply of the older continent after the fifteenth century and became an important factor in the expansion of capitalist civilization. Over half of the agricultural produce raised in the world today comes from plants domesticated by the Indians!

From the first to the fifteenth centuries, the Indians themselves created magnificent, even astounding cultures on the basis of their achievements in agriculture. Agriculture enabled some of the scattered and roving hunting tribes of Indians to aggregate in small but permanent settlements where they supported themselves by growing corn, beans and other vegetables. They also raised and wove cotton, made pottery and developed other handicrafts.

The Incas of the Andes, the Mayans of Guatemala and Yucatan, and the Aztecs of central Mexico, unaffected by European civilization and developed independently, constituted the most advanced of the Indian societies. Their cultures embodied the utmost the Indians were able to accomplish within the twenty-five thousand years or so allotted them by history. In fact, the Mayans had made mathematical and astronomical calculations more complex and advanced than those of the European invaders. They had independently invented the zero for use in their number system — something even the Greeks and Romans had lacked.

Indians progressed as far as the middle stage of barbarism and were stopped there. Whether or not, given unlimited time and no interference from more powerful and productive peoples, they would have mounted all the way to civilization must remain unanswered. This much can be stated: they had formidable obstacles to overcome along such a path. The Indians did not have such important domesticated animals as the horse, cow, pig, sheep or water buffalo that had pulled the Asians and Europeans along toward civilization. They had only the dog, turkey, guinea pig and, in the Andean highlands, llamas, alpacas, and, in some places, bees. Moreover, they did not use the wheel, except for toys, did not know the use of iron or firearms, and did not have other prerequisites for civilizing themselves.

However, history in the other part of the globe settled this question without further appeal. For, while the most advanced Indians had been moving up from wandering hunters' lives to those of settlers in barbaric communities, the Europeans, themselves an offspring of Asiatic culture, had not only entered class society but had become highly civilized. Their most progressive segments along the Atlantic seaboard were passing over from feudalism to capitalism.

This uneven development of society in the Old World and the New provided the historical setting for the second great turning point in American history. What was the essential

meaning of the upheaval initiated by the West European cross-
ing of the Atlantic? It represented the transition from the Stone
Age to the Iron Age in America, from barbaric to civilized
modes of life, from tribal organization based upon collectivist
practices to a society rooted in private property, production
for exchange, the family, the state and so forth.

Few spectacles in history are more dramatic and instructive
than the confrontation and conflict between the Indian representatives of communal Stone Age life and the armed agents
of class civilization. Science fiction tells about visitations to
this planet by Martians in flying saucers. To the Indians,
the first visitations of the white men were no less startling
and incomprehensible.

To the Indians, these white men had completely alien customs, standards and ways of life. They were strange in appearance and behavior. In fact, the differences between the
two were so profound as to be irreconcilable. What was the
root cause of the enduring and deadly clash between them?
They represented two utterly incompatible levels of social organization that had grown out of and were based upon dissimilar conditions and were heading toward entirely different
goals.

Even at its height, Indian life was based upon tribal collectivism and its crude technology. Indian psychology was
fashioned by such social institutions. The Indians not only
did not have the wheel, iron or the alphabet—they also lacked
the institutions, ideas, feelings and aims of civilized peoples
who had been molded by the technology and culture of an
acquisitive society. These conditions had stamped out a very
special kind of human being as the peculiar product of civilization based upon private ownership.

The most highly developed Indians subsisted on agriculture.
But their agriculture was not of the same economic mode as
that of the newcomers. The major means of producing food
by soil cultivation belonged to the entire tribe and nothing
in its production or distribution could be exclusively claimed
by individual owners. This was true of the principal means
of production, the land itself. When the Europeans arrived at
these shores, all the way from the Atlantic to the Pacific there
was not a single foot of ground that a person could stand
on and assert: "This belongs to my solitary private self, or
to my little family—all others keep off and stay out." The
land belonged to the whole people.

It was quite otherwise with the white men, the bearers of the
new and higher type of society. To them it appeared natural

and necessary, as it still does to most citizens of this country, that almost everything on earth should pass into someone's private ownership. Clothes, houses, weapons of war, tools, ships, even human beings themselves, could be bought and sold.

It was in the shiny embodiment of precious metals that private property became not only the cornerstone of worldly existence but even opened up the gates of heaven. Columbus wrote to Queen Isabella as follows: "Gold constitutes treasure and he who possesses it has all he needs in this world as also the means of rescuing souls from purgatory and restoring them to the enjoyment of paradise." This was literally true at that time because rich Catholics could buy indulgences for their sins from the Pope. Cortez is said to have told some natives of Mexico: "We Spaniards are troubled with a disease of the heart for which we find gold, and gold only, a specific remedy."

The doctrine of the European whites was that everything must have its price, whether it pertains to present happiness or future salvation. This idea remains the guideline for the plutocratic rulers of our own day who in their campaigns to dominate the world not only buy up individuals but even whole governments. In their quest for gold and lust for gain, Columbus and the Conquistadors enslaved and killed thousands of West Indians in the islands they discovered. And that was only the beginning.

Viewed from the heights of world history, this turning point in America was characterized by the conjuncture of two revolutionary processes. The first was the shift of maritime Europe from a feudal to a bourgeois basis. Part of this revolutionizing of Western Europe was a push outward as the capitalist traders extended their operations throughout the globe. Their exploring, marketing, pirating expeditions brought the emissaries of the budding bourgeois society in Europe across the ocean and into collision with the Indians. The rape of the ancient cultures of the Aztecs and Incas, the enslavement and extermination of the natives by the Spanish conquerors and others, was a collateral offensive of this European revolution on our own continent.

Through the extension of the revolutionary process, the peoples of the Stone Age here were overcome and supplanted by the most advanced representatives of class civilization. This was not the only continent on which such a process took place. What happened from the fifteenth to the nineteenth centuries in the New World had taken place much earlier in Western

Europe itself; and it was to reach into the most remote sectors of the world, as capitalism has spread over the earth from that time to our own.

The contest between the Stone Age peoples and the representatives of the bourgeois epoch was fiercely fought. Their wars stretched over four centuries and ended in the disintegration, dispossession or destruction of the prehistoric cultures and the unchallenged supremacy of class society.

With the advent of the white Europeans (as well as the enslaved colored Africans who were transported here by them), American history was switched onto an entirely different set of rails, a new course marked out by the needs of a young, expanding world capitalism.

We come now to a most crucial question: What has been the main line of American growth since 1492? Various answers are given — the growth of national independence, the spread of democracy, the coming into his own of the common man, or the expansion of industry. Each of these familiar formulas taught in the schools does record some aspect of the process, but none goes to the heart of the matter.

The correct answer to the question is that despite detours enroute, the main line of American history has consisted in the construction and consolidation of capitalist civilization, which has been carried to its ultimate in our own day. Any attempt to explain the development of American society since the sixteenth century will be brought up against this fact. The discovery, exploration, settlement, cultivation, exploitation, democratization and industrialization of this continent must all be seen as successive steps in promoting the building of bourgeois society. This is the only interpretation of the decisive events in the past 450 years in North America that makes sense, gives continuity and coherence to our complex history, distinguishes the mainstream from tributaries, and is validated by the development of American society. Everything in our national history has to be referred to, and linked up with, the process of establishing the capitalist way of life in its most pronounced and, today, its most pernicious form.

This is commonly called "The American Way of Life." A more realistic and honest characterization would be the capitalist way of life because, as I shall indicate, this is destined to be only a historically limited and passing expression of civilized life in America.

The central importance of the formation and transformation of bourgeois society can be demonstrated in another way. What is the most outstanding peculiarity of American history since the coming of the Europeans? There have been many peculiarities in the history of this country; in some ways this is a very peculiar country. But what marks off American life from the development of the other great nations of the world is that the growth and construction of American society falls entirely within the epoch of the expansion of capitalism on a global scale. That is the key to understanding American history, whether you deal with colonial history, nineteenth-century history or twentieth-century history.

It is not true of other leading countries such as England, Germany, Russia, India, Japan or China. These countries passed through prolonged periods of slave or feudal civilization that have left their stamp upon them to this very day. Look at Mac Arthur's preservation of that feudal relic, the Emperor of Japan, or that Sunday Supplement delight, the monarchy of England.

America, on the other hand, leaped from savagery and barbarism to capitalism, tipping its hat along the way to slavery and feudalism, which held no more than subordinate places in building the bourgeois system. In a couple of centuries, the American people hurried through stages of social development that took the rest of mankind many thousands of years. But there was close connection between these two processes. If the rest of mankind had not already made these acquisitions, we Americans would not have been able to rush ahead so far and so fast. The tasks of pioneers are invariably harder and take far longer to accomplish.

The fusion of the antifeudal revolution in Europe with the wars of extermination against the Indians ushered in the bourgeois epoch of American history. This period has stretched over 450 years. It falls into three distinct phases, each marked off by revolutionary changes in American life.

The first period is that of colonial America, which extended from 1500 to the passage of the U. S. Constitution in 1788-89. If we analyze the social forms and economic forces of American life during these three centuries, colonial America, the formative period of our civilization, stands out as an exceptional blending of precapitalist agencies with the oncoming capitalist forms and forces of production. The tribal collectivism of the Indians was being transformed, pushed back, annihilated; remnants of feudalism were imported from Europe and transplanted here. The ranchos of southern California in the early nineteenth century had been preceded by colonial baronies; entire colonies such as Maryland and Pennsylvania were owned by landed proprietors who had been given title to them by the English monarchy. Big planters exploited white indentured servants and colored chattel slaves who in many places provided the main labor forces.

Alongside them were hundreds of thousands of small farmers, hunters, trappers, artisans, traders, merchants and others associated with the new forms of ownership and economic activity and animated by customs, feelings and ideas stemming from the capitalism which was advancing in Europe and now beginning to flourish on this side of the Atlantic.

The fundamental question posed by this development was — which would prevail, the precapitalist or the capitalist forces? This was the axis of the social struggles within the colonies and even of the incessant wars for possession of the New World among the European nations which characterized the colonial period. The showdown on this front came in the years between 1763 and 1789, the period of the preparation, outbreak, waging and conclusion of the first American Revolution. This was the first stage of the bourgeois-democratic revolution on this continent.

It assumed the form of a war between the rulers and supporters of Great Britain and the colonial masses led by representatives of the Northern merchants, bankers and manufacturers and planters of the Southern slave system, which was an appendage of growing native capitalism. The outcome of the contest determined the next stage in the destiny of American capitalism. If Great Britain's domination had persisted, that may have stunted and perverted the further development of bourgeois society here as it did in India and Africa.

The first American Revolution and its war for independence was a genuine people's movement. Such movements destroy much that has become rotten and is ready for burial. But, above all, they are socially creative, bringing to birth institutions which provide the ways and means for the next surge forward. That was certainly true of our first national revolution which is permanently embedded in the American and international consciousness. So powerful and persistent are its traditions that they are today a source of embarrassment to the capitalist rulers of this country in their dealings with the colonial movements for emancipation.

What were the notable achievements of this first stage of the North American bourgeois-democratic revolution? It overthrew the reactionary rule of the ten thousand merchants, bankers, landowners and manufacturers of Great Britain, who, after helping to spur the American colonies forward, had become the biggest block to their further advance. It gave independence to the colonies, unified them, and cleared away such feudal vestiges as the crown lands which the monarchy held. It democratized the states and gave them a republican form of government. It cleared the ground for a swift expansion of civilization in its native capitalist forms from the Atlantic to the Pacific.

The revolution had international repercussions. It inspired and protected similar movements during the next century in the Latin American colonies and even radiated back to the Old Continent. Read the diary of Gouverneur Morris, a financial leader of the Patriot Party, who became one of the early U. S. ambassadors to France. He was in Paris selling American properties to aristocrats who were threatened with exile by the French revolution. These clients complained to the sympathetic Morris that if only his countrymen had refrained from revolution, the French people would never have had the notion or courage to follow suit.

But even the most thoroughgoing revolution cannot do more than historical possibilities permit. Two serious shortcomings in the work of this first upheaval manifested themselves in the next decades. One was the fact that the revolution did not and could not eliminate the soil in which the institution of slavery was rooted. Many leaders of the time, among them Thomas Jefferson, hoped that slavery would wither away because of unfavorable economic conditions.

The second shortcoming was that although the revolt gave Americans political independence, it could not give thoroughgoing independence to the U. S. in a capitalist sense. This was true in two ways: at home the Northern capitalists had to share power with the Southern slave owners with whom they had waged the revolutionary war for independence and set up the new government; on the international market they remained in economic subordination to the more advanced industrial and financial structure of England.

The leaders of the revolution were aware of these deficiencies. The same Gouverneur Morris wrote to President George Washington from Paris on September 30, 1791:

> We shall . . . make great and rapid progress in useful manufactures. This alone is wanting to compleat our independence. We shall then be as it were a World by ourselves, and far from the Jars and Wars of Europe, their various revolutions will serve merely to instruct and amuse. Like the roaring of a Tempestuous Sea, which at a certain distance becomes a pleasing Sound.

However, a historical freak came along which upset this pleasant prospect. This freak was the result of a double revolution in technology, one which took place in Europe, especially in Europe, especially in English industry, and the other in American agriculture. The establishment of factories with steam-driven machinery in English industry, notably in textiles, its most important branch, created the demand for large supplies of cotton. The invention of the cotton gin enabled the Southern planters to supply that demand.

Consequently, slavery, which had been withering on the vine, acquired a new lease on life. This economic combination invested the nobles of the Southern Cotton Kingdom with tremendous wealth and power. A study of American history in the first half of the nineteenth century shows that its national and political life was dominated and directed by the struggle for supremacy waged by the forces centered around the Southern slaveholders on one side and those of the antislavery elements on the other. The crucial social issue before the nation was not always stated bluntly. But when every other conflict was traced to its roots, it was found to be connected with the question: What are we Americans going to do about slavery?

(A similar situation exists today in relation to capitalism. No matter what dispute agitates the political-economic life of this country, it sooner or later brings up the great social-economic question: What are we Americans going to do about capitalism?)

For the first fifty years of the nineteenth century, the cotton aristocrats of the South undeniably held center stage. They became very cocky about their power and privileges, which they thought would last indefinitely. Then, around 1850, conditions began to change quite rapidly. A new combination of social forces appeared that was to prove strong enough not only to challenge the slave power but to meet it in civil war, conquer and eliminate it.

It is highly instructive to study the mentality and outlook of the American people in 1848. That was a year of revolutions in the principal countries of western Europe. The people in the United States, including its governing groups, viewed these outbursts in an isolationist spirit.

The European revolutions even pleased certain sections of the ruling classes in the United States because they were directed mainly against monarchies. There were no monarchies here to overthrow, although there was a slave aristocracy rooted in the South. Although most of the common people in the United States sympathized with the European revolutions, they looked upon them as no more than a catching up with what had already been achieved in this country. The Americans said to themselves: "We've already had our revolution and don't need any more here. The quota of revolutions assigned to us by history is exhausted."

They did not see even fifteen years into their own future. The bourgeois-democratic revolution still had considerable unfinished business. During the 1850s, it became plainer that the Southern slaveholders were not only tightening their autocracy in the Southern states but were trying to make slaves of the entire population of the United States. This small set of rich men arrogated to themselves the right to tell the people what they could and could not do, where the country should expand, and how the affairs of America should and should not be managed.

So a second revolution proved necessary to complete those tasks left unsettled in the late eighteenth century and to dispose of the main problems that had confronted the American people in the meantime. There had to be thirteen years of preparatory struggles, four and a half years of civil war, twelve years of reconstruction — about thirty years in all, in this intense and inescapable revolutionary upheaval.

What is most important for us now are the net results of that travail. Every schoolchild knows that the slave power was abolished and the Negro population unshackled from chattel slavery. But the principal achievement of this revolution from the standpoint of American and world development was that the last of the internal impediments to the march of American capitalism were leveled, and the way cleared for the consolidation of capitalist rule.

That period saw the conclusion of the contest that had been going on since 1492 between the procapitalist and precapitalist forces on this continent. See what had happened to the peoples representing the diverse precapitalist ways of life. The Indians, who embodied savagery and barbarism, had either been exterminated, dispossessed or herded into reservations. England, which had upheld feudalism and colonial subjugation, had been swept aside and American industrial capital had attained not only political supremacy but economic independence. The Southern plantation owners, who were the final formidable precapitalist force to be pushed out of the road, had been smashed and expropriated by the Civil War and Reconstruction.

The capitalist rulers of the industrial system were then like the Count of Monte Cristo when he burst from prison and exclaimed, with so much wealth and newly gained liberty at

his command, "The world is mine!" And they have been acting on that premise ever since.

I would like now to make several observations on the economic and political development of American society from 1492
to the triumph of the capitalist class. As has already been
pointed out, private property in the means of production was
virtually nonexistent on this continent until the fifteenth century. Thereafter, as the white settlers spread, the dominant
trend was for all the means of production to pass into private
hands and be exploited along such lines. The land, for example, which had been tribally held, was cut up and appropriated by individuals or corporations from one end of the country to the other.

After the victory of the Northern bankers, merchants and
manufacturers in the middle of the nineteenth century, this
process moved on to a still higher plane. The means of production under private ownership became more and more con
centrated in corporate hands. Today an individual might be
able to build a single auto or airplane, but without many,
many million dollars he would not be able to compete in the
market with General Motors or Ford or Lockheed or Douglas.
Even so big a magnate as Henry J. Kaiser found that out
in auto.

Today there is hardly an acre of land without its title deed.
In fact, the Civil War promoted this process through the Home-
stead Act which gave 160 acres to private individuals, and
through other acts of Congress which handed over millions
of acres to railroad corporations. Insofar as the land was
distributed to small farmers, this was progressive because it
was the only way to hasten the development of agriculture
under the given conditions.

It is impossible to detail here the settlement and building of
the West and Middle West, but certain consequences of capitalist expansion deserve mention. First, as a result of this
capitalist expansion, the minds of average Americans, unlike
those of the Indians, have been so molded by the institutions
of private property that its standards can be thrown off only
with difficulty. The Europeans penetrated the America of the
Indians; and their descendants are venturing into outer space.
One extreme, absurd, but for that very reason most instructive, illustration of the effects of capitalist expansion on American consciousness appeared in a press dispatch from Illinois
with the headline: "Who Is the Owner of Outer-Space; Chicagoan
Insists that He Is." This news item followed:

With plans for launching man-made earth satellites now
in motion, the question was inevitable [inevitable, that is,
to Americans believing in the sacredness of private owner-
ship]: Who owns outer space?

Most experts agreed that the question was over their
heads. The rocket scientists said it was a problem for the
international law experts. The lawyers said they had no
precedents to go by. Only James T. Mangan, a fast-thinking
Chicago press agent, has a firm answer to the question
of space sovereignty. Mangan declares he owns outer space.
To back up his claim, he has a deed filed with the Cook
County (Chicago) Recorder. The deed, accepted after the
state's attorney's office solemnly upheld the claim in a
four-page legal opinion, seized "all space in all directions
from the earth at midnight," December 20, 1948.

Mangan declared that the statute of limitations for chal-
lenging the deed expires December 20, 1955, and added:
"The government has no legal right to space without my
permission."

If this be madness, yet there is method in it. That method
is the mainspring of the capitalist way of life. This gentle-
man, Mangan, is only logically extending to the exploration
of outer space the same acquisitive creed which guided our
founding fathers in taking over the American continent. This
particular fanatic of private property thinks the same law
is going to apply no matter how far into space we fly and
no matter how far we go into the future. He differs from other
exponents of capitalism only in the boldness and consistency
of his private-property logic.

The second point I want to deal with is the connection between evolution and revolution. These two phases of social
development are often opposed to each other as unconnected
opposites, irreconcilable alternatives. What does American history teach us about them? The American people have already
passed through two revolutionary periods in their national
history, each the culmination of lengthy periods of social progress on the basis of previous achievements.

During the interval between revolutions, relatively small
changes gradually occurred in people's lives. They consequently
took the given framework of their lives for granted, viewed
it as fixed and final, and found it hard to imagine a different
way. The idea of revolutionary change in their own lives and
lifetimes seemed fantastic or at least irrelevant. Yet it was dur-

ing those very periods of evolutionary progress that often unnoticed accumulations of changes prepared more drastic change.

The new class interests, which grew powerful but remained unsatisfied, the social and political conflicts, which recurred but remained unresolved, the shifts in the relations of antagonistic social forces kept asserting themselves in a series of disturbances until they reached an acute stage. The people of this country were not reckless. They made every attempt to find reasonable compromises between the contending forces, and often arrived at them. But after a while, these truces turned out to be ineffectual and short-lived. The irrepressible conflict of social forces broke out at higher stages until the breaking point was reached.

Look at the American colonists of 1763. They had just emerged — side-by-side with mother England — from a successful war against the French and the Indians. They did not anticipate that within ten years they would be fighting for their own freedom against England and alongside the very French monarchy they had fought in 1763. That would have been considered fantastic. Yet it happened only a little more than a decade later. Dr. Benjamin Rush, one of Pennsylvania's signers of the Declaration of Independence, observed in his *Autobiography* that:

> Not one man in a thousand contemplated or wished for the independence of our country in 1774, and but few of those who assented to it, foresaw the immense influence it would soon have upon the national and individual characters of the Americans.

So, too, the majority of Northerners, who enjoyed the economic boom in America from 1851 to 1857 — the biggest boom in the nineteenth century preceding the Civil War — little reckoned that as the result of domestic processes accelerated by that very prosperity, the country was going to be split on the slave question four years after the depression of 1857. Instead, they reasoned: Hadn't there been a compromise with the slaveholders in 1850 — and couldn't others be arrived at? Indeed, there were attempts at compromise up to the very outbreak of the Civil War, and even afterwards.

Of course, the Abolitionists at one extreme and the Southern "Fire-Eaters" at the other, prophesied a different course of development and, in their own ways, prepared for the coming revolution. But these radical voices on the left and the right were few and far between.

These crucial episodes in American history demonstrate that, under conditions of class society, periods of gradual social *evolution* prepare forces for the *revolutionary* solution of the accumulated and unfinished problems of peoples and nations. This revolutionary cleanup in turn creates the premises for a new and higher stage of evolutionary progress. This alternation is demonstrated with exceptional clarity by American history in the eighteenth and nineteenth centuries.

It is important to note, as a third point in dealing with the consequences of capitalist development in the United States, that our national revolutions stemmed directly from native conditions. Neither was imported by "outside agitators," although some, like Tom Paine, played important roles. They came from the ripening of conflicts between internal social forces. But this is only one side of the matter. The domestic struggles in turn were connected with, conditioned and determined by world economic and social development.

We pointed out earlier that the impetus for the overseas migration that changed the face of America came from the antifeudal bourgeois revolutions, which were transforming Europe; the conquest of our continent was an offshoot of those revolutions. The first American Revolution occurred during the era of commercial capitalism, which was the first stage in world capitalist development. Historically, it forms part of the series of bourgeois-democratic revolutions by which the capitalist class came to power on an international scale. The first American Revolution must be considered a child of the English bourgeois revolution of the mid-seventeenth century and a parent of sorts to the French bourgeois-democratic revolution of the late eighteenth century.

Trade in this era, not simply American but world trade, produced a powerful merchant class in the North, which was backed up by maritime workers and artisans in the coastal cities and by free farmers in the countryside. These became the shock troops of the Sons of Liberty. It is no accident that the bustling seaport of Boston, populated by rich merchants, who wanted to get out from under the thumb of Great Britain, and robust waterfront workers, longshoremen and sailors, stood in the forefront of the fight against Great Britain and that the revolutionary war itself was detonated by the British efforts to gag and strangle Boston.

The second American Revolution took place at the time of

the greatest expansion of industrial capitalism on both sides of the Atlantic. The years from 1848 to 1871, were punctuated by wars and revolutions. These conflicts did not mark the disintegration of world capital, as they do in the present century, but finally gave the capitalist class unmitigated supremacy in a series of countries in America and Europe.

The second stage of the bourgeois-democratic revolution in the United States, the Civil War, placed the Northern industrialists in the saddle. It was the outstanding revolutionary event of the entire period from 1848 to 1871, which began with the abortive French and German revolutions of 1848 and ended with the Franco-Prussian War and the Paris Commune of 1871. The decisive event of that period in world history was the U. S. capitalists' victory in this country, which heralded their ascent to world power.

With these lessons in mind, let us now look at the march of American society from the close of the Civil War period to today. Having reaped the fruits of two successful revolutions, the capitalists began to enjoy them. For them, revolution in America was a thing of the past; the United States would advance by small slow steps. Indeed, there has been a significant evolution of capitalist society on the foundation of the achievements of its previous revolutions. But in the dialectic of our national development, it is the very extraordinary expansion of the capitalist forces of production that has been preparing the elements for another, and this time a final, showdown between class forces that belong to different stages of economic and social evolution.

Since 1878, there have been two major trends in operation in this country. The predominant one to date has been the growing concentration of economic, political and cultural power in the hands of the monopolists. They have occasionally been challenged but never dislodged. Today they are open and insolent in the exercise of power. As Mr. Wilson of the biggest monopoly and the Defense Department has said: "What's good for General Motors is good for the country."

This echoes the assertion by an earlier absolute monarch, Louis XIV: "I am the state." The old regime of France had its funeral in 1789. Everything in this world — and this is especially true of political regimes and social systems under class society — includes within itself its own opposition, its own fatal opposition. This is certainly true of the power of capitalism which breeds its own nemesis in the productive — and political — capacities of wage labor.

The irony is that the greater the wealth of the capitalists, the stronger becomes the social position of the exploited workers from whom this wealth is derived. The United States has witnessed, side-by-side with the rise of monopoly capitalism, the emergence of an ever more strongly organized, centralized and unified labor movement. Ever since the capitalists and wage workers came into existence together, there have been differences, friction, outbursts of conflict, strikes, lockouts, between sections of these two classes. They arise from the very nature of their relations, which are antagonistic.

By and large, up to now, these conflicts have never gone beyond the bounds of the basic political and economic structure laid down by the Civil War. They have been subdued, reconciled or smoothed over. Despite all disturbances, the monopolist rulers have entrenched themselves more firmly in their paramount positions. However, a closer scrutiny of the development discloses that the working class occupies an increasingly influential, though still subordinate, place in our national life.

The question presents itself with renewed force: Will this situation of class stalemate—with the workers in a secondary position—continue indefinitely? The capitalists naturally answer that it can and must be so. Furthermore, they do everything from teaching in school the perpetual existence of the established class structure to passing antilabor laws to insure the continuance of the status quo. The union officialdom, for their part, go along with this general proposition.

Neither the capitalist spokesmen nor the AFL-CIO officialdom will find any precedent in American history to reinforce their expectations of an indefinite maintenance of the status quo. That is one lesson from our national past that the "long view" of socialism emphasizes. For many years, despite occasional tiffs, the American colonists got along with their mother country and even cherished the tie. Then came a very rapid and radical reversal in relations, a duel to the end. The same held true of the long coexistence of the Northern free states and Southern slavery. For sixty years, the Northerners had to play second fiddle to the Southern slave autocracy until the majority of people in the country came to believe that this situation would endure indefinitely. The slaveowners, like the capitalists of today, taught that their "American way of life" was the crown of civilization. But once the new combination of progressive forces was obliged to assert itself, the maturing differences broke out in a civil war which disposed of the old order. The political collaborators of yesterday turned into irreconcilable foes on the morrow.

The upholders of the status quo in this country can find still less support from the main trends of world history in our own time. In 1848, at a time when the capitalist classes on both sides of the Atlantic were toppling monarchies and feudal aristocracies, the pioneer communists first publicly proclaimed their ideas and started the movement of scientific socialism which has become the guide of the world working class in its struggle for emancipation. In 1917, sixty-nine years later, the first working-class state was set up in the Soviet Union. There was no other established for almost three decades.

Then came the second world war, which extended the domain of collectivized property throughout Eastern Europe, and afterwards the victory of the Chinese Revolution, which overturned capitalism in that major power in the East.

All this is tantamount to a colossal advance of world history. The essence of the new stage is that the movement for the advancement of capitalism, which had dominated world history from the sixteenth to the nineteenth centuries, has been succeeded on a world scale in the twentieth century by the anticapitalist movement of the socialist working class and its colonial allies.

Of course, it is not only the hope but the policy of the present capitalist holders of power that the achievements, ideas, and purposes of this revolutionary movement of the workers and colonial peoples can be contained in other parts of the world and crushed there. At any rate, the witch-hunters make every effort to keep its influences from these shores. Just as the British tyrants and the Southern slaveholders, each in their day, mustered all their resources to hold back the oncoming revolutionary forces in this land, so do the agents of the American plutocracy today. Will the monopolists succeed where their forerunners failed? Let us consider this question.

The high point of a revolutionary process consists in the transfer of supreme power from one class to another. What are the prevailing relationships of power in the United States? All basic decisions on foreign and domestic policy are made by the top capitalist circles to forward their aims and interests. Labor may be able to modify this or that decision or policy, but its influence does no more than curb the political power exercised by the monopolists.

However, there is a remarkable anomaly in such a relationship of forces. The now united union movement has about

17 million members. With their families, followers and friends, this movement can muster enough votes to give the political representatives of organized labor majority power in the cities, in the states, and in Washington. This means that the capitalists continue to exercise their sway by virtue of default, that is, a continued default of independent political action and organization by labor, or more precisely by its present leaders. They are failing to use one-thousandth of the power their movement presently and potentially possesses on behalf of the working people.

Organized labor has within its own grasp enough political strength, not to speak of its economic and social capacities, to be the sovereign force in this country. That is why any movement toward the formation of an independent party of labor based on the trade unions would have such highly revolutionizing implications upon the existing setup, regardless of the intentions or announced program of its organizers. Any such move on a massive scale would portend a shift in the power of supreme decision in the United States from capitalist to labor circles, just as the coming to Washington of the Republican Party in 1860 signified the shift of power away from the slaveholders to the Northern industrialists.

The Republican leaders of 1861 did not have revolutionary intentions. They headed a reformist party. They wanted to restrict the power of the slaveholders. But to do this involved upsetting the established balance of class forces. The slaveholders recognized the threat to their supremacy far more clearly and felt it more keenly than did the Northern Republican leaders themselves. That is why they initiated a counter-revolutionary assault in order to retrieve the power they had previously possessed.

The parallel with any national assumption of political power by the labor movement, even in a reformist way, is plain to see. Is such a shift possible? A succession of crucial shifts of power has marked the onward movement of the American people: from Britain to the colonial merchants and planters in the eighteenth century; and from the Southern slavocracy to the industrial capitalists in the nineteenth century. The thrust in the present period of our national history is toward another such colossal shift, this time from the ruling plutocracy to the rising working class and its allies among the oppressed minorities.

The whole course of economic, social and political development in this country in this century points to such a shift in power. Of course, the working class is far from predominant yet, and even less conscious of its historical mission. But, from the standpoint of the long view, it is most important to note the different rates of growth in the economic, social and political potentialities of the respective contenders for supreme power. Reviewing this country's history from 1876 to 1957, together with the rate of growth of the working-class movement on a world scale, the balance of forces has been steadily shifting, despite all oscillations, toward the side of working-class power. Nothing whatsoever, including imperialist war, the Taft-Hartley Act and McCarthyism, has been able to stop the momentum of the U. S. labor movement.

The supreme merit of scientific socialism is that it enables us to participate in this process by understanding it, by striving to influence it through all its stages, by giving it proper direction and speeding it up so that its great aims can be achieved most economically and efficiently. This job can be done in an organized fashion only through a revolutionary leadership and a Marxist party which understands its indispensable educational and organizational functions in the process.

Let us now return to Vincent Sheean, who popularized the phrase "the long view of history," and who was the inspiration for these remarks. Sad to say, this writer held the long view for a very short time. Uplifted by the revolutionary events of the 1920s, and transformed by the widespread radicalism of the 1930s, he had become a well-wisher of the socialist transformation of society, in his own way a partisan of the anti-imperialist cause, and even a sympathizer of Leninism. But, as the backward sweep in the tide of events and of political thought gained strength in this country with the approach of the second world war, Sheean joined the intellectuals in retreat. He slid from the socialist science of Marx and Lenin to the mysticism of Mahatma Gandhi. Let us leave him dozing and dreaming at the spinning wheel about the virtues of passive resistance to evil so long as he doesn't catch hold of any of us and try to pull us back with him.

It was a decisive step in the process of evolution, we pointed out, when the first creature acquired a backbone. There have been many relapses in the movement of history, especially in the world-shaking struggles of our own generation. Many people became frightened by the immensity of the tasks or crushed by adversity to the point of losing their moral and intellectual backbones and of losing sight of the direction of social evolution. This has happened in recent years to many more than Vincent Sheean both in labor and intellectual circles.

This "lost generation" has forgotten, if they ever learned, the supreme lesson of both world history and American history. This is that the forces making for the advancement of mankind have overcome the most formidable obstacles and have won out in the end. Otherwise, we should not be here to tell the tale or to help in making its next chapter.

Our animal ancestors progressed from the fish to the ape; our human ancestors have climbed upward from the ape to Republican President Eisenhower of the United States and conservative President Meany of the AFL-CIO. Along the way, they disposed of recalcitrant master classes, who, like the monopolists, refused to believe their sovereignty would ever end. Is it rational to think that men of their stripe are the ultimate representatives of the American nation and its labor movement or enduring shapers of the world's destiny, or that their reactionary policies and shortsighted outlook will prevail for decades?

The American people will bring forward in the future, as they have at critical times in the past, more audacious men and women with a vision of a new world in the making. These fighting leaders and leading fighters, guided by "the long view" of Marxism, will prove in practice that the socialist prospects of humanity, and of the American nation, are not so distant as they now appear.

3

From Lenin to Castro
The Role of the Individual in History Making

In the third chapter of *The Prophet Outcast,* the final volume of his biography of Trotsky, where he treats of "The Revolutionary as Historian," Isaac Deutscher discusses the role of personality in the determination of social events in a highly instructive context. The problem is raised in connection with Trotsky's appraisal of Lenin's place in the Russian Revolution.

Deutscher holds that Trotsky shuttled between two discordant positions. In the *History of the Russian Revolution,* a letter to Preobrazhensky in 1928, and in his *Diary in Exile,* Trotsky maintained that Lenin was absolutely indispensable to the victory of October. It would not have been achieved without him. Elsewhere, in *The Revolution Betrayed*, says Deutscher, Trotsky reverted to the orthodox view of historical materialism which subordinates the quality of the leadership to the more objective factors in the making of history. Is this a wavering on Trotsky's part?

Marxism does teach that no individual, however talented, strong-willed or strategically situated, can alter the main course of historical development, which is shaped by supra individual circumstances and forces. Therefore, reasons Deutscher, the revolution would have triumphed in 1917 with other leaders even if Lenin had been removed from the arena by some accident. Trotsky himself, or a team of other Bolshevik chiefs, might have filled his place.

Deutscher divines that Trotsky's lapse into a subjectivism bordering on "the cult of the individual" in regard to Lenin was motivated by a psychological need to exaggerate the role of individual leadership as a counterweight to Stalin's autocracy in his mortal political combat with him. He seeks to correct Trotsky by reference to the ideas expressed in Plekhanov's classical essay on *The Role of the Individual in History.* This was a polemic against the Narodnik school of subjective sociology which exalted the hero as an autonomous creator of history at the expense of the masses and other objective determinants of the class struggle. Arguing against the thesis that the collective demand for leadership could be supplied by only one remarkable individual, Plekhanov pointed out that the person hoisted into supreme authority bars the way of others who might have carried through the same tasks, though in a different style. The eclipse of alternate candidates creates the optical illusion of the sole irreplaceable personality. If the objective prerequisites are ripe and the historical demand forceful enough, a range of individuals can fulfill the functions of command.

The Chinese and Yugoslav examples, writes Deutscher, demonstrate how rising revolutions can utilize men of smaller stature than a Lenin or Trotsky to take power. The class struggle can press into service whatever human material is available to fulfill its objectives.

This theme has an importance surpassing Trotsky's judgment on Lenin's significance for the Russian Revolution or Deutscher's criticism of Trotsky's alleged inconsistencies on the matter. The reciprocal action of the objective and subjective factors in the historical process is one of the key problems of social science. It is no less a key to revolutionary practice in our own time.

Historical materialism unequivocally gives primacy, as Deutscher emphasizes, to such objective factors as the level of the productive forces and the state of class relations in the making of history. But there is more to the matter than this.

In the first place, the social phenomena divided into opposing categories are only relatively objective or subjective. Their status changes according to the relevant connections. If the world environment is objective to the nation which is part of it, the nation in turn is objective to the classes, which constitute its social structure. The ruling class is objective to the working class. The party is subjective to the class whose interests it represents, while groups, tendencies, factions and their combinations are subjective to the movement or party that contains them. Finally, the individual has a subjective status relative to all these other factors, although he has an objective existence in relation to other individuals.

In the second place, the multiple factors in any historical process do not, and indeed cannot, have an equal and simultaneous growth. Not only do some mature before others, but certain of them may fail to achieve a full and adequate reality at the decisive moment, or indeed at any point. The coming together of *all* the various factors essential for the occurrence of a particular result in a great historical process is an exceptional or "accidental" event which is necessary only in the long run.

The leadership, collective and individual, embodies the conscious element in history. The influence of an individual in determining a course of events can range from negligibility to totality. The extent of his effectiveness in action depends upon the stage of development of historical conditions, the correlation of social forces, and the person's precise connection with these at a given conjuncture.

There are long stretches of time when the strongest-willed revolutionist cannot in the least avail against the march of events and counts for practically nothing in redirecting them. On the other hand, there are "tides in the affairs of men which, taken at the flood, lead on to fortune."

Ordinarily, individual action takes place somewhere between these two extremes. What individuals do — or do not do — in their personal capacity affects to some limited degree the velocity and specific features of the main line of development.

The question is where and when can an individual exert the maximum weight and become the decisive force in the outcome of a struggle? This can happen only when the individual intervenes at the culminating point of a prolonged evolution, when all the other factors of a more objective sort have come into being. These set the stage for a decisive role and provide the means for carrying through the purposes and program of the movement he or she represents.

The individual who helps start a novel line of development in any field comes as the last link in the concatenation of events. We are all familiar with the straw that breaks the camel's back or the drop that overflows the cup. The individual who makes all the difference serves as the precipitant that transforms quantity into quality in the process whereby the new supersedes the old.

However, the individual must intervene at the critical turning point of development to have so decisive an influence. Such fortunate timing, which does not always depend upon the individual's own awareness, permits him to become the final cause in the cumulative sequence of conditions, which are necessary determinants of the outcome.

The discrepancy noted by Deutscher between Trotsky's observations that Lenin was indispensable for the October victory and that the objective laws of history are far more powerful than the special traits of the protagonists is to be explained by the difference between the short and the long run of history. The calculation of probabilities applies to human history as well as to natural events. Given enough chances in the long run, the forces representing the objective necessities of social progress will break through all obstacles and prove stronger than the defenses of the old order. But that is not necessarily true at any given stage or in any instance along the way. Here the quality of the leadership can decide which of the genuine alternatives growing out of the prevailing conditions will be realized.

The conscious factor has a qualitatively different import over an entire historical epoch than it has in a specific phase or situation within it. When antagonistic social forces vie for supremacy on a world-historical scale, such favorable and unfavorable circumstances as the character of the leadership tend to cancel one another. The underlying historical necessities assert themselves in and through the aggregate struggles and override the more superficial and chance features which can decide the upshot of any particular encounter. Moreover, an ascending class in the long run benefits more than its opponent from the accidents of development, since the receding class has less and less reserve strength to withstand small variations in the relation of forces. The total assets of one increase as those of the other diminish.

Time is an all-important element in the conflict of contending social forces. The indeterminate phase when events can be diverted in either direction does not last long. The crisis in social relations must be resolved quickly one way or the other. At that point, the activity or passivity of dominant personalities, groups, parties and masses can tip the scales on one side or the other. The individual can enter as the ultimate factor in the total process of historical determination only when all the other forces in play are temporarily equalized. Then the added weight can serve to tip the balance.

Almost everyone can recall occasions when his or her own intervention or that of others proved decisive in resolving an uncertain situation. What happens in the small incidents of life applies to big events. Just as the single vote of the chair can decide when the forces on an issue are evenly divided, so the outstanding qualities of great figures are manifested when history arrives at a deadlock. Their decision or decisiveness breaks the tie and propels events along a definite line.

This holds for counterrevolutionary as well as revolutionary tendencies. Hitler was important because he took Germany into fascism and war. But he did not direct German or world history into a qualitatively new channel. He simply helped write a further horrible chapter in the death agony of capitalism.

Lenin's imperishable contribution was the push he gave to opening an entirely new path for Russian and world history, redirecting it from the dead end of capitalism onto the beginning of socialism.

This brings us back to the specific problem Deutscher discusses. He does not question the fact that, in the actual unrolling of the 1917 revolution, Lenin functioned as the final cause in the October victory. The difference between Deutscher and Trotsky concerns the uncertain realm of historical possibilities. Could another revolutionist such as Trotsky, or a combination of them, have assumed Lenin's place?

Trotsky said categorically no. Deutscher objects that if others on hand could not have performed the same job of leadership, then the position of historical materialism on the lawful determination of events must be abandoned. Either the objective or the subjective factors decide; it is necessary to choose between them.

In my opinion, Deutscher here takes a too constricted and one-sided stand on historical determinism, whereas Trotsky employed a more flexible and multisided interpretation based upon the interrelation of mutually opposing categories. He tested his conception, first in practice, then in theory, in the successive stages of the Russian Revolution where the importance of the conscious factors stood out with remarkable clarity.

The type of leadership was very different in the two revolutions of 1917. The February Revolution was not planned or directed from above. Trotsky pointed out in the chapter of his *History of the Russian Revolution*, "Who Led the February Revolution?" that it was led "by conscious and tempered workers educated for the most part by the party of Lenin." As educator and organizer of these key workers, Lenin was to that extent necessary to the February overturn, even though he was not on the spot in person.

Between February and October he became more and more decisive because of his resolute and farsighted positions at a series of crucial moments, starting with the reorienting of the Bolshevik cadres in April and culminating in his insistence on insurrection in October. According to Trotsky, Lenin's role could not have been duplicated. This was not simply because of his personal gifts but even more because of his exceptional standing in the Bolshevik party, which was largely his creation.

The question of leadership in the Russian Revolution had a

dual aspect. While the Bolsheviks led the workers and peasants to victory, Lenin led the Bolshevik party. His paramount role came from the fact that he *led the leaders* of the revolution.

Trotsky knew better than anyone else how Lenin could sway the higher echelons as well as the ranks of his party. His authority was a considerable help from April to October in getting the correct proposals adopted over the resistance of other Bolshevik chiefs. This accumulated capital of prestige was not at the disposal of others, including Trotsky, who had a different organizational history and relations. That was the objective basis for his opinion that the October Revolution would most likely not have taken place unless "Lenin was present and in command."

To be sure, it is not possible, as Deutscher remarks and Trotsky himself recognized, to be utterly categorical on this point. But Trotsky's conclusion, in all his writings after October and before the rise of Stalin, was not based upon a regrettable lapse into subjectivity. It came from applying the Marxist dialectic to the facts as he witnessed and assayed them. If he was wrong, it was not because of any deviation in principle or method induced by unconscious political-psychological motives, which Deutscher considers to be the case, but the result of misjudging the facts.

Sidney Hook has entered this controversy from the opposite end. In a review of *The Prophet Outcast* in the May 11, 1964, *New Leader,* he seizes upon Deutscher's criticism of Trotsky's subjectivism for his own purposes. Instead of condemning, he compliments Trotsky for discarding the dogmas of dialectical materialism and attributing "the most important social event in human history" to the purely personal and contingent circumstance of Lenin's presence in Russia. In his eyes, the October Revolution was the accidental consequence of the work of an individual. Hook repeats the view expressed in his book on *The Hero in History,* cited by Deutscher, that the October Revolution "was not so much a product of the whole past of Russian history as a product of one of the most event-making figures of all time."

Whereas Deutscher in the name of Marxist orthodoxy inclines to make the objective factors virtually self-sufficient and thus underrates the crucial importance of Lenin's leadership, Hook practically nullifies the prior determinants by making the October victory wholly dependent upon a single individual. His approach falls below the standards of the most enlightened liberal historians, who at least placed objective factors on a par with the ideas and intervention of great individuals.

Hook has to falsify Trotsky's standpoint in order to convert him into a pragmatist as superficial as Hook himself. Trotsky's *History* is explicitly devoted to demonstrating the *necessity of the Russian Revolution and its specific outcome* as the result of the whole previous evolution of world capitalism, the backwardness of Russia complemented by its concentrated industrial enterprises and advanced working class, the stresses of the first world war upon a decayed czarist autocracy, the weaknesses of the bourgeoisie, the failure of the petty-bourgeois parties and the bold vision of the Bolsheviks headed by Lenin.

Trotsky delineates the operation of this determinism in living reality by narrating and analyzing the interconnection of the salient events from the February beginning to the October climax. The successive stages of the revolution did not unfold haphazardly; they issued with inexorable lawfulness one from the other in a causally conditioned sequence. The aim of his theoretical exposition was to find in the verified facts of the actual process the effects of the objective necessities formulated in the laws of the class struggle applied to a backward great power under twentieth-century conditions. He had already anticipated and articulated these in his celebrated theory of the permanent revolution.

Trotsky viewed the Bolshevik party as one of the components of this historical necessity, and Lenin as the most conscious exponent and skilled practitioner of the political science of Marxism based on these laws. It was not purely fortuitous that Lenin was able to play the role that he did. He was no chance comer. "Lenin was not an accidental element in the historic development, but a product of the whole past of Russian development." For years he had prepared himself and his party for the task of steering the expected revolution to victory.

There was no foreordination in the preconditions for October extending from the history of Russia to the political foresight and insight of Lenin. Their joint necessity was proved in practice. Nor was the actual course of events realized without the concurrence of many accidental circumstances favorable or unfavorable to both sides.

It was, for example, a lucky chance that the German general staff for its own reasons permitted Lenin to travel from exile in Switzerland back to Russia through Germany in time to redirect the Bolshevik party. It was a historical accident that Lenin remained alive and active throughout the crucial months; it could have been otherwise and, indeed, Lenin thought his murder quite probable. In that case, if we credit Trotsky, the socialist outcome implicit in the situation could not have been achieved in 1917.

This means that the history of the twentieth century, now unthinkable apart from the Russian Revolution in all its consequences, would have been quite different—not in the broadest lines of its development but certainly in the particular course of the irrepressible contest between the socialist revolution and its capitalist antagonists.

There is nothing un-Marxist, as Deutscher seems to think, in acknowledging this. To link "the fortunes of mankind in this century" with Lenin's activity in 1917 is not subjectivist thinking; it is a matter of fact. Conversely, Lenin's absence could well have subtracted that margin of determinism from the conditions required for victory, which would have made the subsequent sequence of developments in the world revolution quite different.

The great fortune of the Russian people and all mankind is that in 1917 *both accident and necessity coincided* to carry the struggle of workers and peasants to its proper conclusion. This has not always happened in the decades since.

Deutscher weakens his case considerably by focusing attention on Russia. The role of Lenin and his party stands out more clearly in light of the defeats suffered by the working class elsewhere in Europe and Asia during the twenties and thirties because of the lack of a collective and individual leadership of Bolshevik-Leninist caliber. The October victory coupled with the post-October defeats convinced the once dubious Trotsky of the decisive role of leadership in an objectively revolutionary situation. These experiences led him to the generalization that was the keystone of the founding program of the Fourth International, adopted in 1938, that "the historical crisis of mankind is reduced to the crisis of revolutionary leadership." That is why he dedicated the last years of his life to the task of attempting to assemble such a leadership under the banner of the Fourth International.

Deutscher's disagreement with Trotsky over Lenin's part in the Russian Revolution is directly connected with his difference with Trotsky over the latter's role in the post-Lenin period. Deutscher regards Trotsky's assertion that the foundation of the Fourth International was "the most important work of my life—more important than 1917, more important than the period of the civil war, or any other . . ." as an aberration. The energy devoted to the Trotskyist groups was largely wasted, he believes, because the objective conditions were not suitable for constructing a new International. In his opinion, Trotsky would have been better advised to remain an interpreter of events instead of trying to change their course by means of a rival world revolutionary organization.

J. B. Stuart undertook to answer Deutscher's criticism of Trotsky's unrealism in connection with the Fourth International in the April 17 and 24, 1964, issues of *World Outlook,* and there is no point in repeating his arguments. Here we are primarily interested in the real rationale behind Trotsky's positions.

Deutscher contends that Trotsky misjudged Lenin's importance in the winning of the Russian Revolution, and his own role in the period of world reaction after Lenin's death, for psychological reasons which ran counter to Marxist objectivity. Trotsky actually derived his position in both cases, it seems to us, from his conception of the demands of the revolutionary process in our time. He thought that all the major objective conditions for the overthrow of capitalism had ripened. What was missing for new Octobers was the presence of leadership of the type supplied by Lenin and the Bolsheviks in 1917. Such cadres had to be created to prevent the incompetent and treacherous bureaucracies heading the different sectors of the workers' movement from ruining more revolutionary opportunities. Thus, world political, rather than individual psychological, necessities accounted for his conclusions.

It is true, as Deutscher points out, that revolutionary power was conquered in Yugoslavia and China with leaderships trained in the Stalinist school which do not match the standards of Lenin's Bolshevism. The 1963 Reunification Congress of the Fourth International took cognizance of this development in its resolution, *The Dynamics of World Revolution Today:* "The weakness of the enemy in the backward countries has opened the possibility of coming to power even with a blunted instrument."

However, the document hastens to add: "The strength of the enemy in the imperialist countries demands a tool of much greater perfection." For the taking of power in the capitalist strongholds as well as the administration of power in the degenerated or deformed workers' states, the building of new mass revolutionary parties and their unification in a new international organization remains the central strategic task of the present period, no less than in Lenin's and Trotsky's day.

This dialectical unity of the objective and subjective factors

in the making of a revolution has been both exemplified and
theorized by Fidel Castro and his close associates. If ever an
historic event could be considered the work of one man, that
was — and is — the Cuban Revolution. Castro is truly its "lider
maximo" [main leader].

Castro has explained, notably in his December 21, 1961,
speech on Marxism-Leninism, that the founders of the July 26
Movement did not wait for *all* the objective conditions required
for revolutionary success to emerge spontaneously. They de-
liberately set about creating the still missing revolutionary
conditions by fighting. Their guerrilla warfare did bring about
the moral, psychological, political changes needed to overthrow
Batista's tyranny.

The transformation of the balance of forces in favor of the
progressive side by the initiative of a small band of conscious
revolutionary fighters in Cuba dramatically demonstrates how
decisive the subjective factor can be in making history. Yet
Castro's intentions would have miscarried and his combatants
would have been rendered powerless without the response they
received, first from the peasants in the mountains and then
from the masses in the rural and urban areas.

Events ninety miles from Cuba have highlighted the twofold aspects of the individual's weight in history-making. Kennedy's assassination in November 1963 did not seriously in-
terrupt any operations of the U. S. government or shift its
course at home or abroad. After assuming executive authority,
Johnson pursued essentially the same policies as his predecessor, albeit with a Texas brand rather than a Harvard accent.
Thus, the abrupt removal of an extremely popular and powerful personality proved to be inconsequential compared to the
automatism of capitalist rulership. Procapitalist individuals
come and go. The system remains.

At the same time, the holder of supreme office in the United
States controls more massive military power than any other
person in human history. On June 4, 1964, Johnson boasted
that the national strength "is stronger than the combined might
of all the nations in the history of the world."

The president can release enough nuclear missiles to destroy
all mankind. Who can question the overwhelming importance
of the individual when one man's decision can terminate human history on this planet? Kennedy was eyeball to eyeball
with this possibility during the 1962 Caribbean crisis.

To be sure, the man in the White House does not act as
an isolated individual. He is the chief executive of the United
States, commander in chief of its armed forces, and more sig-

nificantly, agent of the profiteers who run the economy and government. His personal role by and large accords with the objective necessities of monopolist domination; and, in the last analysis, the fundamental interests of the ruling class determine his political conduct.

But his representative functions do not nullify the fact that he alone is delegated to make the final decision and can give the command to press the H-button.

Personal decision is the crowning expression of social determinism, the last link in its causal chain. The social determinism operative in the world today is divided into two irreconcilable trends, stemming from opposing class sources. One is directed by the capitalist war-makers, whose spokesmen in the United States have stated that they will not refrain from using atomic weapons if necessary. The other is constituted by the masses of the United States and the rest of the world who dread this prospect and have everything to lose if it should occur.

Which of these contending determinisms will prevail? The fate of mankind hangs in the balance of this decision. To dispossess and disarm the atomaniacs headquartered in Washington, a revolutionary movement of tremendous dimensions and determination will have to be built. No single individual will stop them. But victory in the life-and-death struggle for world peace against nuclear annihilation will require the initiative and devotion of *individuals* who, though they may not possess the outstanding leadership capacities of a Lenin, Trotsky or Castro, can act in their spirit.

4

Uneven and Combined
Development in World History

The Uneven Course of History

This essay aims to give a comprehensive explanation of one of the fundamental laws of human history — the law of uneven and combined development. This is the first time, to my knowledge, that this has been undertaken. I shall try to show what this law is, how it has worked out in history, and how it can clarify some of the most puzzling social phenomena and political problems of our age.

The law of uneven and combined development is a scientific law of the widest application to the historic process. This law has a dual character or, rather, it is a fusion of two closely connected laws. Its primary aspect deals with the different rates of growth among the various elements of social life. The second covers the correlation of these unequally developed factors in the historic process.

The principal features of the law can be briefly summarized as follows: the mainspring of human progress is man's command of the forces of production. As history advances, there occurs a faster or slower growth of productive forces in this or that segment of society, owing to the differences in natural conditions and historical connections. These disparities give either an expanded or a compressed character to entire historical epochs and impart varying rates and extents of growth to different peoples, different branches of economy, different classes, different social institutions and fields of culture. This is the essence of the law of uneven development.

The variations among the multiple factors in history provide the basis for the emergence of exceptional phenomena in which features of a lower stage are merged with those of a superior stage of social development. These combined formations have a highly contradictory character and exhibit marked peculiarities. They may deviate so much from the rule and effect such an upheaval as to produce a qualitative leap in social evolution and enable a formerly backward people to outdistance, for a certain time, one more advanced. This is the gist of the law of combined development.

It is obvious that these two laws, or these two aspects of a single law, do not stand upon the same level. The unevenness of development must precede any combinations of the disproportionately developed factors. The second law grows out of and depends upon the first, even though it reacts back upon it and affects its further operation.

The discovery and formulation of this law is the outcome of over 2,500 years of theoretical investigation into the modes of social development. The first observations upon which it is based were made by the Greek historians and philosophers. But the law itself was first brought into prominence and consistently applied by the founders of historical materialism, Marx and Engels, over a century ago. This law is one of Marxism's greatest contributions to a scientific understanding of history and one of the most powerful instruments of historical analysis.

Marx and Engels derived the essence of this law from the dialectical philosophy of Hegel. Hegel utilized the law in his works on universal history and the history of philosophy without, however, giving it any special name or explicit recognition.

Many dialectically minded thinkers before and since Hegel have likewise used this law in their studies and applied it more or less consciously to the solution of complex historical, social and political problems. All the outstanding theoreticians of Marxism, from Kautsky and Luxemburg to Plekhanov and Lenin, grasped its importance, observed its operations and consequences, and used it for the solution of problems that baffled other schools of thought.

Let me cite an example from Lenin. He based his analysis of the first stage of the Russian Revolution in 1917 upon this law. In his *Letters from Afar,* he wrote to his Bolshevik collaborators from Switzerland: "The fact that the [February] revolution succeeded so quickly . . . is due to an unusual historical conjuncture where there combined, in a strikingly 'favorable' manner, absolutely dissimilar movements, absolutely different class interests, absolutely opposed political and social tendencies" (*Collected Works,* Book 1, p. 31).

What had happened? A section of the Russian nobility and landowners, the oppositional bourgeoisie, the radical intellectuals, the insurgent workers, peasants and soldiers, along with the Allied imperialists — these "absolutely dissimilar" social forces — had momentarily arrayed themselves against the czar-

ist autocracy, each for its own reasons. Together, they be-
sieged, isolated and overthrew the Romanov regime. This extraordinary conjuncture of circumstances and unrepeatable combination of forces had grown out of the previous unevenness
of Russian historical development with all its still unsolved
social and political problems exacerbated by the first imperialist world war.

The differences that had been submerged in the offensive
against czarism reasserted themselves after February; and it
did not take long for this de facto alliance of inherently opposing forces to disintegrate. The allies of February 1917 were
transformed into the irreconcilable foes of October 1917.

How did this hostility come about? The overthrow of czarism had in turn produced a new unevenness in the situation,
which may be summarized in the following formula: on one
hand, the objective conditions were ripe for the assumption
of power by the workers; on the other hand, the Russian working class, and above all its leadership, had not yet correctly
appraised the situation or tested the new relationship of forces.
Consequently, they were subjectively unready to take power.
The unfolding of the class struggles from February to October 1917 may be said to consist in the growing recognition
by the working class and its revolutionary leaders of what
had to be done and in overcoming the disparity between the
objective conditions and the subjective preparation. The gap
was closed in action by the triumph of the Bolsheviks in the
October Revolution, which combined the proletarian conquest
of power with the widespread peasant uprising.

This process is fully explained by Trotsky in his *History
of the Russian Revolution.* The Russian Revolution itself was
the most striking example of uneven and combined development in modern history. In his classic analysis of this mo-
mentous event, Trotsky gave to the Marxist movement the
first explicit formulation of that law.

Trotsky, the theoretician, is most celebrated as the originator
of the theory of the permanent revolution. It is likely that his
exposition of the law of uneven and combined development
will come to be ranged by its side in value. He not only gave
this law its name but was also the first to evaluate its full
significance.

These two contributions to the scientific understanding of
social movement are in fact intimately linked. Trotsky's conception of the permanent revolution resulted from his study
of the peculiarities of Russian historical development in the
light of the new problems presented to world socialism in the
epoch of imperialism. These problems were especially acute

and complex in backward countries where the bourgeois-democratic revolution had not yet taken place, at a time when the
proletarian revolution was already at hand. The fruits of his
thinking on these questions, confirmed by the actual developments of the Russian Revolution, prepared and stimulated his
subsequent elaboration of the law of uneven and combined
development.

Indeed, Trotsky's theory of the permanent revolution represents the most fruitful application of this very law to the
key problems of the international class struggles in our own
time, the epoch of the transition from the capitalist domination
of the world to socialism. However, the law itself is not only
pertinent to the revolutionary events of the present epoch but,
as we shall see, to the whole compass of social evolution.
And it has even broader applications than that.

So much for the historical background from which the law
of uneven and combined development has emerged. Let us
now consider the scope of its application. Although having originated in the study of modern history, the law of uneven and
combined development is rooted in features common to all
processes of growth in nature as well as in society. Scientific
investigators have emphasized the prevalance of unevenness
in many fields. All the constituent elements of a thing, all the
aspects of an event, all the factors in a process of development
are not realized at the same rate or to an equal degree. Moreover, under differing material conditions, even the same thing
exhibits different rates of growth. Every rural farmer and
urban gardener knows that.

In *Life of the Past*, G. G. Simpson, one of the foremost authorities on evolution, develops this point:

> The most striking things about rates of evolution are
> that they vary enormously and that the fastest of them
> seem very slow to humans (including paleontologists, I
> may say). If any one line of phylogeny is followed in
> the fossil record it is always found that different charac-
> ters and parts evolve at quite different rates, and it is gen-
> erally found that no one part evolves for long at the same
> rate. The horse brain evolved rapidly while the rest of the
> body was changing very little. Evolution of the brain was
> much more rapid during one relatively short span than at
> any other time. Evolution of the feet was practically at a
> standstill most of the time during horse evolution, but three
> times there were relatively rapid changes in foot mech-
> anism.
> Rates of evolution also vary greatly from one lineage

to another, even among related lines. There are a number of animals living today that have changed very little for very long periods of time: a little brachiopod called Lingula, in some 400 million years; Limulus, the horseshoe "crab" — really more of a scorpion than a crab — in 175 million or more; Sphenodon, a lizard-like reptile now confined to New Zealand, in about 150 million years; Didelphis, the American oppossum, in a good 75 million years. These and the other animals for which evolution essentially stopped long ago all have relatives that evolved at usual or even at relatively fast rates.

There are, further, characteristic differences of rates in different groups. Most land animals have evolved faster than most sea animals — a generalization not contradicted by the fact that some sea animals have evolved faster than some land animals (pp. 137-38).

The evolution of entire orders of organisms has passed through a cycle of evolution marked by an initial phase of restricted, slow growth, followed by a shorter but intense period of "explosive expansion," which in turn settled down into a prolonged phase of lesser changes.

In *The Meaning of Evolution,* G. G. Simpson states, "The times of rapid expansion, high variability and beginning adaptive radiation . . . are periods when enlarged opportunities are presented to groups able to pursue them." Such an opportunity for explosive expansion was opened to the reptiles when they evolved to the point of independence from water as a living medium and burst into landscapes earlier barren of vertebrate life. Then a "quieter period ensues when the basic radiation has been completed" and the group can indulge in "the progressive enjoyment of a completed conquest" (pp. 72-73).

The evolution of our own species has already gone through the first phase of such a cycle and entered the second. The immediate animal forerunners of mankind went through a prolonged period of restricted growth as a lesser breed compared to others. Mankind arrived at its phase of "explosive expansion" only in the past million years or so, after the primate from which we are descended acquired the necessary social powers. However, the further development of mankind will not duplicate the cycle of animal evolution because the growth of society proceeds on a qualitatively different basis and is governed by its own unique laws.

The evolution of the distinctive human organism has been

marked by considerable irregularity. The skull developed its present characteristics among our ape ancestors long before the development of our flexible hands with the opposable thumb. It was only after our prototypes had acquired upright posture and working hands that the brain inside the skull expanded to its present proportions and complexity.

What is true of entire orders and species of animals and plants holds good for its individual specimens. If equality prevailed in biological growth, each of the various organs in the body would develop simultaneously and to the same proportionate extent. But such perfect symmetry is not to be found in real life. In the growth of the human fetus, some organs emerge before others and mature before others. The head and the neck are formed before the arms and legs, the heart at the third week and the lungs later on. As the sum of all these irregularities, we know that infants come out of the womb in different conditions, even with deformations, and certainly at varying intervals between conception and birth. The nine-month gestation period is no more than a statistical average. The date of delivery of a given baby can diverge by days, weeks or months from this average. The frontal sinus, a late development in the primates, possessed only by the great apes and men, does not occur in young humans, but emerges after puberty. In many cases, it never develops at all.

The development of social organization, and of particular social structures, exhibits unevenness no less pronounced than the life-histories of biological beings from which it has emerged with the human race. The diverse elements of social existence have been created at different times, have evolved at widely varying rates, and grown to different degrees under different conditions and from one era to another.

Archaeologists divide human history into the Stone, Bronze and Iron Ages according to the materials used in making tools and weapons. These three stages of technological development have had immensely different spans of life. The Stone Age lasted for around 900 thousand years; the Bronze Age dates from 3000-4000 B. C.; the Iron Age is less than four thousand years old. Moreover, different sections of mankind passed through these stages at different dates in different parts of the world. The Stone Age ended before 3500 B. C. in Mesopotamia, about 1600 B. C. in Denmark, 1492 in America, and not until 1800 in New Zealand.

A similar unevenness in time-spans marks the evolution of social organization. Savagery, when men lived by collecting food through foraging, hunting or fishing, extended over many hundreds of thousands of years while barbarism, which is based upon breeding animals and raising crops for food, dates back to about 8000 B. C. Civilization is little more than six thousand years old.

The production of regular, ample and growing food supplies effected a revolutionary advance in economic development which elevated food-producing peoples above backward tribes that continued to subsist on the gathering of food. Asia was the birthplace of both domestication of animals and of plants. It is uncertain which of these branches of productive activity preceded the other, but archaeologists have uncovered remains of mixed farming communities which carried on both types of food production as early as 8000 B. C.

There have been purely pastoral tribes, which depended exclusively on stock-raising for their existence, as well as wholly agricultural peoples, whose economy was based on the cultivation of cereals or tubers. The cultures of these specialized groups underwent a one-sided development by virtue of their particular type of production of the means of life. The purely pastoral mode of subsistence did not, however, contain the potentialities of development inherent in agriculture. Pastoral tribes could not incorporate the higher type of food production into their economies on any scale, without having to settle down and alter their entire mode of life, particularly after the introduction of the plough, which superseded the slash-and-burn techniques of gardening. They could not develop an extensive division of labor and go forward to village and city life, so long as they remained simply herders of stock.

The inherent superiority of agriculture over stockbreeding was demonstrated by the fact that dense populations and high civilizations could develop on the basis of agriculture alone, as the Aztec, Inca and Mayan civilizations of Central and South America proved. Moreover, the agriculturalists could easily incorporate domesticated animals into their mode of production, blending food cultivation with stockbreeding and even transferring draft animals to the technology of agriculture through the invention of the plough.

It was the *combination* of stockbreeding and cereal cultivation in mixed farming that prepared inside barbaric society the elements of civilization. This combination enabled the agricultural peoples to outstrip the purely pastoral tribes and, in the favorable conditions of the river valleys of Mesopotamia, Egypt, India and China, to become the nurseries of civilization.

Since the advent of civilization, peoples have existed on three essentially different levels of progress corresponding to their modes of securing the necessities of life: the food-gatherers, the elementary food-producers, and the mixed farmers with a highly developed division of labor and a growing exchange of commodities. The Greeks of the classical age were very highly conscious of the disparity in development between themselves and the backward peoples around them who remained at earlier, lower stages of social existence. They drew a sharp distinction between civilized Greeks and barbarians. The historical connection and distance between them was articulated by the historian Thucydides who said, "The Greeks lived once as the barbarians live now."

The unevenness of world historical development has seldom been more conspicuously exhibited than when the aboriginal inhabitants of the Americas were first brought face to face with the white invaders from Europe. At this juncture, two completely separate routes of social evolution, the products of from ten to twenty thousand years of independent development in the two hemispheres, encountered each other. Both were forced to compare their rates of growth and measure their respective achievements. This was one of the sharpest confrontations of different cultures in all history.

At this point, the Stone Age collided with the late Iron and the early Machine Age. In hunting and in war, the bow and arrow had to compete with the musket and cannon; in agriculture, the hoe and the digging stick with the plough and draft animals; in water transportation, the canoe with the ship; in land locomotion, the human leg with the horse and the bare foot with the rolling wheel. In social organization, tribal collectivism ran up against feudal-bourgeois institutions and customs; production for immediate community consumption against a money economy and international trade.

The contrasts between the American Indians and the West Europeans could be multiplied. However, the inequality of the human products of such widely separated stages of economic development was starkly apparent. They were so antagonistic and removed from each other that the Aztec chiefs at first identified the white newcomers with gods while the Europeans reciprocated by regarding the natives as animals.

The historical inequality in productive and destructive powers in North America was not overcome by the Indian adoption of white man's ways and their gradual, peaceful assimilation into class society. On the contrary, it led to the dispossession and annihilation of the Indian tribes over the next four centuries.

But if the white settlers displayed their material superiority over the native peoples, they themselves were far behind their motherlands. The backwardness of the North American continent and its colonies compared with Western Europe predetermined the development here from the start of the fifteenth century to the middle of the nineteenth century. The central historical task of the Americans throughout this period was to catch up with Europe by overcoming the disparities in the social development of the two continents. How and by whom this was done has been the theme of American history for three and a half centuries.

It required, among other things, two revolutions to complete the job. The colonial revolution, which crowned the first stage of progress, gave the American people political institutions more advanced than any in the Old World — and paved the way for rapid economic expansion. Even after winning national independence, the United States had still to win its economic independence within the capitalist world. The economic gap between this country and the nations of Western Europe was narrowed in the first half of the nineteenth century and virtually closed up by the triumph of Northern industrial capitalism over the slave power in the Civil War. It did not take long after that for the United States to come abreast of the West European powers and to outstrip them.

These changes in the international position of the United States illustrate the unevennesses in the development between the metropolitan centers and the colonies, between the different continents, and between countries on the same continent.

A comparison of the diverse modes of production in the various countries brings out their unevenness most sharply. Slavery had virtually vanished as a mode of production on the mainland of Europe before it was brought to America — thanks to the needs of these very same Europeans. Serfdom had disappeared in England before it arose in Russia . . . and there were attempts to implant it in the North American colonies after it was on the way out in the mother country. In Bolivia, feudalism flourished under the Spanish conquerors and slavery languished, while in the Southern English colonies, feudalism was stunted and slavery flourished.

Capitalism was highly developed in Western Europe while only meagerly implanted in Eastern Europe. A similar disparity in capitalist development prevailed between the United States and Mexico.

Disparities in the quantity and quality of social formations in the course of their developments are so conspicuous that Trotsky terms unevenness "the most general law of the historic process" (*History of the Russian Revolution*, p. 5). These inequalities are the specific expressions of the contradictory nature of social progress, of the dialectics of human development.

They occurred even at the lowest stages of social evolution. In *New Light on Ancient America*, the anthropologist Ralph Linton tells us that, in passing over from savagery toward barbarism, the central areas of progress among the American Indians changed places. "As long as the Americans remained in a hunting, food-gathering economy, northern North America was culturally the most advanced part of the continent. None of the preagricultural cultures that have been found south of the Great Plains and Northern Woodland areas compares with those of these areas in richness of content. With the rise of agriculture-based civilizations in Middle America, the situation was reversed. The main line of diffusion was now from south to north, and Middle American influences become increasingly recognizable over the whole area east of the Rockies."

The inequality of development between continents and countries is matched by an equally uneven growth of the various elements within each social grouping or national organism.

In a book on the American working class written by Karl Kautsky early in this century, the German Marxist pointed out some of the marked contrasts in the social development of Russia and the United States at that time. "Two States exist," he wrote, "diametrically opposed to each other, each of which contains an element inordinately developed in comparison with their standard of capitalist production. In one State—America—it is the capitalist class. In Russia it is the proletariat. In no other country but America is there so much ground for speaking of the dictatorship of capital, while the proletariat has nowhere acquired such importance as in Russia." This difference in development, which Kautsky described in the bud, has since become enormously accentuated.

In the opening chapter of his *History of the Russian Revolution*, "Peculiarities of Russia's Development," Trotsky gave a superb analysis of the significance of such unevenness for explaining the course of a nation's history. Czarist Russia contained social forces belonging to three different stages of historical development. On top were the feudal elements: an overgrown Asiatic autocracy, a state clergy, a servile bureaucracy, a favored landed nobility. Below them were a weak, unpopular bourgeoisie and a cowardly intelligentsia. These opposing phenomena were organically connected. They constituted different aspects of a unified social process. The very historical conditions which had preserved and fortified the feudal forces — the slow tempo of Russian development, her economic backwardness, her primitive social forms and low level of culture — had stunted the growth of the bourgeois forces and fostered their social and political feebleness.

That was one side of the situation. On the other side, the extreme backwardness of Russian history had left the agrarian and the national problems unsolved, producing a discontented, land-hungry peasantry and oppressed nationalities longing for freedom; furthermore, the late appearance of capitalist industry gave birth to highly concentrated industrial enterprises under the domination of foreign finance capital and an equally concentrated proletariat armed with the latest ideas, organizations and methods of struggle.

The sharp unevenness in the social structure of czarist Russia set the stage for the revolutionary events which started with the overthrow of a decayed medieval structure in 1917 and concluded in a few months with the rise of the proletariat and the Bolshevik Party to power. It is only by analyzing that unevenness that it is possible to grasp why the Russian Revolution took place as it did.

The pronounced irregularities to be found in history have led some thinkers to deny that there is, or can be, any causality or lawfulness in social development. The most fashionable school of American anthropologists, headed by the late Franz Boas, explicitly denied that there were any determinate sequence of stages to be discovered in social evolution and denied that the expressions of culture are shaped by technology or economy. According to R. H. Lowie, the foremost exponent of this view, cultural phenomena present merely a "planless hodgepodge," a "chaotic jumble." The "chaotic jumble" is all in the heads of these antimaterialists and anti-evolutionists, not in the history or the constitution of society.

It is possible for people living under Stone Age conditions in the twentieth century to possess a radio, though not to manufacture one. But it would be categorically impossible to find such a product of contemporary electronics buried with human remains in a Stone Age deposit of twenty thousand years ago.

It does not take much penetration to see that the activities of food-gathering, foraging, hunting, fishing and fowling existed long before food-production in the forms of gardening or stockbreeding. Or that stone tools preceded metal; speech came before writing; cave-dwellings before house-building; camps before villages; the exchange of goods before money. On a general historical scale, these sequences are absolutely inviolable.

The main characteristics of the social structures of savages are determined by their primitive methods of producing the means of life, which, in turn, depend upon the low level of their productive forces. It is estimated that food-gathering peoples require from four to forty square miles per capita to maintain themselves. They could neither produce nor maintain large concentrations of population on such an economic foundation. The groups usually numbered fewer than forty persons and seldom exceeded a hundred. Their scanty food supply and dispersion of forces set strict limits to their development.

What about the next higher stage of social development, barbarism? The noted archaeologist, V. Gordon Childe, has published in a book called *Social Evolution* a survey of the "successive steps through which barbarian cultures actually passed on the road to civilization in contrasted natural environments." He acknowledges that the starting point in the economic sphere was identical in all cases, "inasmuch as all the first barbarian cultures examined were based on the cultivation of the same cereals and the breeding of the same species of animals." That is to say, barbarism is marked off from savage forms of life by the acquisition and application of the higher productive techniques of agriculture and stock-raising.

He further points out that the final result — civilization — although exhibiting concrete differences in each case, "yet everywhere did mean the aggregation of large populations in cities; the differentiation within these of primary producers (fishers, farmers, etc.), full-time specialist artisans, merchants, officials, priests and rulers; an effective concentration of the economic and political power; the use of conventional symbols for recording and transmitting information (writing), and equally conventional standards of weights and measures, and of measures of time and space leading to some mathematical and calendrical science."

At the same time, Childe points out that "the intervening steps in development do not exhibit even abstract parallelism." The rural economy of Egypt, for example, developed differently from that of temperate Europe. In Old World agriculture, the hoe was replaced by the plough, a tool which was not even known to the Mayas.

Childe concludes from these facts that "the development of barbarian rural economics in the regions surveyed exhibits not parallelism but divergence and convergence" (p. 162). But this does not go far enough. The many peoples that entered barbarism all started from the same essential economic activities, cereal cultivation and stockbreeding. They then underwent a

diversified development according to different natural habitats
and historical circumstances, and, provided they traversed the
entire road to civilization and were not arrested en route or
obliterated, ultimately arrived at the same destination: civilization.

What about the evolution of civilization itself? Is that all
a "planless hodgepodge"? When we analyze the march of mankind through civilization, we see that its advanced segments
passed successively through slavery, feudalism and capitalism
and are now on the way toward socialism. This does not
mean that every part of humanity passed, or had to pass,
through this sequence of historical stages, any more than each
of the barbarians passed through the same sequence of stages.
In each instance, it was necessary for the vanguard peoples
to work their way through each given stage. But then their
very achievements enabled those who followed to combine
or compress entire historical stages.

The real course of history, the passage from one social system to another, or from one level of social organization to
another, is far more complicated, heterogeneous and contradictory than is set forth in any general historical scheme. The
historical scheme of universal social structures — savagery, barbarism, civilization, with their respective stages — is an abstraction. It is an indispensable and rational abstraction which
corresponds to the essential realities of development and serves
to guide investigation. But it cannot be substituted for the
analysis of any concrete segment of society.

A straight line may be the shortest distance between two
points, but we find that humanity frequently fails to take it.
It more often follows the adage that the longest way round
is the shortest way home.

Regularity and irregularity are mingled together in history.
The regularity is fundamentally determined by the character
and development of the productive forces and the mode of
producing the means of life. However, this basic determinism
does not manifest itself in the actual development of society
in a simple, direct and uniform fashion but in extremely complex, devious and heterogeneous ways.

This is exemplified most emphatically in the evolution of
capitalism and its component parts. Capitalism is a world
economic system. Over the past five centuries, it has spread
from country to country and from continent to continent and
passed through the successive phases of commercial capitalism, industrial capitalism and monopoly capitalism. Every
country, however backward, has been drawn into the network

of capitalist relations and become subject to its laws of operation. While every nation has become involved in the international division of labor at the base of the capitalist world market, each country has participated in its own peculiar way and
to a different degree in the expression and the expansion of
capitalism and has played different roles at different stages
of its development.

Capitalism rose to greater heights in Europe and North
America than in Asia and Africa. These were interdependent
phenomena, opposing sides of a single process. The capitalist underdevelopment in the colonies was a product and condition of the overdevelopment of the metropolitan areas at
their expense.

The participation of various nations in the evolution of capitalism has been no less irregular. Holland and England took
the lead in establishing capitalist forms and forces in the sixteenth and seventeenth centuries while North America was still
largely possessed by the Indians. Yet, in the final stage of
capitalism in the twentieth century, the United States has far
outdistanced England and Holland.

As capitalism absorbed one country after another into its
orbit, it increased their dependence upon one another. But
this growing interdependence did not mean that they followed
identical paths or possessed the same characteristics. As they
drew closer together economically, profound differences asserted themselves and separated them. Their national development
in many respects did not proceed along parallel lines but at
angles to one another, and sometimes even at right angles.
They acquired not identical but complementary traits.

The rule that the same causes produce the same effects is
not unconditional. The law holds good only when the historically produced conditions are the same—and since these
are usually different for each country and constantly changing
and interchanging with one another, the same basic causes
can lead to very different, and even opposite, results.

For example, in the first half of the nineteenth century, England and the United States were both governed by the same
laws of industrial capitalism. But these laws had to operate
under very different conditions in the two countries and, in
the field of agriculture, they produced very different results.
The enormous demand of British industry for cotton and cheap
footstuffs immensely stimulated American agriculture at the
same time that these very economic factors strangled farming
in England itself. The expansion of agriculture in the one
country and its contraction in the other were opposite but

interdependent consequences of the same economic causes.

To shift from economic to intellectual processes, the Russian Marxist Plekhanov pointed out in his remarkable work *In Defense of Materialism* that the uneven development of national institutions permits the same stock of ideas to produce very different impacts upon philosophical life. Speaking of ideological development in the eighteenth century, Plekhanov stated:

> The very same fund of ideas leads to the militant atheism of the French materialists, to the religious indifferentism of Hume and to the "practical" religion of Kant. The reason was that the religious question in England at that time did not play the same part as it was playing in France, and in France not the same as in Germany. And this difference in the significance of the religious question was caused by the fact that in each of these countries the social forces were not in the same mutual relationship as in each of the others. Similar in their *nature,* but dissimilar in their degree of development the elements of society combined differently in the different European countries, and thereby brought it about that in each of them there was a very particular "state of minds and manners" which expressed itself in the national literature, philosophy, art, etc. In consequence of this, one and the same question might excite Frenchmen to passion and leave the British cold; one and the same argument a progressive German might treat with respect, while a progressive Frenchman would regard it with bitter hatred (p. 206).

I should like to close this examination of the processes of uneven development with a discussion of the problem of national peculiarities. Marxists are often accused by their opponents of denying, ignoring or underestimating national peculiarities in favor of universal historical laws. There is no truth to this criticism, although individual Marxists are sometimes guilty of such errors.

Marxists deny neither the existence nor the importance of national peculiarities. It would be theoretically stupid and practically reckless because national differences may be decisive in shaping the policy of the labor movement, of a minority struggle, or of a revolutionary party in a given country for a certain period. For example, most politically active workers in Britain follow the Labor Party. This monopoly is a prime peculiarity of Great Britain and the political development of its working people today. Marxists who failed to take this factor into account as the keystone of their organizational orientation would violate the spirit of their method.

Far from being indifferent to national differences, Marxism is the only historical method and sociological theory that adequately explains them, demonstrating that they are rooted in the material conditions of life and viewing them in their historical origins, development, disintegration and disappearance. The schools of bourgeois thought look upon national peculiarities in a different way, as inexplicable accidents, god-given birthrights, or fixed features of a particular people. Marxism regards them as historical products arising from concrete combinations of worldwide forces and intranational conditions.

This procedure of combining the general with the particular, the abstract with the concrete, accords not only with the requirements of science but with our everyday habits of judgment. Every individual has a distinctive facial expression which enables us to recognize him and separate him from all others. At the same time, we realize that this individual has the same kind of eyes, ears, mouth, forehead and other organs as the rest of the human race. In fact, the peculiar physiognomy which produces his distinctive expression is nothing but the outward manifestation of the specific complex of common human structures and features. So it is with the life and the profile of any given nation.

Each nation has its own distinctive traits. But these national peculiarities arise from the operation of general laws as they are modified by specific material and historical conditions. They are at bottom individual crystallizations of universal processes.

Trotsky concluded that national peculiarity is the most general product of the unevenness of historical development, its final result.

But however deep-seated these peculiarities may be in the social structure and however powerful their influence upon national life, national peculiarities are limited. In the first place, they are limited in action. They do not replace the overriding processes of world economy and world politics nor can they abolish the operation of their laws.

Consider, for example, the different political consequences the 1929 world crisis had upon the United States and Germany, owing to their different historical backgrounds, special social structures and national political evolution. In one case, Roosevelt's New Deal came to power; in the other, Hitler's fascism. The program of reform under bourgeois-democratic auspices and the program of counterrevolution under naked totalitarian dictatorship were totally different methods of the respective capitalist classes to save their skins.

The contrast between the American and the German capitalist modes of self-preservation was exploited to the hilt by the apologists for American capitalism who attributed it to the inherently democratic spirit of the American nation and its capitalist rulers. In reality, the difference was due to the greater wealth and resources of U. S. imperialism, on one hand, and the immaturity of its class relations and conflicts, on the other.

However, at the very next stage and before the decade was over, the processes of imperialism drove both powers into a second world war to determine which would dominate the world market. Despite the significant differences in their internal political regimes, both arrived at the same destination. They remained subordinate to the same fundamental laws of capitalist imperialism and could not abolish their operation or avoid their consequences.

In the second place, national peculiarities have definite historical limits. They are not eternally fixed. Historical conditions generate and sustain them; new historical conditions can alter and eliminate them, even transform them into their opposites.

In the nineteenth century, Russia was the most reactionary country in Europe and in world politics; in the twentieth century, it became the most revolutionary. In the middle of the nineteenth century, the United States was the most revolutionary and progressive nation; in the middle of the twentieth century, it has taken Russia's place as the fortress of world counterrevolution. But this role will not be everlasting either, as will be indicated in the next section where we shall deal with the character and consequences of combined development.

Combined Development and Its Consequences

We must now examine the second aspect of the law of uneven and combined development. This law bears in its name indications of the more general law of which it is a special expression — namely, the law of dialectical logic called the law of interpenetration of opposites. The two processes — unevenness and combination — which are united in this formulation, themselves represent two different and opposing, yet integrally connected aspects of reality.

The law of combined development starts from the recognition of unevenness in the rates of development of various phenomena of historical change. The disparities in technical and social development and the fortuitous combination of elements, tendencies and movements belonging to different stages of social organization provide the basis for the emergence of something of a new and higher quality.

This law enables us to observe how the new qualities arise. If society did not develop in a *differential* way, that is, through the emergence of differences that are sometimes so acute as to be contradictory, the possibility for combination and *integration* of contradictory phenomena would not present itself. Therefore, the first phase of the evolutionary process — that is, unevenness — is the precondition for the second phase — the combination of features belonging to different stages of social life into distinctive social formations, deviating from abstractly deduced standards or "normal" types.

Because combination comes about as the necessary outcome of preexisting unevenness, we can see why both are always found together and are coupled in the single law of combined and uneven development. Starting with the fact of disparate levels of development, which result from the uneven progression of the various aspects of society, we will now analyze the next stage and necessary consequence of this state of affairs — their coming together.

We must ask, first of all: What is combined? We can often see that features appropriate to one stage of evolution become merged with those belonging to another and higher stage. The Catholic Church, with its seat at the Vatican, is a characteristically feudal institution. Today the Pope uses radio and television — inventions of the twentieth century — to disseminate Church doctrines.

This leads to the second question: How are the different features combined? Metal alloys provide a useful analogy. Bronze, which played so great a part in the development of early toolmaking that its name has been given to an entire stage of historical development, the Bronze Age, is composed of two elementary metals, copper and tin, mixed together in specific proportions. Their fusion produces an alloy with important properties different from either of its constituents.

Something similar happens in history when elements belonging to different stages of social evolution are fused. The fusion gives rise to a new formation with its own special characteristics. The colonial period of American history, when European civilization, changing over from feudalism to capitalism, met and merged with savagery and barbarism, provided a lush breeding ground for combined formations and furnishes a most instructive field for their study. Almost every kind of social relationship then known to mankind, from savagery to the shareholding company, was to be found in the New World during colonial times. Several colonies, such as Virginia and North and South Carolina, were originally settled by capitalist shareholding enterprises which had been granted charters by the Crown. The highest form of capitalist undertaking, the shareholding firm, came into contact with Indians still living under primitive tribal conditions.

One of the prime peculiarities of American development was the fact that every one of the precapitalist forms of life that grew up here was combined to one degree or another with fundamental features of bourgeois civilization. Indian tribes, for example, were annexed to the world market through the fur trade. On the other hand, the white European colonists, hunters, trappers and pioneer farmers, became partially barbarized by having to survive in the wilds of the plains and hills of the "virgin" lands. Yet the European woodsman who penetrated the wilds of America with his rifle and iron axe, and with the outlook and habits of civilization, was very different from the Red Indian tribesman, however many of the activities of barbaric society the woodsman was forced to adopt.

In his pioneer work, *Social Forces in American History,* A. M. Simons, an early socialist historian, wrote: "The course of evolution pursued in each colony bears a striking resemblance to the line of development that the race has followed" (pp. 30-31). In the beginning, he points out, there was primitive communism. Then came small individual production and so forth right through to capitalism.

However, the conception that the American colonies, or any one of them, substantially repeated the sequence of stages through which advanced societies had traveled before them, is entirely too schematic and misses the main point of their development and structure. The most significant peculiarity in the evolution of the British colonies in America came from the fact that all the organizational forms and driving forces belonging to earlier stages of social development, from savagery to feudalism, were incorporated into, conditioned by, and in the case of chattel slavery, even produced by the expanding system of international capitalism.

There was no mechanical serial reproduction on American soil of outmoded historical stages. Instead, colonial life witnessed a dialectical admixture of all these varied elements, which resulted in the emergence of combined social formations of new and special types. The chattel slavery of the American colonies was very different from the chattel slavery of classical Greece and Rome. American slavery was a bourgeoisified slavery which was not only a subordinate branch of the capitalist world market but became impregnated with capitalist features. One of the most freakish offshoots of this fusion of slavery and capitalism was the appearance of commercial slaveholders among the Creek Indians in the South. Could anything be more anomalous and self-contradictory than communistic Indians, now slaveholders, selling their products in a bourgeois market?

What results from this fusion of different stages of the historical process, then, is a peculiar alloy. In the joining of such different, and even opposing, elements, the dialectical nature of history asserts itself most forcefully. Here, contradiction, flat, obvious, flagrant contradiction, holds sway. History plays pranks with all rigid forms and fixed routines. All kinds of paradoxical developments ensue which perplex those with narrow, formalized minds.

As a further important example, let us consider the nature of Stalinism. In Russia, the most advanced form of property, nationalized property, and the most efficient mode of industrial organization, planned economy, both brought about through the proletarian revolution of 1917, were fused with the most brutal tyranny, which was itself created by the political counterrevolution of the Soviet bureaucracy. The economic foundation of the Stalinist regime historically belongs to the socialist era of the future. Yet this economic foundation became yoked to a political superstructure showing the most malignant traits of the class dictatorships of the past. No wonder this exceptionally contradictory phenomenon has puzzled so many people and led them astray!

Uneven and combined development presents us with a peculiar mixture of backward elements with the most modern factors. Many pious Catholics affix to their automobiles medals of St. Christopher, the patron saint of travelers, who is supposed to protect them against accidents. This custom combines the fetish of the credulous savage with the products of the motor industry, one of the most technically advanced and automated industries of the modern world. These anomalies are, nowadays, especially pronounced in the most backward countries. Such curiosities exist as air-conditioned harems!

"The development of historically backward nations leads necessarily to a peculiar combination of different stages in the historical process," wrote Trotsky in *History of the Russian Revolution* (p. 5).

Carlton S. Coone writes in *The Story of Man:*

there still are marginal regions where cultural diffusion
has been uneven, where simple Stone Age hunters are sud-
denly confronted by strangers carrying rifles, where Neolithic garden-cultivators are trading their stone axes for
steel ones and their pottery water jugs for discarded oil
tins, and where proud citizens of ancient empires, accustomed to getting news some weeks later from camel car-
avans, find themselves listening to propaganda broadcasts
over public radios. In the blue-and-white-tiled city square
the clear call of the muezzin, bidding the faithful to prayer,
is replaced one day by a tinny summons issuing not from
the lips of a bearded man, but from a shiny metal cone
hanging from the minaret. Out at the airport, pilgrims
to the holy places climb directly from the backs of camels to
seats in a DC-4. These changes in technology lead to the
births of new institutions in these places as elsewhere, but
what is born from such travail is often an unfamiliar child,
resembling neither the laggard nor the advanced parent,
and hard for both to cope with (pp. 413-14).

In Africa today, among the Kikuyu in Kenya, as well as
among the peoples of the Gold Coast, ancient tribal ties and
customs strengthen their solidarity in the struggles for social
advance and national independence against the English imperialists. In Premier Nkrumah's movement, a national parliamentary party is linked with trade unions and tribalism —
all three of which belong to different stages of social history.

The blending of backward elements with the most modern
factors can also be seen when we compare modern China
to the United States of America. Today many Chinese peasants in tiny hamlets have pictures of Marx and Lenin on their
walls and are inspired by their ideas. The average American
worker, living in the most modern cities, has, by contrast,
paintings of Christ or photographs of the president on his
prefabricated walls. However, the Chinese peasants have no
running water, paved roads, cars, or television sets, as the
American workers have.

Thus, although the United States and its working class have
in industrial development and in living and cultural standards
progressed far beyond China, in certain respects the Chinese
peasant has outstripped the American worker. "The historical
dialectic knows neither naked backwardness nor chemically
pure progressiveness," as Trotsky put it.

If we analyze the social structure of contemporary Britain,
we can see that it has features belonging to three different

social-historical periods, inextricably interwoven. On top of its political system is a monarchy and an established church, both inherited from feudalism, which serve a capitalist-monopolist property structure belonging to the highest stage of capitalism. Alongside these capitalist-owned industries exist nationalized industries, mighty trade unions, and a Labor Party — all *precursors* of socialism.

It is significant that this particular contradictory combination in Britain sorely perplexes the American. The liberal American cannot understand why the English retain a monarchy and an established church; the capitalist-minded American is puzzled by the British ruling class's toleration of the Labor Party.

At the same time, Britain is being shaken by the most formidable of all the combined movements of social forces in our time, namely, the combination of the anticapitalist movement of the working class with the anticolonial revolution of the colored peoples. These two very different movements, both of them flowing out of opposition to imperialist rule, reinforce one another.

These two movements, however, do not have the same effects in all imperialist countries. They are felt, for example, more directly and forcefully in Britain and France than in the United States. Even in the United States, however, the struggles of the colonial peoples for independence and of the oppressed minorities for self-determination reciprocally influence one another.

The most important outcome of the interaction of uneven and combined development is the occurrence of "leaps" in the process of history. The biggest leaps are rendered possible by the coexistence of peoples on different levels of social organization. In today's world, these social organizations stretch all the way from savagery to the very threshold of socialism. In North America, while the Eskimos in the Arctic and the Seri Indians of Lower California are still in the stage of savagery, the bankers of New York and the workers of Detroit operate in the highest stage of monopoly capitalism. Historical "leaps" become inevitable because retarded sections of society are brought face to face with tasks that can be solved only by the most up-to-date methods. Under the spur of external conditions, they are obliged to skip over, or rush through, stages of evolution that originally required an entire historical epoch to unfold.

The wider the range of differences in development and the greater the number of stages present at any one time, the more

dramatic are the possible combinations of conditions and forces
and the more startling is the nature of the leaps. Some combinations produce extraordinary sudden eruptions and twists
in history. Transportation has evolved, step by step, through
the ages from human to animal locomotion, through wheeled
vehicles on to railways, cars and airplanes. In recent years,
however, peoples in South America and Siberia have passed
directly and at one bound from the pack animal to the use
of planes for transport.

Tribes, nations and classes are able to compress stages,
or skip over them entirely, by assimilating the achievements
of more advanced peoples. They use these, like a pole-jumper,
to soar upward, clear intermediate stages, and surmount obstacles in one mighty leap. They cannot do this until pioneer
countries in the vanguard of mankind have paved the way
for them by prefabricating the material conditions. Other peoples prepare the means and models, which, when the time
is ripe, they then adapt to their own peculiar needs.

Soviet industry, for example, was able to make such rapid
progress because, among other reasons, it could import techniques and machinery from the West. Now China can march
ahead at an even faster pace in its industrialization by rely-
ing not only upon the technical achievements of the advanced
capitalist countries but also upon the planning methods pio-
neered by the Soviet economy.

In their efforts to come abreast of Western Europe, the colonists of the north Atlantic coast quickly passed through "wilderness barbarism," virtually skipped over feudalism, implanted and then extirpated chattel slavery and built large
towns and cities on a capitalist basis. They did all this at
an accelerated rate. It took the European peoples 3,000 years
to climb from the upper barbarism of Homeric Greece to the
England of the triumphant bourgeois English revolution of
1649. North America completed this transformation in 300
years. This was a tenfold speedup in the rate of development.
It was, however, only made possible by the fact that America
was able to profit from the previous achievements of Europe
combined with the impetuous expansion of the capitalist market to all quarters of the globe.

Alongside the acceleration and compression of social development came an acceleration of the tempo of revolutionary
events. The British people took eight centuries to progress
from the beginnings of feudalism in the ninth century to their
victorious bourgeois revolution in the seventeenth century. The
North American colonists took only one and three-quarter

centuries to pass from their first settlements in the seventeenth century to their victorious revolution in the last quarter of the eighteenth century.

In these historical leaps, stages of development are sometimes compressed and sometimes omitted altogether, depending upon the particular conditions and forces. In the North American colonies, for example, feudalism, which flowered in Europe and Asia over many centuries, hardly obtained a foothold. Feudalism's characteristic institutions, landed estates, serfs, the monarchy, the established church and the medieval guilds, could find no suitable environment and were squeezed out between commercial chattel slavery, on one hand, and the budding bourgeois society, on the other. Paradoxically, at the very time that feudalism was being strangled in the North American colonies, it was undergoing vigorous expansion on the other side of the world in Russia.

On the other hand, slavery in the southern colonies of North America sank deep roots, enjoyed such an extensive growth and proved so tough and durable that it required a separate revolution to eradicate it. There are, indeed, still, to this day, significant anachronistic survivals of chattel slavery in the South.

History has its periods of reaction no less than its periods of revolution. Under conditions of reaction, infantile forms and obsolete features, appropriate to bygone periods of development, can be fused with advanced structures to generate extremely retrogressive formations and hinder social advance. A prime example of such a regressive combination was chattel slavery in America, where an obsolete mode of property and form of production belonging to the infancy of class society sprang up in a bourgeois environment belonging to the maturity of class society.

Recent political history has made us familiar with the examples of fascism and Stalinism, which are symmetrical, but by no means identical, historical phenomena of the twentieth century. Both represented reversions from preexisting democratic forms of government which had entirely different social foundations. Fascism was the destroyer and supplanter of bourgeois democracy in the final period of imperialist domination and decay. Stalinism was the destroyer and supplanter of the workers' democracy of revolutionary Russia in the initial period of the international socialist revolution.

Thus far, we have singled out two stages in the dialectical movement of society. First, some parts of mankind, and certain elements of society, move ahead faster and develop farther than others. Later, under the shock of external forces, laggards are prodded along, catching up with and even outstripping their forerunners by combining the latest innovations with their old modes of existence.

But history does not halt at this point. Each unique synthesis, which arises from uneven and combined development, itself undergoes further growth and change which can lead to the eventual disintegration and destruction of the synthesis. A combined formation amalgamates elements derived from different levels of social development. Its inner structure is therefore highly contradictory. The opposition of its constituents not only imparts instability to the formation but directs its further development. More clearly than any other formation, a struggle of opposites marks the course of a combined formation.

There are two main types of combination. In one case, the product of an advanced culture may be absorbed into the framework of an archaic social organization. In the other, aspects of a primitive order are incorporated into a more highly developed social organism.

What effects will follow from the assimilation of higher elements into a primitive structure depends upon many circumstances. For example, the Indians could replace the stone axe with the iron axe without fundamental dislocations of their social order because this change involved only slight dependence upon the white civilization from which the iron axe was taken. The introduction of the horse considerably changed the lives of the prairie Indians by extending the range of their hunting grounds and of their war-making abilities, yet the horse did not transform their basic tribal relations. However, participation in the growing fur trade and the penetration of money had revolutionary consequences for the Indians by disrupting their tribal ways, setting up private interests against communal customs, pitting one tribe against another and subordinating the new Indian traders and trappers to the world market.

Under certain historical conditions, the introduction of new things can, for a time, even lengthen the life of the most archaic institutions. The entrance of the great capitalist oil concerns into the Middle East has temporarily strengthened the sheikdoms by showering wealth upon them. But, in the long run, the invasion of up-to-date techniques and ideas cannot help but undermine the old tribal regimes because they break up the conditions upon which the old regimes rest and create new forces to oppose and replace them.

A primitive power can fasten itself upon a higher one, gain renewed vitality, and even appear for a time superior to its host. But the less developed power leads an essentially parasitic existence and cannot indefinitely sustain itself at the expense of the higher. It lacks suitable soil and atmosphere for its growth while the more developed institutions are not only inherently superior but can count upon a favorable environment for expansion.

The development of chattel slavery in North America provides an excellent illustration of this dialectic. From the world-historical standpoint, slavery on this continent was an anachronism from its birth. As a mode of production, it belonged to the infancy of class society; it had already virtually vanished from Western Europe. Yet the very demands of Western Europe for staple raw materials, such as sugar, indigo, and tobacco, combined with the scarcity of labor for large-scale agricultural operations, implanted slavery in North America. Colonial slavery grew up as a branch of commercial capitalism. Thus, a mode of production and a form of property that had long passed away emerged afresh from the demands of a higher economic system and became part of it.

This contradiction became accentuated when the rise of capitalist factory industry in England and the United States lifted the cotton-producing states of the deep South to top place in American economic and political life. For decades, the two opposing systems functioned as a team. They then split apart at the time of the American Civil War. The capitalist system, which at one stage of its development fostered slavery's growth, at another stage created a new combination of forces that overthrew it.

The combined formation of the old and the new, the lower and the higher, chattel slavery and capitalism turned out to be neither permanent nor indissoluble; it was conditional, temporary, relative. The enforced association of the two tended toward dissociation. If a society marches forward, the advantage, in the long run, goes to the superior structure, which thrives at the expense of the inferior features, eventually dislodging them.

One of the most important and paradoxical consequences of uneven and combined development is the solution of the problems of one class through the agency of another. Each stage of social development inherits, poses, and solves its own specific complex of historical tasks. Barbarism, for example, developed the productive techniques of plant cultivation and animal breeding and husbandry as branches of its economic activity. These activities were also prerequisites for the supplanting of barbarism by civilization.

In the bourgeois epoch, the unification of separate provinces into centralized, national states and the industrialization of these national states were historical tasks of the rising bourgeoisie. But, in a number of countries, the underdevelopment of capitalist economy and the consequent weakness of the bourgeoisie made them unable to fulfill these historically bourgeois tasks. Right in the heart of Europe, for example, the unity of the German people was effected, from 1866 to 1869, not by the bourgeoisie and not by the working class, but by an outmoded social caste, the Prussian Junker landlords, headed by the Hohenzollern monarchy and directed by Bismarck. In this case, a historical task of a capitalist class was carried through by precapitalist forces.

In the present century, China presents another, reversed example — on a higher historical level. Under the double yoke of its old feudal relationships and of imperialist subordination, China could neither be unified nor industrialized. It required nothing less than a proletarian revolution (however deformed this revolution may have been from the start), backed up by a mighty peasant insurrection, to clear the way for the fulfillment of these long-postponed bourgeois tasks. Today, China is unified for the first time and is rapidly becoming industrialized. However, these jobs are not being carried out by capitalist or precapitalist forces but by the working class and under the leadership of the working class. In this case, the unfinished tasks of the aborted capitalist era of development have been shouldered by a postcapitalist class.

The extremely uneven development of society makes necessary these exchanges of historical roles between classes; the telescoping of historical stages makes the substitution possible. As Hegel pointed out, history often resorts to the most indirect and cunning mechanisms to achieve its ends.

One of the major problems left unsolved by the bourgeois-democratic revolution in the United States was the abolition of the old stigmas of slavery and the extension of equality to the Blacks. This task was only partially fulfilled by the industrial bourgeoisie of the North during the American Civil War. This failure of the bourgeoisie has ever since been a great source of embarrassment and difficulty for its representatives. The question now posed is whether the present ultra-reactionary capitalist rulers of the USA can now carry through to fulfilment a national task that it failed to complete in its revolutionary heyday.

The spokesmen for the Democrats and Republicans find it

necessary to say that they can in fact do this job; the reformists of all kinds claim that the bourgeois government can be made to do it. It is our opinion, however, that only the joint struggle of the Blacks and the working masses, against the capitalist rulers will be able to carry through the struggle against the hangovers of slavery. In this way the socialist revolution, combining the struggles of the oppressed nationalities with the anticapitalist movement for workers' power, will complete what the bourgeois-democratic revolution failed to realize.

Those who make a cult of pure progress believe that high attainments in a number of fields presuppose equivalent perfection in other respects. Many Americans automatically assume that the United States surpasses the rest of the world in all spheres of human activity just because it does so in technology, material productivity, and standard of living. Yet in politics and philosophy, to mention no others, the general development of the United States has not yet passed beyond the nineteenth century, whereas countries in Europe and Asia, far less favored economically, are far ahead of the USA in these fields.

In the last few years of his rule, Stalin sought to impose the notion that only "rootless cosmopolitans" could maintain that the West had outdistanced the USSR in any branch of endeavor from mechanical invention to the science of genetics. This expression of Great Russian nationalism was no less stupid than the Westerners' conceit that nothing superior can come from the alleged Asiatic barbarism of the Soviet Union.

The truth is that each stage of social development, each type of social organization, each nationality, has its essential virtues and defects, advantages and disadvantages. Progress exacts its penalties. Advances in certain fields can institute relapses in others. For example, civilization developed the powers of production and the wealth of mankind by sacrificing the equality and fraternity of the primitive societies it supplanted. On the other hand, under certain conditions, backwardness has its benefits. Moreover, what is progressive at one stage of development can become a precondition for the establishment of backwardness at a subsequent stage or in an affiliated field. And what is backward can become the basis for a forward leap.

It seems presumptuous to tell those peoples who are oppressed by backwardness and yearn to cast it off that their archaic state has any advantages. To them, backwardness appears as an unmixed evil. But the consciousness of this "evil" emerges in the first place only after these peoples have come into contact with superior forms of social development. It is the contact of the two forms, backward and advanced, which exposes the deficiencies of the backward culture. So long as civilization is unknown, the primitive savage remains content. It is only the juxtaposition of the two that introduces the vision of something better and feeds the yeast of dissatisfaction. In this way, the presence and knowledge of a superior state becomes a motor force of progress.

The resulting criticism and condemnation of the old state of affairs generate the urge to overcome the disparity in development and drive laggards forward by arousing in them the desire to draw abreast of the more advanced. Every individual who has become involved in the learning process has felt this personally.

When new and imperative demands are made upon backward peoples, the absence of accumulated, intermediate institutions can be of positive value: fewer obstacles are present to obstruct the advance and the assimilation of what is new. If the social forces exist and exert themselves effectively, intelligently and in time, what had been a penalty can be turned to advantage.

The recent history of Russia provides the most striking example of this conversion of historical penalties into advantages. At the start of the twentieth century, Russia was the most retarded Great Power in Europe. This backwardness embraced all strata, from the peasantry to the absolutist Romanov dynasty. The Russian people and its oppressed nationalities suffered both from the heaped-up miseries of their decayed feudalism and from the backwardness of bourgeois development in Russia.

However, when the time came for a revolutionary settlement of these accumulated problems, this backwardness disclosed its advantages in many ways. First, czarism was *totally* alienated from the masses. Second, the bourgeoisie was too weak to take power in its own name and hold it. Third, the peasantry, having received no satisfaction from the bourgeoisie, was compelled to rely upon the working class for leadership. Fourth, the working class did not have any entrenched trade-union and political bureaucracies to hold it back. It was easier for this energetic young class, which had so little to unlearn and so much to learn so quickly, to adopt the most advanced theory, the boldest and clearest program of action and the highest type of party organization. The peasant revolt against medievalism, a movement which in Western Europe had been characteristic of the dawn of the bourgeois-democratic revolutions, meshed with the proletarian revolution against capitalism, which belonged to the twentieth century. As Trotsky explained in *The History of the Russian Revolution,* it was the conjunction of these two different revolutions which gave an expansive power to the upheaval of the Russian people and accounted for its extraordinary momentum.

But the privileges of backwardness are not inexhaustible; they are limited by historical and material conditions. Accordingly, in the next stage of its development, the backwardness inherited from the Russia of the czars reasserted itself under new historical conditions and on an entirely new social basis. The previous privileges had to be paid for in the next decades by the bitter suffering, the economic privations and the loss of liberties the Russian people endured under the Stalinist dictatorship. The very backwardness that had previously strengthened the revolution and that had propelled the Russian masses far ahead of the rest of the world, now became the starting point of the political reaction and bureaucratic counterrevolution, a consequence of the fact that the international revolution failed to conquer in the industrially more advanced countries. The economic and cultural backwardness of Russia, combined with the retarded development of the international revolution, were the basic conditions which enabled the Stalinist clique to choke the Bolshevik Party and permitted the bureaucracy to usurp political power.

For these reasons, the Stalinist regime became the most self-contradictory in modern history, a coagulation of the most advanced property forms and social conquests emanating from the revolution with a resurrection of the most repulsive features of class rule. Giant factories with the most up to date machinery were operated by workers who, serf-like, were not permitted to leave their places of employment; airplanes sped above impassable dirt tracks; planned economy functioned side by side with "slave labor" camps; tremendous industrial advances went hand in hand with political retrogression; the prodigious growth of Russia as a world power was accompanied by an inner decay of the regime.

However, the dialectical development of the Russian Revolution did not stop at this point. The extension of the revolution to Eastern Europe and Asia after the second world war, the expansion of Soviet industry, and the rise in the numbers and cultural level of the Soviet workers, prepared conditions for a modified reversal of the old trends, the revival of the revolution on a higher stage, and the partial overcoming of the scourge of Stalinism. The first manifestations of this forward movement of the masses in Russia and in its satellites, with the working class in the lead, have already been announced to the world.

From the Khrushchev speech to the Hungarian Revolution, there has been a continuous series of events demonstrating the dialectics of revolutionary development. At every stage of the Russian Revolution since 1905, we can see the interaction of its backwardness and progressiveness with their conversion one into the other according to the concrete circumstances of national and international development. Only an understanding of the dialectics of these changes can provide an accurate picture of the extremely complex and contradictory development of the USSR throughout the fifty years of its existence. The dozens of oversimplified characterizations of the nature of modern Russian society, which serve only to confuse the revolutionary movement, derive from a lack of understanding of the laws of dialectics and the use of metaphysical methods in analyzing historical processes.

The law of uneven and combined development is an indispensable tool for analyzing the Russian Revolution and for charting its growth and decay through all its complex phases, its triumphs, its degeneration and its prospective regeneration as the process of de-Stalinization and the movement toward socialist democracy is carried through to the end by the Soviet people.

Disproportions of American Development

The previous section showed how the law of uneven and combined development enables the Marxist to unravel the twisted course of the Russian Revolution. Every socialist today recognizes the supreme importance of arriving at a satisfactory explanation of the degeneration of the Soviet Union and so of reliably estimating the significance of the conflict between the progressive character of nationalized property in the USSR and the reactionary bureaucracy that rules that country. Equal in importance to the Russian question for the international socialist movement is an understanding of the dialectics of the development of the socialist movement in the United States of America, the most highly developed and most powerful capitalist country in the world. How, in essence, has the law of uneven and combined development shown itself in the principal stages in the history of the USA? How does an understanding of this law help us to forecast the course of the class struggle in America?

Prior to breaking loose from British rule, the North American colonies of Britain were certainly underdeveloped in many respects — compared, that is to say, with the mother countries of Western Europe, particularly with Britain herself. The first American Revolution, usually called the "American War of Independence," was a mighty effort on the part of the colonies to come abreast of the Old World.

In preparing, organizing and conducting the War of Independence, the American Patriot Party profited abundantly from the "privileges of backwardness." Its merchant leaders had acquired wealth and power by developing the latest techniques of shipbuilding and the practices of world trade. The people acquired freedom and democracy by taking over those forms of party organization (Whigs and Tories) and governmental forms of legislative representation and local government that had been worked out in England and brought over by the colonists. To justify their demands, the colonists found ready-made theories of natural law in the writings of ideologists of the English revolution of the seventeenth century: Milton, Harrington and John Locke. In addition, the colonists created a new technique of warfare, uniting their experiences of hunting in the wilds of the North American plains and mountains with the potentialities of the musket. These new tactical methods were important in helping the colonists to defeat the British Redcoats of George III. As a result of its victory, America not only caught up with the Old World but, politically, *surpassed* it. This was the first victorious colonial revolution of modern times, and it established what was then the most progressive democracy in the world.

However, the American revolution of the eighteenth century, like the Russian revolution of the twentieth century, could not draw upon unlimited resources. The *political* progressiveness of the Yankee republic became combined with *economic* backwardness. For example, the War of Independence did not, and could not, uproot slavery or curb the power of the slaveowners. The backwardness of the USA in this decisive sphere took its revenge upon the Americans of the nineteenth century.

The American people had for some time to endure the rule of the Southern slaveowners, who later became so reactionary and insolent that they not only prevented further progress but even endangered the democracy and unity achieved by the first revolution. Fortunately a new combination of social forces had been created in the meantime, and this new combined formation proved strong enough to meet and overthrow the slaveholders' counterrevolution.

Historically considered, the second American Revolution (the Civil War) represented, on one hand, the price paid by the

American nation for the *economic* backwardness inherited from its colonial youth. On the other hand, the impetus provided by the Yankee victory in the Civil War jet-propelled the USA once again into becoming the leading nation of the world. After all the precapitalist forces and formations, from the Red Indian tribes to the slavery of the Southern states, had been disposed of, American capitalism was able to leap forward with mighty strides, so making the USA today the most advanced capitalist nation and the paramount world power.

This dominant position was not achieved all at once but in two revolutionary leaps separated by an interval of gradual progress and political reaction.

What are the penalties of progressiveness and the privileges of backwardness in the USA today? American technical know-how is the most advanced and American industry and agriculture, the most productive in the world. This not only enriches the capitalist monopolists but showers many benefits upon the American people — ranging from an abundance and variety of foodstuffs to a plethora of television sets, refrigerators, automobiles and other "luxuries." This is one side of the picture. On the other side, the American monopolists are the most efficient of all the capitalists in the world in exploiting both their own working people and the rest of the toilers of the world. While the American worker enjoys the highest standard of living of any worker in the world, he is also the most heavily exploited. This tremendously productive working class gets back for its own consumption a smaller part of its output and hands over in the form of profit to the capitalist owners of the instruments of production a greater part of its output than does either the English or the French working class.

The greatest unevenness of America's social development is that its economy is so advanced that it is fully ripe for collective ownership and planned production (that is, it is ripe for socialism) and yet this economy remains in a strait-jacket of capitalist and nationalist restrictions. This contradiction is the main source of the social insecurity of our age and of the main social evil of our time, not only in the USA but throughout the world.

The high productivity of the American economy, along with the privileges of the dominant position of American capitalism in world economy, is primarily responsible for another phenomenon of American life, and one that always impresses foreign observers — the extraordinary backwardness of American politics in general and the backwardness of the political ideology of organized labor in particular. In this field, it may be said, a colonial cottage is standing upon foundations suitable for skyscrapers. The workers and even the farmers of Britain, or even for that matter the peasants of China, are today influenced and, to some extent, guided by socialist ideas, while the working people of America remain captive to the crudest bourgeois ideas and organizations.

This is the second outstanding feature of unevenness in the social structure of the USA. The political life of America lags far behind that of most of the rest of the world and even further behind the economic and social development of the country itself. This lag is, ironically enough, part of the price America is paying for the successes of its two previous revolutions and for its resulting outstanding achievements in industry and agriculture. The third American revolution, the socialist revolution, is being retarded precisely because its forerunners accomplished so much.

Unevenness also prevails in other sections of the American social consciousness. The ideology of the American ruling class is one of the most highly developed in capitalist history. This ruling class not only has a militant, positive philosophy to justify its privileges, a philosophy that it assiduously disseminates inside the USA and internationally, but it is also simultaneously engaged in an unceasing offensive against the ideas of communism and socialism, even though Marxist ideas have spread amongst the people of America to the most limited degree. This anticommunist, antisocialist crusading zeal, together with its acute class sensitivity and consciousness of the class struggle, expresses the American ruling class's forebodings about its own future. In contrast to the class consciousness of the capitalists, the American working class has not yet reached the level of generalizing its own particular class interests, even in the form of the most elementary social-reformist notions. This indifference to socialist ideology is one of the most pronounced peculiarities of the American worker. This is not to say that the American worker is devoid of class feeling and initiative. On the contrary, the American working class has asserted itself time and time again as an independent fighting force, especially in the industrial field — often with brilliant results. But these experiences have not led to the establishment of a conscious and permanent challenge to the capitalist order — to a mass socialist movement.

The hyperdevelopment of bourgeois ideology in America and the corresponding underdevelopment of working-class consciousness are the inseparable products of the same historical conditions. They are interdependent aspects of the present stage of social and political development in the USA.

Today, the political complexion of the whole world reflects the unevennesses of American society — one in the domain of production, another in political organization and a third in social consciousness. The gap between the economy's ripeness for socialization and its capitalist-monopolist ownership and administration, and the gap between the high level of labor's trade-union organization and its political and ideological immaturity, are the most striking peculiarities of American life. This situation poses the most difficult theoretical and practical problems for all socialists, especially for those who have to operate in such an environment. To the whole world of labor, these gaps in American social life sometimes look like bottomless pits into which the peoples of the whole world must be dragged to their nuclear destruction. Sometimes it seems impossible to imagine that forces could ever come into existence to bridge the abyss.

But will things remain like this forever or even for the remainder of this century? Will the contradictions in America's social life persist indefinitely without essential changes? Will the gaps between the level of American economic development and the forms of ownership, between the present weaknesses and the potential power of the American working class, remain as they are today? The capitalists, the reformists, the liberals, the pragmatists and pseudo-Marxists of all kinds not only think they will but try also to induce everyone else to share their convictions.

But all these people reckon without the movement of world history, a movement which has been considerably speeded up in our time. They reckon without the contradictions of the capitalist system on a world scale; and these contradictions will, in time, generate new and more devastating crises. They reckon without the development of the class conflicts in our own time. Above all, they underestimate the creative capacities of the American working class. Not being Marxists, they leave out of their calculations the operation and effects of the law of uneven and combined development.

Let us see how the law of uneven and combined development can help us to penetrate below the surface and to expose the kernel of present realities. As we have seen, this is certainly not the first time in the history of America, nor is America the only place in the world in the twentieth century, where economic relations, political structures and social ideas have lagged far behind the development of the forces of production. The undeniable facts of history are that, in the past, the only way in which major disparities have been resolved, and unevenness eliminated, has been through revolutionary upheavals whose function, on each occasion, has been to place new progressive forces at the head of the nation. In our time, only the working class can perform this historically necessary function. There is no adequate reason for believing that, whatever else intervenes, the extreme contradictions in American life can be resolved in any other way.

At this point, an astute critic may object that according to the law of uneven and combined development, and this exposition of it, events do not necessarily reproduce themselves in the same way even within the same social system, but, under a different set of circumstances, the course of events may take a different line of development. Why then does the USA have to follow the same revolutionary path in the twentieth century as it did in the eighteenth and nineteenth centuries? Why must the USA necessarily follow the course taken by the backward countries like Russia and China in our own time? Is it not possible for America to make a detour around the socialist revolution and by easy and gradual stages arrive at a higher form of social organization and a better life?

It is certainly true that no historical precedent, however superficially apposite, can properly replace the direct analysis of the concrete situation; precedents can only guide and supplement specific investigation. Of course, it would be more advantageous for the peoples of the whole world if the transition from capitalism to socialism in America (or, indeed, in Britain or anywhere else) could be effected by mutual agreement between the classes. Marxists have never denied this nor desired otherwise. But this pious wish, unfortunately, does not dispose of the problem. The question then arises: Is this ideal and desirable prospect a realistic one? Should it be made the basis for practical socialist politics in Britain or in the USA? The same question has once more been raised in the British and American Communist parties in the "great debate" that has followed the Twentieth Congress of the Soviet Communist Party.

The "peaceful" road to socialism in America presupposes that American capitalism can proceed without further devastating economic convulsions, social crises and wars, and that if these do occur, the rulers, discredited by these catastrophes, would step aside and voluntarily relinquish their power, property and privilege in answer to the demands (and perhaps votes) of an aroused people.

Can it be realistically expected that the most profound social

conflict in all history, the conflict that involves the abolition
of exploitation of one section of humanity by another will, in
the advanced capitalist countries of "Western democracy," be
resolved through diplomatic negotiations between the classes,
backed up by peaceful forms of mass pressure and by count-
ing votes? Incidentally, there are no precedents for such "revolutions" in British, French, German or American history. It
can be shown that the most powerful reasons exist indicating
why the capitalist-monopolists of today, in the USA and elsewhere, are even less likely to relinquish voluntarily their ruling
position, to act against their material interests and to commit
"social suicide" than were the courts of Charles I, George III
and Louis XVI, the slaveholders of the Southern states or,
for that matter, the court of Czar Nicholas II.

The powerful financial and industrial magnates who rule
America today have long been accustomed not only to rule but
to believe in the rightness and eternity of their rule. Moreover,
they realize that they would not merely be relinquishing their
own supremacy but also that of capitalism on a world scale.
For, should the American workers assume state power, this
would not be just a minor shift of power within a single social
system. It would represent the decisive act in the most fundamental and far-reaching of all the transformations of society.
Nothing less would be involved than the worldwide historical
coup de grace to capitalism and the passing of decisive sections of humanity to a higher social system, to socialism. Fundamentally, the fate of two world historical systems, capitalism
and socialism, are at issue in the struggle between the American capitalists and the American working class. The recognition
of this key position of the American working class is of fundamental importance for the socialist movement in every country.

With so much at stake, the reflex action of the American
capitalists to the threat of displacement by the working class
would most likely be, as McCarthyism indicated, a sharp turn
toward military dictatorship or fascism. In any event, it would
be unrealistic and irresponsible for a serious Marxist to count
only upon the most favorable development and to ignore the
probability that, instead of facilitating the transition to socialism, the representatives of capitalism will try to throw up
new barriers against socialist advance and to fight to retain
their sovereignty, however illegal and "undemocratic" their resistance might be.

However, if this last stronghold of world capitalism, the
USA, is the least likely of all countries to escape the ne-

cessity for revolutionary struggle on its road to socialism, this certainly does not mean that the pattern of struggle will duplicate precisely the path taken in other countries, say, for example, Russia. It is an elementary proposition of Marxism, which, to suit their own temporary aims, the Stalinists are now busy "rediscovering," that the revolutionary class in each country will proceed in its own peculiar way in achieving state power and in building socialism.

After decades of the most discouraging delay, the American workers won their industrial organization in one mighty leap during the thirties through the CIO. They compressed several stages of development in this leap. The American auto workers did not proceed through craft unionism to industrial unionism, but went at one bound from a state of nonorganization to the highest form of industrial organization, skipping the intervening craft stage, which industrial workers in Britain had found necessary to pass through.

Similar spectacular leaps will most probably be repeated in the forthcoming political development of the American working class. The value of the law of uneven and combined development consists in helping to anticipate such leaps. When Britain lost its paramount position on the world market around the beginning of the twentieth century, the most progressive elements of British labor began to draw the necessary political deductions by turning away from the Liberal Party and establishing their own class party around a program of social reform — albeit social reform supplementing and expressing itself through a quasi-socialist ideology. American labor has yet to reach the point reached by the British workers over half a century ago. The American trade-union movement remains politically attached to the Democratic Party, the American equivalent of the old and now obsolete Liberal Party in Britain.

How are the American working masses likely to respond to radical changes in their economic and political conditions? Can they be expected to follow in the footsteps of the British workers? A Marxist, dialectical thinker can only answer — yes and no. The American worker will follow the British worker but only in the most general way. He will certainly find it imperative to cut loose from the capitalist parties and to create an independent class outlook and organization, just as the workers of Britain have done. But the specific forms, the special features and the rate of political development of the American workers *need* not and most certainly *will* not simply duplicate the features of British development because

the world historical conditions under which they will set up
their class political party will be vastly different from those
under which the British Labor Party was created.

When the British working class launched itself into independent politics at the turn of the century, world capitalism was
still ascending and no country had yet overthrown capitalist
rule. Today, capitalism on a world scale is on the defensive,
while the anticapitalist powers and the socialist and colonial
movements have become a mighty reality.

Nor is the America of today, internally, anything like the
Britain of the first half of the twentieth century. Today, America is the last stronghold of capitalism and, unlike the British capitalists of Edwardian days, the American capitalists
have little room for strategic retreat. These differences will
ensure that there will be great differences between the British
Labor Party and the American Party of Labor, which still
remains to be created. Accordingly, the American working
class will enter this new chapter of American political events
in a mood very different from that of their British predecessors.

Furthermore, these struggles will be preceded and accompanied by powerful mass movements of the insurgent nationalities, students and rebellious youth, feminists and other radicalized sectors of the oppressed.

In the USA, it will take a very acute crisis to jerk labor
loose from the old moorings, rather than the sort of chronic
long-drawn-out crisis that characterized Britain. The impact
of these social shocks will hit the stunted political development
of the U. S. working class at a time when capitalism is on
the defensive and the anticapitalist forces on the offensive in
the rest of the world. The offensive of the working class will
not only collide with intensified resistance from the capitalists,
but also with the inertia and shortsightedness of the trade-
union bureaucracies — as it has already done in Britain. But
the American reactionary trade-union bureaucracies will also
have to operate under far different conditions from those which
obtain in Britain. The critical situation will, on one hand,
dictate the most radical measures. On the other hand, the bureaucrats will be challenged for the leadership of the militant
workers by a strong and solid revolutionary socialist organization.

Such a combination of an organized, highly cultured and
newly radicalized working class with a leadership equipped
with the most advanced theory and farseeing policies, as is

in the process of gestation in the USA today, will have extraordinary explosive power.

At such a juncture in world history, the penalties of backwardness from which the American socialist movement now suffers will be certain to show their other, more hopeful side. The American workers will be receptive to the boldest revolutionary prospects and will be prepared to assimilate them readily and to act upon them.

New species, it was noted earlier, have experienced "explosive expansion" when they have broken into virgin territories under favorable conditions. An analogous acceleration in development can be expected when the American workers enter the field of independent class political action and take possession of the ideas of scientific socialism and the methods of Marxism. In such days of grave social crisis, this amalgamation of a previously politically backward but potentially powerful working class with the science of society and of political action, that is, with Marxism, can effect the greatest leap forward any society has yet achieved — greater than any leap forward in American history — and, by this single act, raise the whole of humanity by a head.

How to Apply a Law of Sociology

[The first three sections of this chapter first appeared in the January and March-April 1957 issues of the British socialist journal *Labour Review* under the title "The Law of Uneven and Combined Development." The publication of these articles led to the following exchange between a British Marxist and George Novack.]

George Novack's series "The Law of Uneven and Combined Development" must have been very stimulating to British Marxists. In the complex and rapidly moving world of the twentieth century a formal notion of eternal sequences for the development of societies is as useless as the idea that there are no law-governed processes at all in social life. Novack therefore does a service in highlighting that aspect of materialist dialectics which explains the result of a clash between, or a combination of, phenomena at different levels of development, e.g., American technical efficiency with semi-feudal — or recently tribal — economies and the accompanying customs.

The place of this law of uneven and combined development requires a systematic treatment as part of the dialectical method;

meanwhile one question seems to be raised from Novack's own material. A scientific law should outline the particular sets of conditions which give rise to a typical result in the given sphere of investigation. In sociology, a law of this kind is the law that the productive forces develop to a point where they demand a change in, first, the economic structure and then the political and ideological superstructure of a society. A definite dependence of one set of facts on another set is clearly stated. Can the law of uneven and combined development be seen in the same way? It states that factors developed to an uneven extent, either between societies or within one society, combine to form single formations of a contradictory character. If this generalization is to be accorded the status of a law it should give clear guiding lines to the following problem, among others. Will the processes at work give rise to a dialectical leap forward in history, as in the October Revolution in Russia, or will they give rise to degenerative processes, as in the bureaucratic distortions of Stalin's regime, or the destruction of the Tasmanian aborigines? One does not expect of course an answer to all questions which will be a substitute for analysis of each particular case, for that is the essence of the scientific method. But a law should state the characteristics of progressive as against regressive combinations. If this point can be cleared up, then other fruitful controversial problems can be raised later.

C. S.

REPLY BY GEORGE NOVACK

I do not clearly see why C. S. hesitates to accord the law of uneven and combined development the status of a law. Lawfulness is derived from ascertaining materially conditioned, necessary connections among phenomena. Laws formulate such necessary relations among the factors in a certain sector of reality in a generalized way. In natural science, for example, the early physicists, Boyle, Charles, Gay-Lussac and Avogadro, established simple relationships connecting the volume, temperature and pressure of gases which they formulated in elementary empirical laws.

Because different aspects of reality have their own laws, different laws do not operate on the same level of generality, nor do they have the same degree of necessity. The broadest laws are formulated in the materialist dialectic of being and becoming, which embraces universal processes and modes of development. The law of the interpenetration of opposites belongs in this class. On the other hand, there are particular laws that apply only within the limits of specific social-economic formations — as, for instance, the law of the growing concentration of capital, which pertains exclusively to the capitalist system.

The law of uneven and combined development stands midway between these two types in its scope of operation. It belongs not to philosophy nor to political economy, but primarily to the science of sociology, which seeks to discover the general laws of human evolution. It formulates certain important aspects of the historical tendencies of social development. It is more concrete than the law of the interpenetration of opposites, of which it is a specific expression, and less limited than the law of the concentration of capital.

1. Historical materialism starts from the factual premise that humans cannot exist without eating, drinking, etc. This is the supreme law of life.

2. The inescapable physical contradiction between hunger and survival, which animals overcome by direct appropriation and consumption of food, is solved by mankind through labor activities.

3. The development of society is determined by the development of the productive forces.

4. These productive forces give rise to certain definite relations of production which shape the rest of the social structure.

5. The further development of the productive forces eventually comes into conflict with the existing relations of production, initiating a revolutionary period which, if progressively resolved, results in the establishment of a higher social-economic order.

These are the main links in the chain of necessity that governs social development and in the logical reasoning of the scientific socialism which explains it. The law of uneven and combined development enters the chain at the following point: the productive forces, which are the mainspring of the entire social movement, developed unevenly from one time and place to another, from one people to another, and from one social formation to the next. These differences in the degree of development in turn produce disproportion not only between different segments of society but also among the various elements in any given social structure.

The fundamental lawfulness of the phenomena theoretically expressed in the law of uneven development comes from the observed, verifiable fact, running throughout history, that disproportions of various types emerge from the different rates of economic development. Given these disparities, certain consequences inescapably follow in the subsequent unfolding of the social process.

To prove the contrary, that is, the lack of historical necessity in this law, it would have to be demonstrated that society proceeds in a different way; that the productive forces develop evenly and that the resultant social organizations and cultural superstructures consist of harmonious elements perfectly proportioned to one another.

From this starting point, the process goes on to a second stage, formulated in the law of combined development, which supplements the first. The diversely developed elements are united, not in simple homogeneous structures, but in complex, heterogeneous and sometimes highly contradictory ways.

The contradictory characteristics of the combinations do not depend only on the fact that the various formations and factors have evolved independently of one another and coexist on different levels of social development. The manner and consequences of the merger also depend upon the historical period in which they come together. It can make considerable difference whether the elements are united in precapitalist times, during the capitalist period, or under postcapitalist conditions.

After such combinations are brought into being, the process passes over to a still higher stage in which the emergence of new unevennesses in the situation leads to the conflict and dissociation of the previously synthesized, contradictory factors.

This sociological law, whose operations and effects can be observed throughout the course of history, has attained its maximum strength and scope under capitalism and during the period of transition to socialism because all the accumulated contradictions and disproportions of historical development inherited from past ages come to a head at this juncture.

The single difficulty raised in the remarks of C. S. is that the law of uneven and combined development ought to indicate without ambiguity what the specific outcome of its operation is going to be. It should enable us to foretell whether the combination of factors at different levels of development will culminate in a leap forward or retrogression.

The law cannot do that because its action and results do not depend upon itself alone as a theoretical formulation of general tendencies, but more upon the total situation in which it functions. The latter is decisive. What determines the specific outcome of its operation are the material factors in their totality: the living structure of a society, the dynamics of its inner forces, and their historical and international connections.

One and the same law can give different results at different stages in the development of the same economic system, as the objective conditions of its operations change. The law of value, the supreme regulator of the capitalist system, energetically promotes the productive forces in its progressive period — and then in its further operation leads to the constriction of the productive forces in its declining monopolist-imperialist stage.

The law of uneven and combined development likewise leads to different results according to the specific circumstances of its operation. Under certain conditions, the introduction of higher elements and their amalgamation with lower ones accelerates social progress; under other conditions, the synthesis can retard progress and even cause a retrogression. Whether progress or reaction will be favored depends upon the specific weight of all the factors in the given situation.

Advanced elements cannot, in and of themselves, guarantee a comprehensive and uninterrupted forward movement unless and until they reach down into the foundations of the social system, revolutionize and reconstruct them. Otherwise their efficacy can be restricted and distorted.

Consider in this light the evolution of the Soviet Union since 1917, as Trotsky explained it in *The Revolution Betrayed* with the aid of the law of uneven and combined development. Trotsky pointed out that, in the first place, "the law of uneven development brought it about that the contradiction between the technique and property relations of capitalism (a universal feature in its death agony) shattered the weakest link in the world chain." The Russian Revolution was, as he stated elsewhere, a national avalanche in a universal social formation. "Backward Russian capitalism was the first to pay for the bankruptcy of world capitalism."

Trotsky then observed that in general "the law of *uneven* development is supplemented throughout the whole course of history by the law of *combined* development."

What was its specific result in Russia? "The collapse of the bourgeoisie in Russia led to the proletarian dictatorship — that is, to a backward country's leaping ahead of the advanced countries." As we know, this caused a lot of grief to the schematic theorists in Russia and Western Europe who insisted that the workers could not and should not take power until capitalism had elevated the national economy.

But it also brought much genuine grief to the Russian people, as Trotsky went on to explain. "However, the establishment of socialist forms of property in a backward country came up against the inadequate level of technique and culture."

That is, new types of unevenness emerged on the basis of the preceding achievements and on a higher historical level. "Itself born of the contradictions between high world productive forces and capitalist forms of property, the October Revolution produced in its turn a contradiction between low national productive forces and socialist forms of property."

Although the achievements of the revolution—the nationalized property and planned economy—exercised a highly progressive action upon the Soviet Union, they were themselves subjected to the degrading influence of the low level of production in the isolated workers' state. From this fundamental condition flowed all the degenerative effects witnessed in the Soviet state under the Stalinist regime, including that regime itself. The most advanced ideas and progressive productive relations could not prevail against the inadequacy of their economic substructure, and suffered debasement as a result.

Thus, unevenness prevents any simple, single straight line of direction in social development. What we have instead is a complex, devious and contradictory route. The theoretical task is to analyze the dialectical interplay of action and reaction of the contending forces in their connection with the historical environment.

Now the progressive tendencies and now the reactionary counterforces assert themselves and come to the fore.

This dialectical interplay can be observed in the contradictory consequences of the same historical factors in the neighboring countries of China and Japan. Both of these formerly isolated and backward countries felt the impact of capitalist forces upon them in the nineteenth century. Western capitalism invaded China, penetrated its economy, and established political and military control. Only the rivalry of the contending imperialisms saved China from outright division among them.

Although the intrusion of capitalism, with the latest techniques in production, transport, commerce, finance and knowledge, mangled and shook up China, these instruments of modern capitalism did not, on the whole, modernize Chinese life nor emancipate China. On the contrary, entrenched imperialism propped up the most archaic institutions, such as the feudal landholding system, and helped the compradore bourgeoisie, landlords, officials and militarists prolong precapitalist forms of social organization. Its grip prevented China from passing through a genuine bourgeois-democratic renovation and from having any independent capitalist development.

In the same period that these capitalist influences were stunting Chinese development, they were stimulating Japan. There, the introduction of Western capitalist civilization promoted from the top a reorganization of the country's precapitalist structure without revolutionary convulsions from below. Along with the Meiji Restoration, the capitalist agencies of change strengthened new classes of industrialists, merchants, financiers, who developed large-scale industry, trusts, banks and military power after the most advanced Western models. Instead of being a victim of Western imperialism, Japan became the supreme embodiment of Eastern imperialism, avidly flinging itself upon China for its share of the spoils.

Thus, in the first stage, under the given historical conditions, the law of uneven and combined development led to the degradation and subjugation of China, while Japan experienced a tremendous surge of national energy and achievement under capitalist auspices. Little wonder that in Japan nationalism poured into imperialist channels, while across the China Sea nationalism had to seek other outlets along anti-imperialist lines.

However, as we know, the world historical process swung in a different direction following the first world war and the Russian Revolution, and this affected the trend of development in the Far East.

Even during the first period of the merger of Western capitalism with Far Eastern life, tendencies emerged that ran counter to the dominant direction of development in both countries. In Japan, the imperialist regime — product of the highest stage of world and national evolution — was headed by an emperor cult carried over from prefeudal times. Its capitalist structure bulged with bizarre combinations and extreme disproportions. Modern factories and workshops sprang up in the cities while feudal relations in the countryside remained unaltered. Light industry was overdeveloped, while the heavy industry, from which contemporary mastery is derived, remained underdeveloped. The military, equipped with the latest weapons, remained animated by feudal traditions. Because of its reformation from above, instead of revolutionization from below, democracy was feeble and parliamentary life flimsy. The incomplete modernization of Japan's social structure culminated in a supreme disproportion: the imperialist program imposed upon that latecomer by the needs of national capitalist expansion and world competition were beyond the capacities of its forces and resources. The result was the debacle suffered by Japanese militarism in the second world war.

Meanwhile, China's backwardness under imperialism built up the impetus for its forward leap at the next stage. Along with the venal compradore bourgeoisie, represented by Chiang Kai-shek, the westernization process created a modern proletariat. The unsolved but pressing problems of national unification and independence, agrarian revolution, industrialization, etc., which imperialism blocked and Chiang's regime could not tackle, gave an explosive force to the popular movements for their solution.

After the Russian Revolution, world historical factors of a higher order intervened in the Far East and with special force in China. The influences emanating from the October Revolution and the Soviet Union permeated China more effectively than the capitalist ideas and forces of Western imperialism had penetrated Japan. Thanks to the power of these influences on an international and national scale, China, so long dragged down by imperialism and its servitors, rose up after the second world war. In the process of tackling the long-postponed historical tasks, the movements of the proletarian and peasant masses lifted the country over native capitalism into the first stage of a workers' state.

This mighty leap reversed the relations between China and Japan. Under the pressures of world capitalism, Japan had climbed from feudalism to imperialism in a couple of generations, while China was held down by the same forces. Then, at the next stage, under the combined pressures of reactionary imperialism and progressive socialism (mixed with Stalinism) China vaulted beyond capitalism and took the lead from Japan.

Thus, each of the two series of historical influences, the first issuing from capitalism in the nineteenth century, the second from postcapitalist movements in the twentieth century, had very different impacts upon the development of the two neighboring countries. This demonstrates that the consequences of the law of uneven and combined development depend upon the action and reaction of the new forces upon the old; the concrete reality at any given stage is a resultant of the dynamic interplay between them. These can acquire the most divergent forms.

A sociological generalization, such as the law of uneven and combined development, can serve only as a guide to the investigation and analysis of the processes at work in a given social environment. It can help us understand the peculiarities of past history and orient us with respect to the peculiarities of unfolding social processes. But it cannot categorically tell us in advance what will issue from its further operation. The specific results are determined by the struggle of living forces in the national and international arenas.

The law of uneven and combined development expresses certain features of the dialectics of history. The dialectic is "the algebra of revolution" and evolution. That is to say, it formulates certain necessary aspects, relations or tendencies of reality in a general form, extracted from specific conditions. Before its abstract algebraic qualities can be converted into definite, "arithmetic" quantities, they have to be applied to the substance of a particular reality. In every new case and at every successive stage of development, specific analysis is necessary of the actual relations and tendencies in their connection and continual interaction. The dialectical formulas are abstract but "the truth is concrete."

5

The Uneven Development
Of the World Revolutionary Process

All social formations and their component parts have undergone irregular development. This is a universal feature of history and a fundamental law of its dialectical process, which has its ultimate material source in the variable growth of the forces of production.

The disproportions that have accumulated in all sectors of society through the ages have been coalesced, accentuated, and brought to a head under world capitalism. The totality of their effects is being manifested during this system's decline, which overlaps the first stage in the transition to socialism.

The extremely variegated growth of capitalist relations and power in different parts of the globe is the underlying historical cause for the contradictory course of the socialist revolution. From the sixteenth to the twentieth centuries, indigenous capitalism rose to its full stature only in Western Europe, North America, and Japan. It was retarded in Eastern Europe and the Iberian peninsula, and barely got off the ground in Asia, Africa, the Middle East and Latin America.

The disparity of capitalist development decisively shaped the march of events in the nineteenth and twentieth centuries. The older, richer, and more favored capitalist powers carved up the planet for themselves, stunted and distorted the growth of the less advanced nations, and blocked their progress.

By 1914, the world had been split into a few plutocratic giants enjoying a monopoly of industrial capacity, wealth, and power, with the majority of humankind suffering from both precapitalist stagnation and imperialist depredation. Their confrontation set the stage for the first round of revolutions in which those peoples who had lagged far behind the industrialized metropolises began to turn the tables and deal staggering blows to the imperialist system.

Those who bemoan the crawling pace and jagged path of the proletarian struggle for power need reminding — if ever they knew — that the mass democratic movements that marked the formative stages of capitalism and gave hegemony to the bourgeoisie went through an even more protracted and twisted development. It took more than three centuries for the anti-feudal forces to unfold their full potential and for the Western magnates of capital to gain mastery.

The first period of bourgeois-democratic revolutions was inaugurated by the uprising of the Low Countries against Spanish dominion in the late sixteenth century and culminated in the two English revolutions of the seventeenth century. One hundred years later, bourgeois revolutionary energies reached their peak with the American War of Independence, the first victorious colonial revolt of modern times, and the decisive French Revolution, which broke the spine of the European feudal order. The era came to a close during the series of wars and revolutions from 1848 to the Paris Commune of 1871, with the Civil War in the United States the foundry in which the present colossus of world capitalism was forged.

The progressive camp and its plebeian elements experienced many setbacks during this upward climb. The big bourgeoisie, which was the ultimate victor, at times saw the political power it had won slip from its grasp into the hands of its rivals. That happened, for instance, when the Northern merchants, bankers and manufacturers of the United States were shoved aside at Washington by the Southern cotton planters and their accomplices in the decades before the Civil War.

Even after three hundred years of struggle for republican democracy, political regimes the world over were not transformed as much as the social structures. As late as 1848, monarchy, either absolute or constitutional, remained the most common mode of governing states, except on the American continent—and even there Brazil had an emperor. The crowned heads were not removed from Germany, Austro-Hungary and Russia until the first world war and the advent of the first proletarian revolution.

Nevertheless, the precapitalist order was overthrown and its major institutions eliminated by these successive endeavors spanning the centuries. The basic acquisitions of the revolutionary process proved enduring; the reverses transitory. The "new men of power" had taken over the civilized world by the last quarter of the nineteenth century.

But the bourgeoisie did not everywhere conquer *political* sovereignty. It is widely believed that a capitalist democracy, headed by the captains of industry, trade and finance, is an obligatory stage in the political advancement of all enlightened nations. This preconception is strongest in the United States. Actually, the bourgeoisie has managed to win and retain political preeminence largely in the most privileged capitalist nations. Elsewhere, this possessing class arrived too late and with too little to dislodge its rivals to the right or its challengers on the left, to concentrate state power in its own hands.

This default was first and most evident in Russia. Up to 1917, the Russian bourgeoisie had to bow before the czar and the landlords. Its representatives could not wield power in their own right between February and October and lost the last chance of taking command of the state when the worker-peasant revolt led by the Bolsheviks kicked out the Provisional Government and set up the first Soviet Republic. The impotence of a belated bourgeois rulership has been subsequently demonstrated in China and elsewhere.

Because the democratic revolution was able to reorganize the social and political structures of only a restricted number of countries along progressive bourgeois lines, the rest of humanity, tormented by backwardness, has been driven in this century to find other ways and means of hacking a path to modernity. The unevennesses, inequities and iniquities of capitalist development have transmitted to the next epoch of world revolution the unfinished historical tasks of bringing the more backward countries into the mainstream of civilization. This is directed not to the expansion and consolidation of capitalism, but to its constriction and abolition.

The lopsided evolution that characterized the four centuries of bourgeois-democratic revolution has been extended in exaggerated form to the first stages of the international proletarian revolution. Over the past century and a half, the prerequisites for the socialist revolution have come into being and matured in an extremely dispersed and disparate manner. On one hand, this irregularity has served to weaken the latent strength of the anticapitalist camp, hamper its forward march, and impart anomalous forms to its development. But it has also had positive results by bringing together unusual alignments of social forces that have exerted tremendous power, speeded up the revolutionary process at certain conjunctures, and secured unexpected victories over the class enemy.

The heterogeneity of its different national sections was already evidenced in the infancy of the working-class movement. Although during most of the nineteenth century the wage workers were more numerous and strongest in England, France and the United States, their class consciousness and ideological level were low.

Marxism, the scientific method of socialist thought and action, did not originate in the industrially advanced countries but in the more retarded environment of Germany. Marxist ideas made their way haltingly and superficially among the socialist vanguard in France during the last quarter of the century. The discrepancy between the theoretical equipment and the latent social power of the workers in England and the United States has been far from mended to this day. Fabian empiricism and insularity still dominate the British labor movement, while the crassest pragmatism and opportunism prevail across the Atlantic.

When Marx and Engels published the *Communist Manifesto* in 1848, Western Europe was the exclusive theater of proletarian revolutionary activity. Russia and the United States — the two titans of the twentieth century — were given only marginal mention in the original text of that epoch-making programmatic document. The shifts in the revolutionary center of gravity since then indicate that the imbalance in the distribution of the forces ready for socialism has persisted.

Both the First and Second Internationals, the earliest political organizations of the world working class, had their seats of strength entirely in Western Europe. The outlying regions did not count for much in that preliminary phase of the mobilization of the proletarian forces.

Although the Labor and Socialist International rested on a mass base, it was predominantly a white man's organization that had few ties and little concern with the colonial masses. The most radical sections came from the perimeter of Europe: Russia and Poland. Its mainstay and model, the German social democracy, was the undisputed leader of the workers, a close partner of the unions, and performed a prodigious work of organization and indoctrination. But its leaders' talents in these fields were not equaled by foresight, courage, revolutionary will or internationalism. These deficiencies proved to be the undoing of German social democracy and the Second International in August 1914 and thereafter.

Although the Russian working class was not so large and cultured and could not create such powerful mass organizations as the German, it had since 1903 acquired something far more precious and decisive: a firm, farsighted and audacious leadership in the Bolshevik team. When the strains and disasters of the first world war provoked the insurrection of the Russian masses, Lenin's party was able to make the most of the opportunities it offered for the overthrow of the old order.

In the first chapter of *The History of the Russian Revolution,* "Peculiarities of Russia's Development," Trotsky has explained how the conjoined proletarian and peasant uprisings grew out of the unequal development of capitalist imperialism, which imposed objectives upon the backward state and society of Russia, exceeding the strength and endurance of all its possessing classes, from the landed nobility to the weak bourgeoisie. Under the mounting stresses of the czarist government's participation in the imperialist dogfight, the most vulnerable pillar of world capitalism collapsed and the revolutionary epoch burst in through the most weakly barricaded door. Trotsky wrote in *The Revolution Betrayed:*

> Russia took the road of proletarian revolution, not because her economy was the first to become ripe for a socialist change, but because she could not develop further on a capitalist basis. Socialization of the means of production had become a necessary condition for bringing the country out of barbarism . . . (p. 5).
> [Thus,] the law of uneven development brought it about that the contradiction between the technique and property relations of capitalism shattered the weakest link in the world chain. Backward Russian capitalism was the first to pay for the bankruptcy of world capitalism (pp. 299-300).

It turned out that the Russian people likewise had to pay a terrible price for their primacy in the order of socialist revolution. The very unevenness of historical development that propelled Russia ahead of the more advanced countries, enabling it to install the first workers' government and nationalize the means of production, took its revenge subsequently. The new economy moved forward by fits and starts, now dragging along, now spurting ahead, at the cost of tremendous sacrifices, but all too slowly to bridge the enormous gap between the low level of productive power and the elementary needs of the people.

Because of the isolation and national backwardness of the Soviet Union, its revolutionary vanguard was thrown back and crushed. "The establishment of socialist forms of property in the backward country came up against the inadequate level of technique and culture. Itself born of the contradictions between high world productive forces and capitalist forms of property, the October Revolution produced in its turn a contradiction between low national productive forces and socialist forms of property" (Trotsky, *The Revolution Betrayed*).

The political regression was consummated by Stalin's bureaucratic despotism. The counterrevolutionary conservatism that sapped the Russian Revolution was itself a consequence of the arrested development of the international struggle for workers' power. The revolutionary movements from 1918 to 1923 failed to overthrow capitalism in any of the highly industrialized countries of Western Europe. The isolation of the Soviet Union was reinforced by the ensuing stabilization of world capitalism, the train of defeats suffered by the socialist forces, and the spread of fascism in the years before the second world war.

It appeared to many that the proletarian revolution was doomed to remain indefinitely locked within the borders of the USSR. This belief was the psychological source of the conception of building socialism in one country, improvised in 1924 by Stalin to justify the usurpation of power by the Soviet bureaucracy and the subjugation of the international Communist movement to its narrow national dictates. The theory and practice of autarchic socialism expressed both the ideological and political relapse of the revolutionary process in Russia and the episodic but drawn-out retardation of the world socialist revolution.

The next wave of revolutionary victories, which surged up from 1943 on, shattered the objective basis for upholding one-country socialism. At the same time, the struggles after World War II extended to the more backward areas of the world the anticapitalist revolutions initiated by the October 1917 overturn. The peoples most meagerly developed along capitalist lines became the most eligible candidates for socialist revolution. The storm center of revolution shifted to the East rather than to the West—from Eastern Europe to China, Vietnam, and Korea.

The colonial world became the hearth of revolutionary activity, while the most highly industrialized and richest parts of world economy remained in the clutches of imperialism. This turn of events lifted the state of siege from the Soviet Union and opened bright new vistas to the colonial masses. But the split between East and West kept the postcapitalist regimes confined to the least developed countries.

Thus, on a more magnified scale and higher historical plane, the workers' states, separately and together, continued to be ringed by world imperialism. The unremitting pressures exerted by the class enemy had injurious effects upon the new revolutionary regimes; they could not avoid being deformed from birth to one degree or another by their own material and cultural backwardness and the influence of Stalinism. These deformations were strongest in Eastern Europe and China.

The interweaving of the favorable and unfavorable effects of uneven development can be discerned in the unfolding of the socialist revolution in Cuba. This island was the last country in Latin America to be liberated from Spanish domination; it was the first to be liberated from capitalist exploitation. The decadence of world Stalinism discredited the Cuban Communist Party as the fresh young leadership of the July 26 Movement was stimulated to take the helm of the popular revolution and propel it forward.

Unfortunately, its example has yet to be duplicated in Latin America. This has kept the Castro regime isolated in the Western Hemisphere and imperiled by Washington's economic blockade and threat of intervention, despite the aid received from other workers' states. The extension of the socialist revolution through Latin America is, as Havana recognizes, imperative both for the salvation of the peoples of that continent and the healthy internal growth of the new Cuba itself.

The disabilities arising from the disproportionate tempos in diverse zones of the revolutionary process are more conspicuous today than ever. Fifty years after the October victory, the Third World pulses with revolutionary ardor and energies, while opportunist conservatism dominates the Soviet bloc. The working-class movements and parties in the major capitalist countries remain largely unresponsive to the demands of the world struggle for socialism. The political atomization of the masses in the Communist countries, coupled with the passivity of the workers in the strongholds of imperialism, deprive the revolutionary elements in the colonial lands of their most powerful potential allies, permitting the imperialists and their native accomplices to bolster neocolonialism and impede liberation movements from the Congo to Southeast Asia.

While the antidemocratic features of the bureaucratized workers' states reduce the attractiveness of socialism for the Western masses, the unequal economic levels among the Communist countries embitter their mutual relations. This is one of the root causes of the Sino-Soviet split.

Official Soviet sociologists maintain that, whereas capitalism is subject to the law of uneven development, the existing workers' states operate under the opposite law of even development. Thus, G. Glazemann writes in *The Laws of Social Development:* "Revisionists ignore the basic fact that the law of uneven economic and political development has ceased to operate within the framework of the world socialist system, that the socialist countries are now governed by a new law, the law of the evening out of their economic and cultural development" (p. 238).

Such an assertion "ignores the basic facts" about the USSR itself, where the growth of heavy industry has outstripped that of light industry, services, and agriculture. It is certainly untrue of the political evolution of the Soviet Union where Soviet and party democracy was destroyed by Stalinist despotism, a relapse which, despite the reforms and economic and cultural advances of recent years, has still to be overcome.

No less unfounded is the pronouncement that a general law of proportionate development prevails among Communist countries. Planned economy does contain the potential of a balanced growth, especially if it is combined with control by the working people over economic and political policy. But, singly or collectively, the workers' states remain a long way from such symmetry. Most flagrant is the contrast between the Soviet Union and China, which today stand at opposite ends of the scale in economic development.

Soviet aid was a boon to China's economic progress in the first period of the revolution, and its withdrawal was reprehensible. But even with closer and continued cooperation, the two major Communist countries cannot command enough resources to overcome the wide gap in their economic levels and march side-by-side to socialism. That is a global revolutionary task.

Sino-Soviet relations have been adversely affected more than their leaders wish to admit by the still restricted scope of the world revolution which reinforces the deficiencies inherited from past backwardness. These *objective* sources of friction have been considerably irritated and intensified by the narrowly nationalistic outlook and overbearing bureaucratic behavior of their respective leaderships.

It is the paramount task of the entire transitional period from capitalism to socialism to iron out the vast disproportions between the rich and poor sectors of humanity along with the inequalities within each country. It is imperative to acknowledge the gravity and explain the difficulty of this problem and publicly discuss what short-term and long-range measures are required for the best available solutions. But the false orientations of the Soviet and Chinese Communist parties have kept them from bringing this fundamental issue into the spotlight. It would puncture the illusory perspective of constructing socialism or communism in a single country and pose sharply and squarely the indispensability of spreading the revolution to the centers of capitalism. To make such a preoccupation central smacks too much of the "heresy" of Trotskyism, even though it accords with the views of Marx and Lenin.

Three main processes today contribute to the promotion of the world revolution—the actions and reactions of their driving forces serve either to accelerate or delay its development. These are the colonial revolution, the political revolution aiming at the democratization of the degenerated or deformed workers' states, and the proletarian revolution in the imperialist countries.

Their complex interaction is delineated as follows in the resolution on the "Dynamics of World Revolution Today," adopted by the Reunification Congress of the Fourth International, June 1963:

> The delay of the proletarian revolution in the imperialist countries has in general undoubtedly prevented the colonial revolution from taking the socialist road as quickly and consciously as would have been possible under the influence of a powerful revolutionary upsurge or victory of the proletariat in an advanced country. This same delay also retards the maturing of the political revolution in the USSR, especially inasmuch as it does not place before the Soviet workers a convincing example of an alternative way to build socialism. Finally, the upsurge of the colonial and political revolutions, hampered by the delay of the proletarian revolution in the West, nevertheless contributes in helping the proletariat in the imperialist countries to overcome the delay.

The major tendencies competing for the allegiance of the class-conscious workers offer quite different answers to the problems presented by the disparity of development among these three sectors of the struggle for socialism. Since 1956, the Moscow leaders have vigorously propagated the conception, first promulgated by Stalin, that the advancement of the international revolution is no longer the aim of the anticapitalist camp. They preach that in the course of time the Soviet Union, which has supposedly already reached socialism and is on the way to communism, would provide such an alluring showcase of the splendors and benefits of the new society that the peoples still under the capitalist yoke will cast it off like an outworn cloak—and almost as easily.

Meanwhile, peaceful coexistence between Communist and capitalist governments in the international arena, implemented by class collaboration with "peace-loving, progressive elements" among the imperialist and neocolonialist bourgeoisies, is to be the principal guideline for Communist strategy.

This is utopianism of the purest hue. Just as Owen, Fourier and their like believed that the example and achievements of model cooperative communities would win over or neutralize the big property owners, draw all reasonable citizens to them, and spread by imitation in a peaceable way, so Khrushchev, Kosygin, Brezhnev and their followers suggest that the shining example of Soviet progress will come to prevail without the necessity for intransigent revolutionary struggle. They envisage the bad example of force being replaced by the force of good example.

The Stalinist line disorients and demoralizes the world struggle against capitalism in two ways. First, its advice to rely upon alliance with the "progressive" elements of the bourgeoisie disarms the masses and aids their enemies. This has been demonstrated by catastrophic defeats since 1964 in colonial countries from Brazil to Indonesia. Its folly was shown by the support accorded President Johnson by the American CP in the 1964 presidential campaign on the grounds that he would be less "trigger-happy" in Vietnam than his Republican opponent.

Second, it proposes to leave the task of disarming the monopolists and militarists to "summit" negotiations and diplomatic pacts between Washington and Moscow. No governmental agreements between the "Big Two" can guarantee world peace. Like the partial nuclear test ban of 1963, they can even be tacitly directed against the sovereign rights of the People's Republic of China. The atomaniacs heading the United States can be permanently deprived of their power to work evil and annihilate the human race with their H-bomb arsenal only if the American working people are organized in a movement to take economic, political and military control of the country away from them.

The Maoists advocate, at least in words, a more militant strategy for world revolution than do their adversaries in the Kremlin. Yet they have displayed serious shortcomings in theory and practice. Even in countries closest to them in Asia, they have not consistently advised the independent mobilization of the masses for the taking of power, but have fostered reliance upon bourgeois leaders, like Sukarno, who may be friendly to Peking. This attitude led to tragic consequences in Indonesia.

Contrary to the teachings of Marx and Lenin, the Maoists regard the colonial revolution not as the area of most intense and important revolutionary activity and accomplishment at the present stage, but as the paramount force in the world movement for socialism. They depreciate or dismiss the factor that shapes the prevailing international balance of forces and can bring about the successful outcome of the world revolution: the class relations in the imperialist strongholds.

Thus, in an editorial article commemorating the first anniversary of Defense Minister Lin Piao's celebrated programmatic document, "Long Live the Victory of a People's War," the newspaper *Jenmin Jih Pao* wrote in September 1966 that the big battle between people who accounted for more than 90 percent of the world's population and United States imperialism was the "decisive battle between revolution and counterrevolution on which hinges the future of the world." It was also said to be the decisive battle between "socialism and capitalist imperialism."

Both for its benefits to the most oppressed nations and the blows it delivers to imperialism, the colonial revolution has colossal historical significance and class consequences. But it would be incorrect for a Marxist to regard its course and outcome as *ultimately decisive* in the world struggle for workers' power and socialism.

The superiority of the program and perspectives of the Fourth International, which views the dynamics of the revolutionary process in its entirety through all its historical twists and turns, is demonstrated on this crucial issue. It never loses sight of the truth that the development of the proletarian struggle for supremacy *within the imperialist countries* is of cardinal importance for the world revolution. The economic, military and diplomatic successes scored by the existing workers' states and their colonial allies are mighty spurs to progress, and foundation stones of socialism. But the key to permanent peace and the construction of a democratic socialist society of abundance on a global basis lies within the capitalist centers, above all in the United States. The missile crisis of 1962 and the escalation of the war in Southeast Asia should have driven home this lesson.

The international revolution and the social structures issuing from it promise to be as full of incongruities and imbalances in the second half-century of the breakup of the old order as in the first. How are these pronounced disproportions to be dealt with?

Marxism teaches that the inescapable contradictions of the period of transition from capitalism to socialism can be lessened and overcome only by broadening and deepening the revolutionary processes. Any national state, no matter how great its resources, is too narrow a framework for the building of a harmonious socialist society that will be in all decisive respects superior to and stronger than the most advanced capitalist countries. The only way out of its internal difficulties and external dilemmas will be found in the international arena. This is the principal lesson to be derived from the economic and political experiences of the Soviet Union during its first fifty years — and it is also the gist of the theory of the permanent revolution.

The workers in the highly industrialized countries have an indispensable role to play in easing and eventually eliminating the multiple deficiencies and distortions engendered by the paucity of productive power in the less-developed areas. Their conquest of power would remove the terrible threats and pressures exerted by the ever-aggressive imperialists. On the other hand, they can, through international planning, supply essential material aid for arriving most quickly at effective solutions to the excruciating problems presented by the restriction of the anticapitalist revolutions to the poorer parts of the world.

The underlying assumption of the Kremlin's policy of peaceful coexistence — and of social-democratic reformism — is that national and world politics will be more calm, peaceful and reasonably regulated in the decades ahead than between 1917 and 1967. This might be — if there were not as many explosive elements lodged in international and class relations as in military technology. The diversity of crises inherent in the contradictions of a hard-pressed capitalist system can produce abrupt and deep-going shifts in the balance of class forces which will considerably speed up the timetable of revolution — and counterrevolution — in unexpected ways and places. Who thought in 1950 that Cuba would enter the path to socialism by the end of the decade?

The drawbacks of disproportionate development are not one-sided. If they favor the opponents of socialism at one point, they can seriously cripple them at another. In the showdown, the defenders of capitalism in Russia, Yugoslavia, China and Cuba found themselves without sufficient means to save their sources of power and became casualties of the operation of the law of uneven and combined development.

Disproportions in historical development create as many opportunities as obstacles for the forces of progress. They lay the groundwork for the emergence of unusual conjunctures of circumstances and combinations of elements that can give rise to startling novelties and sharp reversals of fortune. Thus, in the last part of the nineteenth century, Japan burst from feudal isolation and rushed into a feverish capitalist career which culminated in catastrophe for its overambitious imperialists. Meanwhile, China remained shackled by backwardness, the victim of subjugation and division by foreign powers, including Japan.

Then, under the shocks of the Japanese invasion and the second world war and through the catapult of their third revolution, the Chinese people vaulted beyond capitalism and outstripped defeated Japan in their social and political regime. Is it warranted to assume that the dialectical differentials in the evolution of these neighboring countries have now been brought to a halt? Or will the further dynamics of history see resurgent Japanese capitalism stumble once again and enter so severe an internal crisis that its workers and farmers will be impelled to throw off monopolist rule and leap ahead of Communist China in their economy and political democracy?

Or consider the revolutionary prospects of the Southern Africans who may be among the last on that turbulent continent to be freed of their oppressors. They cannot win political independence and self-determination except by waging as harsh and long an armed struggle as in Algeria. Once launched on a mass scale, the liberation movement, which has been so long delayed and suppressed, may well pass to a high ideological and political level precisely because it must contend against so ferocious and formidable a foe and comes after so many diverse revolutionary and counterrevolutionary experiences in Africa and elsewhere.

South Africa is the most industrially advanced country on the continent. Its several million Black workers are closely associated with the peasantry in the reserves. In the absence of any Black bourgeoisie or even a substantial urban petty bourgeoisie, a neocolonialist evolution along native capitalist lines is a most unlikely alternative.

Under such conditions, an alignment of social forces arrayed against the unyielding regime of the white exploiters and determined to overthrow it at any cost would provide the objective basis for a revolutionary alliance of workers and peasants on the Russian model. With leadership such as the Bolsheviks gave, the program, outlook and achievements of the South African freedom movement could make a gigantic leap beyond any thus far attained on the continent, break sharply with all capitalist interests, and become the vanguard of socialist revolution in Africa.

An alert revolutionary leadership should foresee and prepare for "quantum jumps" in the relations of class forces which result from preceding disproportions of development, and utilize them for the conquest of power. Will such qualitative changes be confined to the colonial and neocolonialist countries?

This has become an article of faith with many anticapitalists whose outlook is based on the assumption that the practical struggle for socialism in our time is the exclusive prerogative of the Third World. They see little or no chance of the working class under neocapitalist affluence becoming a history-making force.

Because every successful revolution in this century has taken place in the less-developed lands, they conclude that this persistent pattern will not be violated or complicated by the outbreak of revolution and the establishment of workers' power in any major capitalist country. They have converted into its opposite Marx's expectation that the socialist revolution would begin in the most advanced countries. They prescribe that henceforward it must travel undeviatingly from the extremities to the heartlands of imperialism or, as the Maoists put it, from the peoples' war in the countryside to the cities.

They have a short memory. From 1943 to 1947, the masters of capitalism were alarmed by the imminent prospect of working-class uprisings in Western Europe. The danger to their rule was removed thanks to timely aid from Stalin and the Communist parties and then by the reconstruction and reinforcement of the capitalist economy. But the revolutionary potential lurks below the surface and can rise up again, as the May-June 1968 general strike in France indicated.

The neat diagram of universal priorities that fixes the labor movement of the West at the end of the revolutionary line can also be upset by sudden turns in the class struggle. The coming decades should provide some surprises for both the foes and the friends of socialism. The different sectors of neocapitalism may not be quite so impervious to the consequences of class antagonisms as they appear during the exceptionally prolonged postwar expansion.

The supreme testing ground will of course be the United States. As the richest, strongest, most stable sector of capitalism, it has long been considered immune to structural transformation: the Gibraltar of imperialism would stand fast in the future regardless of the storms raging elsewhere.

However, it is open to question whether the United States is destined to remain indefinitely separated from the world-historical movement toward socialism, when it is up to its ears in every other important international development. Indeed, the consequences of its reckless and far-ranging activities in safeguarding a declining capitalist system against socialism promise to accelerate an eventual internal radicalization.

The administrators of the ruling class have pledged unlimited resources against the advance of the anticapitalist forces on all fronts. Will Washington be able to carry out this gigantic historical assignment seccessfully — or will the incalculable obligations involved exceed the capacities of the colossus of capitalism and boomerang?

In projecting their revolutionary strategy for Latin America, the Cuban leaders have insisted on the vulnerability of an overextended Yankee imperialism. It will not have, they predict, the necessary strength to check all the uprisings of the oppressed peoples.

> It has had to employ 245,000 men in order to confront the heroism of the people of a country as small as Vietnam. [The number reached 525,000 early in 1968.] How many divisions and how many men will they need to confront a whole continent? How many situations similar to that of Vietnam can imperialism face simultaneously? What will happen when not one but several, and even the greater part of the peoples of the Continent, take the road of revolutionary action? How many U. S. soldiers will have to die in the mountains or on the plains of the Americas defending a system of exploitation which is not theirs and which oppresses them as well, and which has in addition gained universal reprobation?

It is already evident that the American nation is not one reactionary bloc solidly united behind the monopolists and militarists, as it appeared in the heyday of McCarthyism. The escalation in Southeast Asia has not only provoked differences on the commanding heights but generated deep antiwar sentiment that has spurred radical students and intellectuals into protest and that is seeping into the conscript army. One of the major potential anticapitalist forces, the twenty-two million Afro-Americans, has embarked on a struggle for Black power and liberation.

The most inscrutable and anomalous element in American society is the working class, which is unique in world labor history. It numbers tens of millions, is highly skilled, powerfully unionized, and capable of tremendous militancy. Yet, because of special historical circumstances and privileges, its political and ideological development lags far behind the ripeness of the American economy for socialization and the consciousness of its fellow workers in other lands. The American labor movement remains without any independent political organization or socialist inspiration.

Conservative mentalities, including many in left circles, conclude from its present condition that the American working class must be dismissed as a revolutionary factor. Marxists have the opposite outlook. They anticipate that this giant will be roused from slumber, and that when it manages to break loose from antiquated ideas and attachments and launches a large-scale offensive against big business and its government, the virile new generation of labor militants can rush through or skip over intervening stages of social-democratic or Stalinist politics that workers elsewhere have tarried in for prolonged periods. They can more easily and quickly arrive at radical conclusions in theory, organization and action because they may be less impeded by traditional political formations and receive more assistance from principled revolutionaries.

The social and political stability of the most solid monopolist regime in the world can be upset once revulsion against the costly aggressions of the military machine, the irrepressible thrust of Black Americans for emancipation, and the alienation of rebel youth from bourgeois society coalesce with the upsurge of a sizable segment of aroused industrial workers.

Victory hinges upon a timely meshing of revolutionary openings with the right kind of leadership. The unfolding of the struggle for socialism cannot avoid being marked by pronounced irregularities because all the requirements for successful revolution on a national or international scale seldom come together simultaneously. The objective and subjective factors in the revolutionary process mature at different rates and in varying measures. This is especially true in the earlier stages of a revolutionary epoch when an ascending social force, such as the world working class, must take its first experimental steps in political organization, social reconstruction, and cultural renewal under the most difficult conditions.

The handicaps arising from the grave disproportions between the objective and subjective factors in the making of a revolution can be tackled from opposite ends. Fidel Castro has been foremost in emphasizing that a certain degree of immaturity in the objective conditions can be made good by the resolute action of politically enlightened, armed guerrillas who know how to weld unbreakable bonds first with the rural, then with the urban masses. Such a tactical line, as the Cuban

Revolution has shown, may be suited to certain colonial countries where the tasks of the democratic revolution are unsolved and the regime is corrupt, hated, and without popular support.

However, the most constant and crucial contradiction in the world situation over the past fifty years has not arisen from immaturity in the objective conditions for the overthrow of capitalist rule, but rather from the unreadiness or unwillingness of the leaderships of the workers' organizations to shoulder that task. Since 1918, the crises of the capitalist regime and the tensions of class conflict have created one prerevolutionary situation and revolutionary chance after another, which have been missed or ruined because of the opportunist character, treacherous role, or conciliatory policies of the old parties.

At the present point, two gigantic disproportions hang like leaden weights upon the progress of the world revolution. One is the perilous gap between the revolutionized but industrially backward East and the unrevolutionized but economically advanced West. The other is the urgent need of the workers and rural masses for correct guidance in their fight for power and the incapacity of the established leaderships to provide it.

These conditions define the historical function and set the supreme task of the Fourth International: to assemble and train a leadership that can close these gaps and assure definitive victory to the forces of socialism.

6

Hybrid Formations

Hybrid Formations and the Permanent Revolution in Latin America

The following three questions on topics of special interest to Latin American revolutionists were addressed to George Novack by some members of the Grupo Comunista Internacionalista, a Mexican Trotskyist organization. They deal with the relations between the theory of the permanent revolution and the law of uneven and combined development and their application to the problems of Latin American history and politics.

What is the relation between the theory of permanent revolution and the law of uneven and combined development in history? Why have you written that the first theory is founded upon the second?

The law of uneven and combined development is a general law of the historical process of which the theory of permanent revolution is a particular expression limited to the period of transition from the capitalist system to socialism.

During the second half of the nineteenth century, the idea of evolution flourished in the western world largely in the form of gradualism. In social and political thought, it was believed that in the ascent of humanity from savagery through civilization there was a prescribed uniform sequence of stages that every people was obliged to follow. No part of this orderly procession could be mixed up, shifted around, telescoped, or skipped over.

This sort of neat schematizing even acquired a biological basis. It was known that the early embryonic forms of different animals from the same general group resemble one another much more closely than the adult form of the same species. Evolutionary naturalists like the German Ernst Haeckel elevated these parallels between the embryo and their predecessors into a general law that "ontogeny recapitulates phylogeny," that is, that during development any embryo passes through a succession of forms which represent its adult ancestors in their evolutionary order. Biologists have since discovered that while this observation does reflect certain features in some species, the supposed law has too many exceptions to be accepted as generally valid. [1]

The embryology of social formations was interpreted along similar lines by vulgar evolutionists. The apostles of capitalist progress maintained that all forward-moving peoples would eventually step up from their benighted precapitalist state to the enlightenment of free competition, bourgeois liberalism, parliamentarism, and their attendant institutions in the same order and in much the same way as the pioneer capitalist nations had done.

Twentieth-century events have shown that there was a fatal flaw in their method of reasoning. They failed to take into account the accumulated effects of the most fundamental and inescapable feature of world capitalist development, its extreme irregularity. This aspect of the workings of the first part of the law of uneven and combined development dictated that the further course of historical progress was not to be so smooth and simple.

Capitalist commerce, banking and industry, capitalist power, capitalist relations and their benefits were for the most part concentrated and developed in classical forms in only one small portion of the planet, Western Europe and the United States, while the majority of mankind remained stuck fast or were forcibly held in more backward conditions by the overseas exploiters.

The pronounced unevenness of economic, social, political and cultural growth on a global scale laid the groundwork for a drastic and unexpected upset in the norms of development that had characterized the earlier stages of capitalism. The stunted forms of bourgeois life and labor, yoked together with archaic precapitalist relations, prevented the bourgeois strata, which had performed such progressive services in revolutionizing the old order in Western Europe and the United States, from filling a comparable historical role in the colonized areas.

The theory of permanent revolution proceeded from a recognition of the fact that the roles of the social classes were to be vastly different in the declining stage of capitalism than they had been in its progressive period. The main tasks of the democratic revolution in the bourgeois era were the achievement of national independence and unification, agrarian reform, secularization, equal rights for women, self-determination for subjugated nationalities, the creation of a democratic state, industrialization and modernization of the economy. These tasks, which had been solved with more or less success by the radical and liberal bourgeoisie in the West, had barely been broached on the continents where the majority of mankind lived.

Because of the deficiencies arising from the unequal development of capitalist civilization, neither the big nor the little native bourgeoisie in the underdeveloped lands could shoulder these tasks and lead the masses in a thorough renovation of the old regime along democratic lines. What then was to be done? This has been the paramount question posed to the revolutionary vanguard in the backward countries since the turn of the century.

Through an analysis of the social structure of semifeudal, semicapitalist Russia and the dynamics of the class forces revealed during the defeated 1905 revolution, Trotsky drew the following conclusions: the liberal bourgeoisie had become impotent and politically bankrupt; when the chips were down, it would go over to the counterrevolution. The peasantry and intellectuals could only play auxiliary roles in the revolutionary process. The sole available candidate for revolutionary leadership to carry the struggle for democracy to its conclusion was the proletariat, the peculiar product of the capitalist industrial revolution.

The unique alignment of social forces produced by the evolution of world capitalism as it entered upon its imperialist phase had prepared the conditions, Trotsky deduced, for a combined development of historical stages in the revolutions of the twentieth century.

This correlation had two major aspects. First, because the anticapitalist working class was the leading political force in the upheaval, the democratic tasks appropriate to a belated antifeudal revolution inevitably became intertwined with the tasks of the socialist revolution. The latter tasks included the conquest of power by the proletariat at the head of the insurgent masses, the abolition of capitalist private property, the collectivization of agriculture, the creation of a planned economy and the state monopoly of foreign trade, the development of a socialist democracy. These institutions could promote the most rapid growth of the economy and lead to higher levels of consumption and culture, the abolition of inequalities, the gradual elimination of the differences between mental and manual labor, between the city and the countryside, and the uprooting of alienation in social life. The overriding task was the extension of the world revolution through the establish-

ment of workers' power in the most advanced industrial countries, where the most highly developed productive forces and
the seats of imperialist power were located.

Second, both sets of tasks, one belonging to the dawn, the
other to the sunset of capitalist society, had to be carried out
by a revolutionary alliance of the workers and peasants in
mortal combat against the property and power of the native
bourgeoisie, the precapitalist proprietors, and the foreign imperialists.

In collaboration with Parvus (A. L. Helphand), Trotsky originated this conception of the revolutionary process and its
socialist strategy in the epoch of imperialism as early as 1906,
while considering the orientation of the proletarian struggle
in Russia. It was adopted in principle by Lenin and the Bolsheviks in April 1917. It guided their policy leading to the
October overturn.

Trotsky's theory of the permanent revolution has been confirmed since that time by the Yugoslav, Chinese, Cuban, and
Vietnamese revolutions. It has been confirmed in the negative
by the inability of those colonial peoples that have not combined their struggle for national independence with a victorious onslaught against capitalist property and power, to
achieve either a stable democratic regime or an escape from
the yoke of imperialism. Witness the continent of Latin America today from Argentina to Mexico.

In addition to illuminating the road to power and to liberation from imperialism, the theory of the permanent revolution
contains two other theses pertinent to the law of uneven and
combined development. It asserts that while the socialist forces
can be victorious in a single backward country without wait-
ing for any others, as happened in Russia in 1917 and Cuba
much later, the revolution cannot realize its full program and
be consummated in a socialist order unless workers' power
has been achieved in the most highly industrialized sectors
of the globe. This revolutionary internationalist position is
squarely counterposed to the Stalinist national-bureaucratic
dogma of building socialism in a single country.

It further stresses that a victorious socialist revolution does
not equally and all at once eradicate all the relations and
customs of the past, but only overthrows those economic, political, and legal institutions at the root of capitalist domination. After the conquest of power, the worker-peasant revolution is obliged to tackle and remove inherited obsolescences
as fast as conditions permit.

This historical assignment is especially arduous and protracted in those postcapitalist countries that, because of their backwardness, have had to cope simultaneously with the unsolved tasks of the democratic revolution and the tasks involved in building socialism. Without a vigilant, firm, and highly conscious political leadership and, above all, without breaking the imperialist encirclement through the extension of proletarian power to the advanced countries, the backward workers' states run the risk of suffering retrogression and deformation along bureaucratic lines. The record of the Soviet regime under Stalin and his successors is the most forceful and appalling evidence of this danger.

It should be pointed out that the interconnection of the theory of the permanent revolution with the law of uneven and combined development can be seen in the fact that Trotsky himself came to formulate the wider law of historical development only after elaborating the more restricted conception (much as Einstein around the same time first presented the restricted and then the general theory of relativity). Although the seeds of the law of uneven and combined development can be discerned in his previous thinking, they did not flower until after the October revolution when he delved more deeply into the reasons, contrary to the expectations of Marx, that the proletariat could and did take power in one of the less developed countries sooner than in the more developed ones.

Here, the results of experience fructified and stimulated a profounder understanding of the dialectics of history. The successive stages in Trotsky's intellectual enlightenment can be studied in his two works, *Results and Prospects,* written in 1906, and the first chapter of the masterful *History of the Russian Revolution,* written in the early 1930s.

Some authors such as Andre Gunder Frank believe that the formula of uneven and combined development cannot be applied to Latin America since it is nothing but a Trotskyist schema. What do you think of the interpretation of Latin American development presented in his work which contraposes the Marxist method to the Trotskyist law of uneven and combined development?

The first questions focused upon the passage from a well-developed capitalism to a postcapitalist society. The subject now concerns the earlier period of transition from precapitalist to capitalist formations.

Despite Frank's contention, there is no opposition between the Marxist method of approach and the application of the law of uneven and combined development to the problems involved in this historical process. The two are identical. Indeed, the complexities of the colonial period cannot be unraveled without resort to the law of uneven and combined development.

As capitalism spread from its center in maritime Europe to create the world market, it encountered and penetrated all sorts of precapitalist formations and relations. These early forms ranged from primitive food collectors through a gamut of intermediate types of social organization to feudalism.

The forces of capitalism could not immediately wipe out these archaic social relations, especially in the field of production. Quite the contrary. Just as the feudal proprietors of Western Europe had made use of slavery and peasant households along with the dominant serfdom in the rural regions and the merchants and guildsmen in the towns, so the original emissaries of capitalist trade and manufacture sought to harness precapitalist institutions and put them to work for their own profit.

The mercantile elements went so far as to re-create overseas antiquated modes of production which they had already outgrown at home. The most conspicuous case was the large-scale implanting of chattel slavery in the New World long after it had come to play a marginal role in Europe. This mode of production was exported to the semitropical zones of the New World as the most lucrative and feasible type of labor for growing such staple crops as sugar, tobacco, rice, indigo, etc., and for mining precious metals.

However, the slavery introduced into the Americas was not a mere replica of classical slavery. Although it had the same economic form, it acquired very different features and functions owing to the circumstances of its birth, the more advanced epoch in which it grew, and the specific part it played as an agricultural branch of the expanding capitalist world market. From its origins, it was a commercialized and bourgeoisified chattel slavery. The slave trade was itself one of the principal forms of commercial enterprise.

This combined type of slavery was perfected in the Cotton Kingdom of the Southern United States during the first half of the nineteenth century, and functioned as the main agricultural appendage of industrial capitalism in the international social division of labor. In *The Poverty of Philosophy,* Marx termed it "the pivot of bourgeois industry."

The fusion of capitalist with precapitalist relations gave rise to an assortment of combined economic forms and incongruous social formations in the age of commercial capitalism.

In North America, the Indian trappers, who traded skins and furs with the French, English and Dutch trading companies, were thereby annexed to the circuit of capital even though they retained their tribal structure and customs.

Marx mentions in the *Introduction to the Critique of Political Economy* that the corporate form which dominates the monopolist stage of capitalism first appeared in the joint-stock companies that engaged in far-flung colonizing and trading enterprises.

One of the most bizarre was the Carolina Plantations. This joint-stock company sought to set up on the Atlantic seaboard a purely feudal society in line with the blueprint of a constitution drafted by its secretary, the eminent empirical philosopher John Locke. The charter decreed that landlord-serf relations would be enforced in perpetuity among the settlers. This experiment turned out to be more quixotic than empirical. It quickly ran aground because the socioeconomic conditions in the wilderness, where labor was sparse and land plentiful, militated against the growth of medieval forms of production.

Slavery flourished, however, in the Southern English colonies, the Caribbean and Latin America during the colonial era. Feudal and semifeudal relations of production experienced a more uneven growth. They found the most favorable seedbed in South America. The colonizing process on that continent was the result of forces coming from two very disparate levels of development: the Spanish and Portuguese conquerors, who were passing over from feudal to bourgeois conditions, and the indigenous population, which preserved the communal tribal relations of the Stone Age. Their interaction gave rise to a wide variety of intermediate forms. The question is: What was their socioeconomic nature?

According to Andre Gunder Frank, they were essentially capitalist. In *Capitalism and Underdevelopment in Latin America,* he writes: "Capitalism began to penetrate, to form, indeed *fully* to characterize Latin American and Chilean society as early as the sixteenth century" (emphasis added). This postulate of his analysis of their development cannot stand up against either the historical facts or the method of Marxism for the following reasons:

1. In the sixteenth century, capitalism itself was just beginning to take shape in Western Europe. The industrial revolution, which established the specifically capitalist mode of production, did not take off until the nineteenth century. How, then, could backward Latin America have become "fully" capitalist that early?

2. The chief colonial power, Spain, had itself barely begun

to crawl out of medievalism. The country was still as much feudal as bourgeois. It was ruled by an absolute monarchy attended by an inquisitorial church, and resembled an Asiatic despotism more than the progressive royal regimes of the rest of Western Europe. It rested upon a decadent economy whose relations with the New World did far more to enrich the more advanced powers beyond the Pyrenees than to revolutionize its own social structure. "As late as the eighteenth century the strength of the higher nobility and the pre-eminence of the grandees rested firmly on their command of land and labor, and four great families reputedly owned one-third of all the land under cultivation in Spain."[2]

The Spanish merchants served as intermediary agents for the French, English and Dutch producers and powers. How could the Spaniards and the Portuguese have instituted forms of economic organization in Latin America superior to their own in Europe between the sixteenth and nineteenth centuries? It is well known that the economic underdevelopment of Spain in relation to the other great maritime mercantile nations of Europe was partly attributable to the overdevelopment of its colonial holdings. This in turn was a considerable factor in perpetuating backwardness in the possessions it ruled and robbed.

3. Spain and Portugal created economic forms in the New World that had a combined character. They welded precapitalist relations to exchange relations, thereby subordinating them to the demands and movements of merchant capital.

During the colonial period, diverse forms of forced rather than free labor prevailed in the main areas of production such as mining, ranching and agricultural enterprises. The subjugated native population toiled under serfdom (the *mita*), outright slavery, peonage or debt servitude, and sharecropping. Wage labor cropped up here and there but was exceptional, marginal and stunted. The *encomiendas,* which were the principal source of wealth and power, were a feudal, not a bourgeois form of property and method of production, and the landed aristocrats who held them were as feudalized as their counterparts on the Iberian peninsula.

What, from the standpoint of Marxism, are the sources of Andre Gunder Frank's errors?

1. He fails to see the distinction between the existence of certain capitalist forms of economic activity, such as money-lending and merchant capital, and a matured capitalist system of economic relations. The more primitive and superstructural forms of capital can coexist with precapitalist con-

ditions before capitalist entrepreneurs take command of the processes of production. They did in fact coexist from ancient times to the industrial revolution.

2. He fixes attention upon the relations prevailing in the sphere of exchange to the exclusion of the relations of production which, for a historical materialist, are decisive in determining the nature of an economy and its corresponding social structure. Commodities can be produced under precapitalist as well as capitalist and even postcapitalist conditions. Mercantile capital, viewed in either its domestic or foreign operations, is not identical with the capitalist system of economic relations. This form of capital antedates the creation of capitalist production per se and is its precondition. As Marx explained, the capitalist mode of production acquires its adequate and appropriate technical basis only with the advent of large-scale factory industry under the command of industrial capital.

3. He does not understand the role of combined formations in the period of transition from a precapitalist to a capitalist economy. He thereby misses the very peculiar character — the special form of exploitation — that characterized the colonial system: the exploiting of *precapitalist* conditions of production by the colonial powers for the benefit of the rising *capitalist* system. Capitalist exploitation can thus take place before capitalism takes over the system of production at the base of social life.

When gold, silver, and diamonds were mined by slaves or enforced laborers rather than wage workers and then brought to market, this was a combined economic activity from the standpoint of historical evolution. The precious metals produced by precapitalist methods were converted into commodities, then into money, and eventually into capital, contributing mightily to the prosperity and power of the commercial kingdoms on the way to bourgeoisification. But the weighty role of these commodities in promoting capitalism does not negate the fact that they originated within precapitalist forms. The cotton grown on the Southern slave plantations was produced in a noncapitalist manner even though it was the principal export commodity of the United States before the Civil War and was tied to the capitalist textile industries of both Old and New England.

4. On the level of Marxist theory and method, Frank does not grasp either the highly contradictory character of such transitional formations or the dynamics of their development.[3] The European civilization that was grafted upon the aborig-

inal population of Latin America not only produced biological half-breeds like the *mestizo* but sociological hybrids that were as much feudal as bourgeois. The trouble with Frank's theory is that he seeks to rule out hybrids in economics and sociology.

Frank considers it imperative to "elaborate a unitary dialectical theory of the process of capitalist development. . . ." Yet he calls into question "the supposed coexistence of feudalism and capitalism" (Frank, *Capitalism and Underdevelopment in Latin America,* p. 268). He insists that one should have nothing to do with the other, when in historical fact these contrary economic categories have not only coexisted but have been fused, above all, in the backward colonial lands.

Frank ignores the dialectical law of the unity or interpenetration of opposites which, in sociohistorical terms, presupposes the possibility of the coexistence, at least for a certain time, of feudal and capitalist relations in the evolution of class societies. In the test case of Chile, they did so coexist in the *encomiendas* and mines where the products of forced labor were sold on the capitalist market. The coexistence of precapitalist with mercantile relations is still clearer in regard to the sugar plantations of Brazil which were cultivated by slave labor. At the end of the colonial period, two-fifths of the people in that country were Black slaves.

Frank's approach to the socioeconomic development of Latin America is highly oversimplified. It leaves no room for complex historical situations, combined class relations, and contradictory socioeconomic formations. A scientific investigator cannot work efficiently without the proper tools. Frank could have avoided his one-sided conclusions if he had assimilated and learned how to apply the law of uneven and combined development. This theory is one of the most valuable additions to scientific socialism in the twentieth century and is indispensable for analyzing transitional periods and formations, especially those characterizing the colonial world.

Andre Gunder Frank, in our opinion, correctly states that the historical development of Latin America is complex and cannot be explained by blueprints. Nonetheless, in his polemic with the Stalinists, he has maintained that the conquest of America by the European powers was capitalist in its essence. This view is shared by Luis Vitale in Chile, Alonso Aguilar in Mexico, and other Marxists. What is your position in this controversy?

The viewpoint represented by Frank and the others mentioned

is prompted by revolutionary motives and directed against far more erroneous and dangerous positions.

The myth of a *purely* feudal past is put forward by liberal and proimperialist U. S. scholars in order to defend the path of capitalist development as a dynamic "democratic alternative" to Latin American stagnation and its traditional institutions. It is likewise championed by the ideological followers of the Moscow-oriented Communists to bolster their opportunist conception of a two-stage revolution in colonial countries in which priority over the mass struggle for socialism is assigned to a separate and independent democratic revolution. (Many Maoists likewise share this conception, which is derived from Menshevism, not Bolshevism.)

This false and pernicious schema enables the reformists and Stalinists to justify supporting the allegedly "progressive" and "anti-imperialist" wings of the native bourgeoisies against the reactionary landed interests. In practice, the policy comes down to subordinating and sacrificing the revolutionary class struggle for workers' power.

However, praiseworthy political intentions do not excuse crude sociological analysis and superficial historical insight. One can hardly refute the reformists and Stalinists by matching their erroneous conception of a purely feudal society with the mistaken view of a purely capitalist one in defiance of the historical realities. One view is only a mirror image of the inadequacy of the other. [4]

Both can be avoided if the law of uneven and combined development is properly used to clarify the actual course of Latin American socioeconomic development. More than a theoretical or academic question is at issue. Since the answer involves serious political and strategical consequences for the revolutionary vanguard throughout Latin America today, a correct and comprehensive approach to the problems is essential.

The theory of permanent revolution explains why the belated Latin American bourgeoisie has been unable to carry through the basic tasks of the democratic revolution and why the proletariat is the one social and political force that can complete these tasks as part of the anticapitalist struggle.

The two most important democratic tasks facing the Latin American peoples are the achievement of genuine liberation from imperialism and agrarian reform. But it will take a socialist revolution to realize these aims.

Frank's theory cannot explain why the agrarian question, which is one of the vestiges of feudalism or the slave system, plays so central a role in the contemporary revolutionary process.

How is it that this requirement of the democratic revolution, which was taken care of by the bourgeoisie of the United States in its two revolutions, weighs so heavily upon Latin America? And how is it to be solved? The theory of the permanent revolution provides the clearest explanation and the most realistic approach to its solution from the revolutionary Marxist point of view.

In confronting the Stalinists, one ought to examine their position in accordance with the Marxist method. This requires, among other things, studying its origin. Not much effort is needed to uncover the fact that the Stalinist theory of "revolution in two stages" and the possibility of the capitalist class or a sector of it playing a "progressive role" in such a revolution, did not originate in Latin America. It is a mere application in Latin America and elsewhere of a theory advanced by Stalin after the bureaucratic caste had usurped power in the Soviet Union.

A little further research will reveal, not unexpectedly, that Stalin only revived a theory that had been thoroughly discussed in the Marxist movement in Russia in the early part of the century and before. This was the theory of the Mensheviks, who held that the revolution in Russia would come in two stages, in the first of which the Russian bourgeoisie would play a leading role.

The debate of the Russian Marxists over this question is highly pertinent to the current discussion, inasmuch as they were confronted with the problem of making a revolution in a land where very palpable vestiges of feudalism existed. It is hardly worthwhile to reexamine that debate from the vantage point of Frank's theory, but it would seem obvious that Trotsky's contribution of the theory of permanent revolution would, of course, be rejected out of hand, as would the basic position of Russian Marxism, including that of Plekhanov and Lenin, since all of the Russian Marxists, whatever their differences on other questions, agreed that the tasks historically belonging to the bourgeois democratic revolution had not yet been achieved in Russia.[5] Against the Marxists, a Russian revolutionary committed to the equivalent of Frank's theory would have said that the country was already capitalist and that the question of feudal vestiges was only diversionary. What was imperative was to discard "the received dualist view" of "the supposed coexistence of feudalism and capitalism" and "to elaborate a unitary dialectical theory of the process of capitalist development."

The Russian prototype of Frank would also be hard put to explain the origin of the agrarian question, why a thoroughgoing agrarian reform was of paramount importance, and why Lenin insisted on working out a correct program so as to assure leadership of the revolution to the proletariat.

Andre Gunder Frank can argue that this is absurd. Naturally, in the case of Russia he agrees that the Marxists of those days were correct in holding to a "dualist view," and correct in viewing agrarian reform as a bourgeois-democratic task that had fallen to the workers to carry out.

However, that ought to lead him logically to admit the following possibility: if feudal vestiges do exist in Latin America today, this does not stand in the way of making a successful revolution. In fact, from the standpoint of both theory and practice, it can facilitate the revolutionary process. The example of the Russian Revolution proves it.

The reality is that this *is* the situation. The semifeudal, semibourgeois nature of Latin American development has created a contradictory state of affairs in the amalgamation of feudal with capitalist relations that only the conquest of power by the revolutionary working class, leading all sections of the oppressed, including the landless and impoverished peasantry, can resolve. Just as the structure of Latin American society intermingles precapitalist with capitalist elements in an indissoluble unity, so the solution of its inherited democratic tasks are inseparably linked with the socialist tasks of the coming revolution. This is the gist of the teaching of the permanent revolution. It is no less Marxist than Trotskyist.

The law of uneven and combined development is indispensable for understanding the development of Latin America over the past four centuries. It can illuminate both the earliest stage, when precapitalist were meshed with capitalist relations, and the present stage, when the tasks of democratization, belonging historically to the bourgeois epoch, have become an integral part of the proletarian revolution of the twentieth century.

That is also why Frank's attempt to divide Marxism from Trotskyism and contrapose one to the other does not hold water. The theoretical formulations of the Trotskyist movement are not only solidly rooted in scientific socialism but are the most penetrating expressions of Marxist thought available today.

Law of Uneven and Combined
Development and Latin America

[The following is a response to David Romagnolo's article, "The So-Called Law of Uneven and Combined Development," which appeared in the spring 1975 issue of *Latin American Perspectives*. Novack's article appeared in the spring 1976 issue of the same journal.]

*   *   *

David Romagnolo makes two main criticisms of the law of uneven and combined development. First, it supposedly disregards the leading principle of historical materialism that the mode of production determines the nature of a social formation. It thereby bases itself upon the superficial peculiarities, the exceptional features, of historical development instead of its general and fundamental ones. Second, the law of uneven and combined development focuses on exchange rather than productive relations, thus lapsing into the errors of the vulgar bourgeois economists.

Neither contention is factually correct. The law of uneven and combined development proceeds from the premise that the mode of production, constituted by the level of the productive forces and the corresponding relations of production, is the underlying determinant in all social structures and historical processes. Nor does the law subordinate the relations of production to exchange relations, although it recognizes that in the generalized commodity relations intrinsic to capitalism exchange relations have far greater importance than in precapitalist societies, where the sale and purchase of products is economically marginal.

However, these two elementary Marxist principles only provide the points of departure and serve as guidelines for analyzing historically developed social formations in their full concreteness. With their aid it is necessary to go forward and explain why a particular mode of production manifests itself in such different ways and develops to such disparate degrees under different circumstances. How is it, as Marx pointed out, that "the same economic basis" shows "infinite variations and gradations of appearance?" This can be ascertained, he tells us, "only by analysis of the empirically given circumstances." In this case we must ask: what empirical circumstances account for the variations and gradations of appearance of the modes of production in Latin America after its conquest and colonization?

The law of uneven and combined development formulates the general reason, the underlying causes, for the differential growth of a given mode of production within a concrete social formation. It may grow normally, like nineteenth-century British capitalism; or in stunted fashion, like feudal relations in the North American English colonies; or luxuriantly, like slavery in Brazil. The specific nature and level of its development depends upon the environing conditions and influences.

A mode of production does not come into the world, or a continental part of it, ready-made and fully fledged; it goes through a complex course of evolution from start to finish. In the process of origination, expansion, disintegration, and destruction, its relations with other modes of production of an inferior or superior order have a great deal to do with the rate, extent and quality of its own development. They mold its special characteristics. These distinctive features arising from its actual career in life are incorporated and cannot be separated from it or ignored in defining or assessing its real nature.

The principal issue of historical theory in the so-called dependency debate is: what caused the relative backwardness of Latin America with all the fateful consequences of its underdevelopment? Collaterally, why have the Latin American bourgeoisies had so feeble and stunted a development, and played so limited a progressive role, compared with their North American and Western European counterparts?

The law of uneven and combined development can help clarify these problems along the following lines. Up to the sixteenth century the Old World and the New, cut off from each other, experienced very different paths of development, which placed them on different levels. The maritime powers of Western Europe were passing over from feudalism to capitalism at a time when the original inhabitants of the Americas were still far behind them. This immense disparity in their grades of development predetermined the predominance of the one over the other and shaped the further destinies of Latin America from the conquest to the present day.

Romagnolo insists that "the focus of historical materialism is upon internal development, while that of the law of uneven and combined development [is] upon external relationships" (p. 18). Such a rigid dichotomy between internal and external relationships is unwarranted for the era of capitalist expansion which unfolded on a worldwide scale. It is most inappropriate in connection with the development of Latin America in post-Columbian times when external forces directed by the Iberians invaded the continent, subjugated and plundered its inhabitants, and radically altered previous economic and social relationships. The collision and conjunction of their modes of life and labor set an indelible stamp upon the whole of Latin America.

The new and higher relations that the Spanish and Portuguese introduced into the Western Hemisphere from Mexico to Chile did not evolve organically out of the pre-existing social order, as in Western Europe, where the rising bourgeois forces flourished to the point where they demanded a higher form of social economy and political regime. To the contrary, commercial capital penetrated by various channels into the New World as its representatives broke up the ancient communal institutions and reconstructed human relations in hitherto unknown ways. For instance, the cities as trading centers did not grow out of the countryside as in Western Europe but were independently founded by the commercial colonizers under the patronage of the crown, whence a nascent Creole bourgeoisie proceeded to change rural life.

The law of uneven and combined development operates with special force and can be most relevantly applied to such periods of transition when old conditions are being uprooted and transformed, or deformed, and new ones are in the formative stage.

Romagnolo writes:

> The extension of commodity circulation can provide an impetus to the development of a mode of production but does not initiate a change in the form of social production. The internal contradictions of the mode of production do not emanate from the "fortuitous combination of elements," i.e., externally; rather, they are inherent in the social form of production and characterize the essential relationship between the forces of production and the social relations of production [p. 18].

This categorical assertion skips over the fact that before a mode of production can function in accord with its own immanent laws, it must be brought into being. Chattel slave, feudal and capitalist relations, along with other institutions, customs and values of civilization, did not exist in the New World until they were imported from overseas. The commodity circulation of the world market and the lust for precious metals that propelled the Spaniards and Portuguese westward in the first place did far more than "give an impetus" to the existing form of social production; it implanted and fostered all the characteristic modes of class exploitation in Latin America except mechanized industry. Whether slavemasters or feudalists, its mine owners, entrepreneur planters and ranchers produced and sold commodities for the world market. The precious metals extracted by forced labor promoted the formation, circulation, and accumulation of capital abroad.

Rosa Luxemburg stated in *The Accumulation of Capital*: "Capital, impelled to appropriate productive forces for purposes of exploitation, ransacks the whole world; it procures its means of production from all corners of the earth, seizing them, if necessary by force, from all levels of civilization and from all forms of society."[1] Capitalist accumulation in all its stages has depended to one or another extent upon access to means of production and subsistence produced under precapitalist or noncapitalist conditions. In doing so, it annexes precapitalist forms of production as tributaries to its economic operations. Brazilian sugar earlier played the same role in this respect as Southern cotton cultivated by slaves and Russian wheat raised by serfs.

Indeed, the Brazilian plantations, which had a precocious growth as the world's chief exporter of sugar, provide an impressive case of uneven and combined development. Their predominance imposed an extreme lopsidedness upon the economy during the colonial period.

The crop was cultivated and processed by slave-labor, the most primitive kind of extensive agricultural labor. While the sugar barons directly profited from the surplus labor of their workforce, their type of operation was not the same as the classical slavery based upon a natural economy. It was a commercialized slavery which originated and developed as an offshoot of the capitalist world market.

Although the plantation (*fazenda*) was a self-sustaining, isolated production unit outside the money economy, where the opulent landowning families disported themselves like lords and ladies on the backs of their slaves, it was geared into the vast machinery of commerce. The labor supply came not from the local Indians but, as in the Caribbean, from African traders who dealt in slaves as a commodity.

The sugar mills required a sizeable capital investment. The luxury staple was marketed by monopolistic companies, carried on Portuguese ships alone, sold in Portugal and exchanged for goods from the mother country. Consequently, unlike the Spanish towns, the few underdeveloped seaboard centers were little more than places for the transhipment of goods.

This symbiosis of slave production with international commerce gave a combined character to the Brazilian economy. It resulted from and embodied the mutual penetration of factors belonging to two different historical species: slavery, which was characteristic of the first stage of class society; and the market and monetary relations that were ushering in its climactic capitalist form.

Of course, once Black slavery was established on a large scale (six to eight million slaves were brought into the colony from the late sixteenth to the early nineteenth century), it was actuated by its own internal laws. But this mode of production, beset by a twofold contradiction, had a twin-motored dynamic. Its development was regulated not only by its own momentum but even more by outside conditions and forces. The export economies were not self-determined but shaped and misshaped by the social division of labor bound up with the centralized imperial system, and they have to be analyzed and appraised in their organic connection with the money economy of the world market.

This linkup was evidenced in the cyclical pattern of Brazilian trade, the "boom and bust" cycles expressed in the rise and decline of the sugar crop and other commodities such as lumber, precious metals, cotton, and later, rubber and coffee, which depended upon the fluctuations in foreign demand and competitive conditions in the world market. The expansion and contraction of these branches of production have been responsible for its onesided, backward and dependent development.

The distortion of Latin America's economic and social development under the pressures of the world market and domination by foreign forces is one of the prime peculiarities of its history from which the continent suffers to the present day. The subordinate role clamped upon Latin America as a supplier of raw materials and foodstuffs in the international capitalist division of labor enabled the more advanced metropolitan powers to exploit and rule over its peoples, first under the colonial system and later through the more refined methods of monopoly capitalism.

This unevenness manifested itself, in Latin America as in other parts of the colonialized world, in the emergence and endurance of a broad spectrum of combined forms in which precapitalist relations of one kind or another were fused with capitalist relations. In this way the various precapitalist modes of production were conscripted to serve the demands and interests of the monied men overseas and at home. In the transitional period from the dominance of one mode of production to the maturity of its deplacement by another, Romangnolo does not allow for the existence of such mixed modes with contradictory characteristics that give a peculiar twist to the social structure of a country.

Two articles in the same issue of *Latin American Perspectives* that Romagnolo's article appears in pinpoint successive stages in the process of combination. The first step whereby institutions of a lower and weaker order were subjected to the influence of a higher and more powerful one is described in the paper by Karen Spalding on the reorganization of social relations in Peru under the Spanish colonial rulers.[2] The *ayllu*, the ancient unit of the Inca community based on kinship, was transmuted when the Andean population was relocated and concentrated into villages controlled by representatives of the Spanish authorities. Although the Indians retained the right of using the land, it became the legal property of the Spanish state.

Here the traditional kinship form of social life, with its communal possession, was subordinated to the rule of the exploiters and oppressors, who exacted tribute from the people. The old communal possession was amalgamated with the new state property in a servile formation under the impulsion of the European exchange economy. Even more brutal was the parceling out of the Indians to the proprietors of the *encomiendas*, who exacted forced labor from them.

The prevalence of subsequent combined formations is excellently documented by Kyle Steenland in his "Notes on Feudalism and Capitalism in Chile and Latin America."[3] He distinguishes four stages in the economic development of postconquest Chile: 1) the direct enslavement of the native population; 2) the growth of semifeudal relations of production; 3) the appearance of wage labor toward the end of the nineteenth century with agriculture remaining semifeudal; 4) the dominance of capitalist relations from the 1930s on. In none of these stages did the Chilean economy have a fully capitalist or a purely precapitalist character. It was, he pointed out, a composite—a singular mixture of one and the other. While agriculture and mining, the main sectors of production and sources of wealth, were carried on under servile or feudal conditions, these branches of the economy were hooked into commercial capitalist relations that were responsible for their rise or decline, as happened with the Brazilian sugar crop. The precapitalist forms of labor ministered to the needs of the world market dominated by merchant capital.

Steenland poses the problem very clearly when he writes: "One cannot define as capitalist an economy which produces predominantly for the market but in which labor is not free. . . . On the other hand, it is clear that an economy which produces for the market, in which the main goal of the landowners or farmer is commodity exchange, cannot be called feudal."[4] The solution to this contradictory situation is to acknowledge that Chile during this period was "semifeudal," he says. That is, its economy blended precapitalist productive relations with commodity ties to the local and world market.

That is correct. The Chilean economy did not have a homogeneous but a heterogeneous nature. It was, in fact, a combined formation in which primitive features were synthetically unified with more advanced ones.

When Romagnolo criticizes the law of uneven and combined development for focusing on exchange rather than productive relations, he fails to understand the peculiar and decisive feature of the colonial period in Latin America—and of the era of commercial capitalism as such. Under the colonial system the backward countries were exploited by their metropolitan masters precisely through "the external relations of exchange and commerce" that they instituted and operated for their benefit. The Board of Trade in London that monopolized the commerce of the British colonies for the crown government, exciting the North American War of Independence, had its counterpart in the Trade House at Seville, which regulated foreign trade even more strictly.

Romagnolo faults the law of uneven and combined development for implying that "the capitalist mode of exploitation can take place, it would seem, under any conditions of production, be they capitalist or precapitalist" (p. 20). His irony is misplaced. He writes as though industrial production is the exclusive method of exploitation available to the capitalist. This is not so. Money lending and merchant capital employ the method of exploitation characteristic of capital without engaging in the distinctive capitalist mode of production. Wage labor is the essential mode of extracting surplus value from the work force in a matured capitalism. But even under monopoly capitalism the worker can be exploited not only as a producer but as a consumer, through installment loans from the moneylender. Here the primary exploitation in the production process is supplemented by the secondary exploitation of the usurer.

Romagnolo forgets that, on top of the direct exploitation of one class by another, there exists the economic, political, military and cultural domination of one country—and even one continent—by another. These two types of exploitation are inseparably united under the colonial system and its imperialist successor. Before the capitalists arrived at their own mode of technical production based on mechanized industry, the bankers, merchants and manufacturers of the more advanced powers practiced diverse methods of extorting wealth from the backward peoples of the earth. Marx describes these ways and means in *Capital* under the heading of "The So-Called Primitive Accumulation."[5]

The Old World enriched itself at the expense of the New not only by direct exploitation through the process of production but indirectly through state and commercial relations. The globe was divided into oppressive and exploitative powers and oppressed and exploited nations. The maintenance of feudal relations in Latin America on its export plantations was indispensable both for the accumulation of international capital and the prosperity of the native landowners. These conjoined ruling-class necessities have held the continent in their grip for centuries.

It is strange that Romagnolo objects to the application of the law of uneven and combined development to Latin America when he admits the possibility of the "simultaneous presence of more than one mode of production" (p. 15), and says that "backward Russia [was] characterized by a combination of semifeudal and capitalist relations" (p. 12). When two qualitatively different sets of economic relations commingle, as they did in tsarist Russia and Latin America, they constitute a combined formation.

Romagnolo does not deny the presence of uneven development; structural inequality is all too obvious. He further admits the possibility of combined formations. However, he refuses to take the next logical step of putting the two historical phenomena together in their necessary correlation. That is what the law of uneven and combined development does.

*　　　*　　　*

There is an excess of abstraction and a dearth of concreteness in his strictures on the law of uneven and combined development. This is not excusable even in discussion of theoretical and methodological questions. The method of historical materialism yields the most fruitful results, not from constant reiteration of its formulas, but when these general truths are wedded to the concrete realities of history. While Marxism approaches the particular through the general, it simultaneously views the general in and through its specific embodiments in the given facts.

Both the generality and the particularity of the real historical process are embraced in the law of uneven and combined development. Far from negating or denying any of the principles of historical materialism, this law has enriched and extended them by theoretically explaining the wealth of variety in the concrete and changing expressions of any given mode of production. The same economic system has multiform manifestations, not a uniform course of evolution. Romagnolo could extricate himself from his one-sided outlook if he resorted to this law in considering the course of the economic and social development of Latin America since the sixteenth century, instead of misunderstanding and misinterpreting it in the manner of Maoism.

The "Second Serfdom" in
Central and Eastern Europe

The transition from one social formation to the next brings forth a variety of anomalous phenomena in which features belonging to an earlier, more primitive stage of development are fused with those representative of the new order in the making. These extremely contradictory forms grow out of the operation of the law of uneven and combined development.

Such hybrid forms necessarily appear because the superior economy remains attached to the inferior conditions of labor until it acquires strength enough to stand firmly upon its own productive foundations and let loose its full energy. Before it becomes autonomous, the new stage of economic organization grows at the expense of its predecessors but in reliance upon them.

This law of the historical process asserted itself with great vigor during the rise of capitalism from the sixteenth to the nineteenth centuries. The co-mingling of capitalist relations with precapitalist forms characterizes this epoch on a world scale. The expansion of capitalism not only displaced, disintegrated, and destroyed precapitalist arrangements, but penetrated, annexed, impregnated, and merged with them, creating a wealth of paradoxical economic, social, and political institutions that had a combined character.

In the Americas, the Western Europeans from the Spanish to the English implanted and fostered chattel slavery, which had been unknown until the time of Columbus. This type of labor exploitation, installed to grow such staple crops as sugar and tobacco for the widening world market, amalgamated the most rudimentary mode of class production with the most advanced commercial relations of that era.

The nature of slavery itself was transformed. In its archaic patriarchal form, slavery was the pedestal of a self-contained natural economy producing use values for the master's family estate. In the New World, from the start it was a subordinate branch of the developing capitalist system, producing commodities for its commerce.

Marx explained the effects of such combinations of the new and the old upon the direct producers in *Capital* when he discussed "the greed for surplus labor" among the owners of the means of production. "As soon as people whose production still moves within the lower forms of slave-labor, corvée labor, etc., are drawn into the whirlpool of an international market dominated by the capitalistic mode of production, the sale of their products for export becoming their principal interest, the civilised horrors of overwork are grafted on the barbaric horrors of slavery, serfdom, etc."[1]

At the same time that this "werewolf's hunger for surplus labor" was taking hold in the Americas, a parallel phenomenon emerged in Central and Eastern Europe. Under the pressure of West European commerce, the agrarian relations in that backward area of the continent were transformed. But the result of the infiltration of trading relations with the West into the old order and their melding with a lower form of labor was very different in content and consequences from that across the ocean.

Whereas previously nonexistent modes of exploitation, notably chattel-slave and feudal relations, were introduced and imposed by the European conquerers and settlers in North and South America, the indigenous rulers and large property owners of Central and Eastern Europe, avid for monetary gain, extended and intensified serfdom in the most brutal and thoroughgoing fashion. This product of uneven and combined development was analyzed in various connections by Marx and Engels, who designated it as "the second edition of serfdom."

A collection of articles entitled "Le Deuxième Servage en Europe Centrale et Orientale," dealing with this historical phenomenon, was issued by *Recherches Internationales á la Lumiére du Marxisme*, Numbers 63-64, 1970, with a foreword by the French Communist historians Antoine Casanova and Charles Parain. Many of my references to this topic, which has been debated by scholars for the past hundred years, are taken from the studies by Soviet and East European authorities translated for this symposium.[2]

From the fifteenth to the twentieth centuries, Western Europe was the birthplace and remained the center of world capitalism. The preconditions for its origination there, rather than elsewhere, were rooted in the exceptionally high degree of development of the potentialities of feudal society and culture. The artisans and merchants of the medieval towns and cities, especially those carrying on extensive trade, developed the productive forces that provided the starting points and set free the elements for promoting the manufactures, overseas commerce, home market, and collateral economic processes that enriched the bourgeoisie and undermined the feudal regime.

England presented the perfected model of the primordial transition from feudal to capitalist conditions. As early as the last part of the fourteenth century, serfs had been converted into independent yeomen and landless cottagers on that island. Later the demands of the bourgeoisie for wool for the manufacture of fabrics led to driving the peasants from the land, which was taken over for raising sheep. The dispossession of the rural cultivators benefited all sections of the ruling classes, who were aided by a powerful and centralized monarchical state. The evictions gave the landed proprietors the necessary supply of agricultural laborers for capitalist farming on a large scale, in which the city bourgeoisie also invested its accumulated wealth. They placed levies of wage workers at the disposal of the capitalist manufacturers in the cities and countryside and provided sailors and soldiers for navigation and the armed forces of the kingdom.

A bourgeoisified aristocracy, the "gentry," replaced the old aristocracy which had been exterminated in the War of the Roses. This new nobility came to live, not upon feudal tribute, but upon capitalist money rent derived from its agricultural enterprises. Thanks to their common economic interests, they coexisted politically in close alliance with the rising bourgeois forces. This reconstruction of its economy enabled England to build its colonial empire and achieve domination of the world market, first in trade, afterwards in industry.

During this same period the regions of Central and Eastern Europe, including Germany, especially east of the Elbe, experienced another path of development which gave birth to very different economic, social, and political forms. Social relations in general, and feudalism in particular, which lasted with modifications throughout Europe until the end of the eighteenth century, were far less developed in that part of the continent than in the West. The state power, though autocratic, was relatively weak in relation to the nobility. Until the sixteenth century the peasants had managed to retain or regain communal rights to the land in the villages (the mir and the mark) and kept family possession of their allotments. They owed tolerable obligations as tenants of the landed proprietors, and enjoyed considerable acquired personal rights. The lords of the manor did not feel an overwhelming urge to turn from brigandage, compete with the patrician bourgeoisie, and amass monetary wealth by selling sizable amounts of surplus produce from their domains.

The feudal mode of production pivots around the payment of tribute in diverse forms to the liege-lord by the direct producers (serfs or peasants). The first edition of feudalism, like patriarchal slavery, was based upon the supremacy of a

natural economy in which the feudal domain was a self-sufficient whole. Most of the agricultural output was consumed
by the people living on the estate and only a small surplus
was exchanged or sold on the nearby market.

While the cultivators were attached to the land, this tie endowed them with that indispensable means of production. They
owed fealty to their lord and paid their dues to him in kind
or in labor. The serf or peasant worked the soil on an extremely low level of traditional technique, using the crudest
implements. However ample the lord's holdings, they were
cultivated by a multiplicity of small farming units. Under
these conditions the amount of surplus labor extracted from
the free peasants or bondsmen was circumscribed. The weak-
ening of the feudal dependence of the peasantry in many
places during the thirteenth and fourteenth centuries further
eased their situation.

The entry of capitalist influences from the end of the fifteenth century on changed this situation from top to bottom.
The increased demand for agricultural products by Holland,
England, Scandinavia, and other countries, coincided with
a revolutionary rise in prices that doubled and tripled the
price of commodities in the sixteenth century, impelled the
nobles in Central and Eastern Europe to embark on a new
course. They strove to enlarge their domains, deprive the
peasants of their family and communal lands and rights, and
intensify serf corvée labor in order to export large quantities of grain and other agricultural products abroad, maintain their extravagant courtly style of living, and buy new
articles of consumption to vie with the wealthy merchants.

The lords of the land became transformed from feudal barons
into entrepreneurs engaging in large-scale undertakings of the
commercial type. For this kind of exploitation they required
greater territory and more forced labor. So they proceeded to
acquire both of these necessary means of production at the
peasants' expense.

In various ways and by devious means free peasants were
ousted from their allotments of land, which were amalgamated
with the lords' domains. The cultivators were converted from
tenants, owing payment in kind or money to the seigneur, into
full-fledged serfs. Their corvée labor became the basis of this
second edition of serfdom. This type of tribute that had formerly
been minor became major.

Corvée in general comprised obligatory services of an economic, social, or military kind rendered to a lord or a king.
More precisely, it was the labor performed by the vassals, not

for themselves on their own land, but for the lord on his portion of the manorial demesne. The peasant had to divide his working week between labor on his own fields and labor on the lord's land.

Labor rent (corvée), rent in kind (in agricultural or artisan products), and money rent were the three successive forms of feudal rent. As the peasants lost their rights and autonomy and fell under the unrestrained sway of the lord, the more developed forms of supplementary imposed labor, realized in kind or in money, were replaced by the most elementary form. In reverting to personal servitude the serf became subjected to the most brutal exploitation under the corvée. Work for the lord rather than for his own account took up a larger and larger part of the year. It rose from two to three to four days a week until the grasping lord claimed there was no limit to the obligations he could exact from his tenants.

As the corvée gained control over social production, the whole existence of the cultivators changed for the worse. At its extreme the serf was no better than a slave. He could be bought and sold like a chattel with or without the land, which was not customary in earlier centuries. Although corvée labor had existed from the beginning of feudalism (serfdom in fact sprang out of the corvée), it was not so harsh and omnivorous until the landed proprietors, their lust for gain incited by the prospects of export trade, "grafted the horrors of civilized overwork" upon this type of labor. Overwork took the form of more days of labor for the lord.

The Belgian historian Pirenne describes the result of these arbitrary measures in this way: "The descendants of the free colonists of the thirteenth century were systematically deprived of their land and reduced to the position of personal serfs (Leibeigene). The wholesale exploitation of estates absorbed their holdings and reduced them to a servile condition which so closely approximated to that of slavery that it was permissible to sell the person of the serf independently of the soil. From the middle of the sixteenth century the whole of the region to the east of the Elbe and the Sudeten mountains became covered with Rittergüter exploited by Junkers, who may be compared, as regards the degree of humanity displayed in their treatment of their white slaves, with the planters of the West Indies."[3]

These developments greatly augmented the wealth and power of the landed nobility, which concentrated economic, juridical, and clerical functions in their hands, giving them virtually total command over the lives and minds of their bondsmen.

This intensified oppression and robbery by the landlords was fiercely resented and contested by the peasants, who time and again rose in insurrection. Their resistance, which was spread out for more than a century from the Peasants War in Germany of the early sixteenth century to the Thirty Years War, was pitilessly crushed. The defeat of the peasant insurgency sealed the fate of the rural toilers, leaving them in a state of helpless servitude. Except for some "free" villages surviving in protected pockets here and there, the subjugated village communities disintegrated and disappeared. Thus the second edition of serfdom was consolidated on the expropriation and coercion of the peasantry, just as serfdom was instituted in Latin America on the forced labor of the aboriginal population and slavery on the importation and bondage of the African peoples.

The second serfdom, oriented to the production of commodities for the international market, was not a mere replica of the first, which was based on the growing and making of products for local consumption. It was a reversion in form but not in substance. Whereas the serfs originally created use values according to custom, the overworked bondsmen of the new dispensation had to produce more and more exchange values. Far from reproducing the pristine state of affairs, the second serfdom was a novel combination with dual characteristics, imposed by the higher laws of social development that forcibly merged an old mode of production with a new form of exchange.

The second serfdom, whereby the surplus agricultural product entered the European market, was a product of the uneven development of capitalism in its rise and feudalism in its decline. It was a specific phenomenon that could take root and flourish only in essentially backward agrarian countries with an underdeveloped social division of labor and a dispersed rural population, lacking a strong central authority or thriving commercial centers to which the peasants and serfs could flee and be absorbed. Such a feudalized society in Eastern Europe was suitable for economic annexation by the more advanced countries of Western Europe with a high degree of commodity production, exchange, and monetary relations.

Capitalism preserves and uses for its own purposes all forms of labor, provided they remain subordinate to its mastery. The combination of capitalist relations with precapitalist methods of production that took place on all continents during the transition from feudalism to capitalism presupposed the coexistence of social formations on disparate levels of historical development. This was not an unprecedented phenomenon. After all, feudalism itself had originated as a composite of the decayed remains of Roman civilization and Germanic barbarism integrated with the technological innovations, particularly in agriculture, of the early Middle Age.

So too the North American Indian trappers living in collective tribal conditions hunted and exchanged their skins and furs for goods, firearms, whiskey, and money offered by the great trading companies or their factors. In Latin America the colonial powers and landed aristocrats subjugated native peoples and reduced them to serfdom, instituting feudal relations of production and forms of ownership in the service of mercantile and money-lending capital. Such hybrids are inevitable when backward societies come under the sway of higher ones, wherever, that is, disproportionate historical and social development is present and active.

Similar crossbreeds arose in industry as well as agriculture. Whereas manufacture, the primary stage of capitalist industry, was carried on in Western Europe in cottage industry or by wage labor, in the Russia of the eighteenth and early nineteenth centuries many manufacturing enterprises employed serf labor. Indeed, as Trotsky pointed out, "The landlords who owned factories were the first among their caste to favor replacing serfdom by wage-labor."[4]

History exhibits manifold variations even within a single mode of production. There were not only two editions of feudalism east of the Elbe but, as we have indicated, pronounced contrasts between the feudal societies of Western and Eastern Europe. The rich and diversified urban activities of the former gave it a progressive character that led on to the independent evolution of capitalism. The retarded urban and industrial development, the stunted growth of the bourgeoisie, the lack of differentiation among the peasantry, and the generally adverse political and cultural conditions gave a sluggish and reactionary stamp to Eastern Europe that facilitated the imposition of the second serfdom upon it.

In the Western Hemisphere the vigor of bourgeois relations in the British colonies of the North American seacoast gave an impetus to their advancement along capitalist lines that eventuated in revolutionary consequences. On the other hand, the weakness of bourgeois forces coupled with the strength of feudal and semifeudal institutions under the Spanish and Portuguese conquerors stunted the development of capitalist relations in Latin America and perpetuated its backwardness.

As A. Casanova and C. Parain note in their introduction, the second edition of serfdom itself passed through very uneven phases of development from place to place and from one century to another. This phenomenon, they write, involved "a lengthy process, extending from the sixteenth to the eighteenth centuries, unrolling at paces and in forms and stages that differ for Germany (where the essential stages are the Peasants War and the Thirty Years War), Poland, Russia, Hungary or still more Rumania (where the expansion of the system is complicated and relatively late)." As Rumania demonstrated, even parts of the same nation were unequally developed.

After the breakup of primitive collectivism it is rare to find a "pure and simple" social formation without weighty carry-overs from earlier forms of life and labor. The distinguished French medievalist Marc Bloch observed: ". . . Feudal Europe was not all feudalized in the same degree or according to the same rhythm and, above all . . . it was nowhere feudalized completely . . . No doubt it is the fate of every system of human institutions never to be more than imperfectly realized."5

Every concrete, actually existing, civilized society incorporates more archaic institutions, customs, and ideas into its own dominant economy and culture. The blending of past conditions of social production with the new functions of capital was especially evident throughout the rise of capitalism.

Moreover, no method of production evolves in a harmonious, symmetrical, all-sided manner. It is constrained by inherited and environing conditions to follow a more or less erratic and lopsided course. This inescapable irregularity of development forbids any rigidly schematic interpretation of the historical process. The analyst has to take into account the deviations from the norm produced by uneven and combined development. The passage from one stage to another moves not along a straight line but a complicated curve.

As capitalism expanded, the laws of the market pervaded all countries regardless of their degree of development and no matter what the distances between them. However, the consequences of these laws differed considerably, depending upon the given historical conditions.

The heterogeneity in the socioeconomic development of Central and Eastern Europe and Western Europe in the infancy of the capitalist system left its imprint upon the entire subsequent course of European and world history and had fateful consequences for its peoples. Indeed, the key to the evolution of Eastern Europe and Russia from the sixteenth to the twentieth centuries is to be found in the role played by the second serfdom.

It saddled an onerous backwardness upon these nations from

which they have still not fully recovered. The corvée remained intact in Russia until the Reform of 1861, and even then this moribund system of economy hung on. In his first major work, *The Development of Capitalism in Russia,* Lenin devoted a chapter to "The Landowners' Transition from Corvée to Capitalist Economy," which contained the following pertinent paragraph.

"Thus capitalist economy could not emerge at once, and corvée economy could not disappear at once. The only possible system of economy was, accordingly, a transitional one, a system combining the features of both the corvée and the capitalist systems. And indeed, the post-Reform system of farming practised by the landlords bears precisely these features. With all the endless variety of forms characteristic of a transitional epoch, the economic organisation of contemporary landlord farming amounts to two main systems, in the most varied combinations — the labour-service [in a footnote Lenin explains that this is another term for "corvée." — G.N.] system and the *capitalist* system. . . . The systems mentioned are actually interwoven in the most varied and fantastic fashion: on a mass of landlord estates there is a combination of the two systems, which are applied to different farming operations. It is quite natural that the combination of such dissimilar and even opposite systems of economy leads in practice to a whole number of most profound and complicated conflicts and contradictions, and that the pressure of these contradictions results in a number of farmers going bankrupt, etc. All these are phenomena characteristic of every transitional period."[6]

The backward condition of Europe east of the Elbe in turn determined its mode of transition from feudalism to capitalism. In Western Europe and the United States this changeover took place in a thoroughgoing way by virtue of the successful bourgeois democratic revolutions. Central and Eastern Europe on the other hand experienced no such bourgeois-democratic reconstruction and had to crawl toward capitalism by way of a compromise between the feudal and bourgeois forces.

Lenin pointed out that agriculture could develop along two very different lines in the transition from feudalism to capitalism. It could either continue to rely on servile labor or go over to small freehold farm production. He wrote: "Either the old landlord economy, bound as it is by thousands of threads to serfdom, is retained and turns slowly into purely capitalist, 'Junker' economy. The basis of the final transition from labour-service to capitalism is the internal metamorphosis of feudalist landlord economy. The entire agrarian system of the state becomes capitalist and for a long time retains feudalist features. Or the old landlord economy is broken up by revolution, which destroys all the relics of serfdom, and large landownership in the first place."[7]

Lenin designated the first possibility of development as "the Prussian way" and the second as "the American way" in accord with the patterns set in these two countries. The former, based on an impoverished and oppressed class of dependent laborers, was highly conservative; while the latter, based on the emancipation of the peasants as independent proprietors and producers, was the most progressive within the framework of bourgeois relations.

The reactionary combination of semifeudal with capitalist relations that prevailed from eastern Germany to Czarist Russia up to the twentieth century shaped the peculiar path of development there. History sooner or later demands payment on its unfulfilled obligations, and however circuitous the route it takes from one turning point to the next, it cannot be cheated in the end.

The failure of these countries to achieve the objectives of a democratic revolution in the preceding centuries paved the way for the occurrence of a novel type of revolution in the twentieth century. This joined a peasant uprising, characteristic of the beginning of bourgeois development, with the conquest of power by the proletariat, which sought to realize both the democratic tasks of the former and the socialist measures of the latter, a combination that marked the process of permanent revolution.

Thus in historical perspective, the second serfdom in its death agony was a component of the combined character of the Russian Revolution of 1917, just as the commercialized slavery in the cotton kingdom led to the Civil War that consummated the democratic revolution in the United States. It might be further noted that the survivals of four centuries of Black bondage, combined with the contemporary miseries of proletarian existence as an oppressed nationality under monopoly capitalism, is bound to be one of the most explosive factors in the coming American revolution.

The dialectics of the historical process, expressed in its contradictory phases, movements, and manifestations, is not an invention of the imagination or a Hegelian sophistication foisted upon scientific socialism. It exists in social reality and can be verified in concrete cases. The second edition of serfdom, initiated at the end of the sixteenth century, was preceded by an emancipation of the serfs under medieval conditions in the thirteenth and fourteenth centuries. And it was followed in the post-Reform period of Czarist Russia by a transitional form in which corvée labor was intermingled with hands hired by the year, season, or day.

Contrary to the mechanical thinkers, a given cause can have very different effects, depending on the context. The radiation of forces that led to the formation of slave and feudal tributaries of commercial capitalism in the Americas simultaneously produced capitalist farming in England and intensified serfdom east of the Elbe. A spectrum of three complementary variations! The spread of capitalism that suppressed feudalism in Western Europe re-created and reinforced it in Eastern Europe.

The specific course, consequences, and outcome of new economic relations depend upon the given historical context and circumstances in which these forces must operate. There was, for example, a general tendency of increased economic energy by the nobility throughout Europe during this epoch. Yet their activities acquired dissimilar forms in the East and the West. The landlords in England transformed themselves into a bourgeoisified gentry profiting from capitalist agricultural enterprise; whereas the landed proprietors in the East became beneficiaries of the unlimited corvée, ruling their agricultural districts like absolute monarchs.

The gentry-entrepreneurs constituted a more progressive type of landed proprietors than the nobility of East Prussia, Poland, and Russia, who clung to the way of life proper to feudal barons and resisted the subversive introduction of bourgeois culture. To be sure, at a later stage the Junkers themselves more and more approximated the category of landlord-entrepreneurs, as did the cotton planters of the Southern slave states.

The ruling classes of both parts of Europe expropriated their peasantry — but with very different results. In the one case, the dispossessed peasants were degraded into serfs; in England they became landless and propertyless proletarians, raw material for capitalist exploitation as wage workers in agriculture or manufacture.

The efficient cause for the strengthening of serfdom as the fundamental form of labor organization in Central and Eastern Europe came from the influences exerted by foreign commercial capital. But this economic driving force had to find the existing social structure susceptible to its penetration. While natural, geographical, technological, and other factors played a role in the process, its outcome was determined by the alignment of the class forces engaged in struggle.

The correlation between the noble landlords and the agrarian population was most decisive. But their respective strengths were conditioned by the presence or absence — and the active intervention — of other social forces on the arena. Here the peasants were immensely disadvantaged. The state backed up the nobility. There was no strong and oppositional urban bourgeoisie or aggressive petty bourgeoisie to give aid and leadership to the rural rebels, as in the West. The rich merchants allied themselves by and large with the feudal re-action. The isolated and scattered peasants could not prevent the lords from suppressing their defensive efforts and reducing them to abject servitude.

At all stages of its development, capitalism has produced inequalities between the imperial powers and the less developed peoples they directly or indirectly subjected. Outside Europe these were incorporated into their colonial systems. Within Europe the backward peoples of the East on a lower economic level labored for the benefit of the West. Just as contemporary imperialism blocks and holds back the economic and cultural progress of the colonial world, so Dutch, English, and West European capital took the feudalists into tow, upheld their power, and deformed and checked the development of their countries along capitalist lines. Not the city and its culture but rather the village and the manor acquired supremacy, consolidated themselves, and dictated the further mode of development. There was a comparable contrast between the slaveholding South and the free North in the United States.

*   *   *

The phenomenon of the second serfdom in Europe casts light upon the issues involved in the contemporary debate over the relations between capitalism and feudalism in Latin America from the sixteenth to the twentieth centuries. Two positions have been defended in this discussion. One is the liberal, proimperialist view, shared by the reformists and Stalinists, of a purely feudal past that has to be overcome by a bourgeois-democratic renovation. The opposite conception, held by scholars on the left like Andre Gunder Frank, is that capitalism fully characterized Latin American society as early as the sixteenth century. Both are one-sided and incorrect. (The two tendencies draw corresponding sets of political conclusions for the current situation from their premises. The liberals stand for reforms to be undertaken by the capitalist regimes, a position grading into the Stalinist revival of the Menshevik theory of a two-stage revolution — first a democratic revolution in which the national bourgeoisie is assigned a progressive role, then in the distant future a socialist revolution. Those who agree with Andre Gunder Frank exclude any transitional phases in the development of the socialist revolution. Both schools, of course, deny the validity of Trotsky's theory of permanent revolution.)

Just as economic pressures from Western Europe produced the second serfdom in the East, similar pressures created a first edition of serfdom in Latin America. Both of these formations had a combined character resulting from the adaptation of a primitive culture to the more advanced one. They amalgamated a precapitalist mode of production based on the forced surplus labor of serfs (or slaves) for the landlords and planters with the exploitative relations of merchant capital to which they were economically subordinated. [8]

The further development of a hybrid formation proceeds in a dialectical manner. Just as the master and the slave are bound together, so the superior system needs the lower to exploit, while the inferior one becomes even more dependent upon the more advanced economy for survival and prosperity — until changing conditions bring them to a parting of the ways.

Merged within the combined form, the two opposing trends progress at varying rates and extents, depending upon the totality of circumstances. For an entire period, the reinstated lower economic formation may be reinforced, retarding the overall development of the society, while the more advanced productive forces, assimilated in a debased and disfigured form, may be relatively subordinated.

But that is not the end of the road. Where a more progressive system is active at home and abroad in the next phase, the higher forces, however sublimated at first, feeding on a more advanced technique and culture, grow stronger and will break through more extensively, corroding the hybrid formation to the detriment of the old conditions.

This fate befell the second serfdom. It established itself not in the ascending epoch of feudalism in Europe but in its descending phase. Like slavery in the New World, it was a historical anomaly that was essentially opposed to the major forces shaping the bourgeois world. As a mixed offspring of capitalism in its rise to world supremacy, corvée labor burned brightly before it suffered extinction. Born in Russia at the end of the sixteenth century, it flourished for the next two centuries until it was illegalized by Alexander II's reform in 1861. Austria abolished the last corvée in that part of Europe in 1848. This feudal relic therefore had a run of about three and a half centuries, about the same as commercialized slavery.

This differential growth of the old forms and the new in backward countries where precapitalist systems of economy are first implanted and invigorated, and thereafter devitalized and eliminated, exemplifies the contradictory pattern of historical progress, the essence of its dialectic. The antagonistic coexistence of the two systems could be resolved in the long run only by the triumph of the more efficient one. What was done in the West by the bourgeois-democratic revolutions had to be carried through in the East by dual popular revolutions in which the socialist proletariat led the insurgent peasantry demanding possession of the land.

It is significant that none of the articles in the *Recherches Internationales* collection mentions the law of uneven and combined development. Since all the writers live in Eastern Europe or the Soviet Union, they may never have heard of it. They recognize and describe manifestations of uneven development, a phenomenon that is not only visible on the surface of events but has been certified by such authorities as Marx, Engels, and Lenin (Stalin, too, approved it.)

However, the authors do not go beyond this point of empirical observation to a profounder theoretical insight into the main features of the transition from feudalism to capitalism that have a combined character. In this respect the scholars of the Soviet bloc are no better equipped than their counterparts in the bourgeois universities, who are likewise ignorant of this valuable tool of analysis generalized and named by Trotsky in the 1930s.

This deficiency demonstrates the degree to which able minds educated under the restrictions of Stalinism suffer from lack of knowledge of the contributions of Trotskyism to Marxist theory, not only in contemporary politics, but in the explanation of social processes and the understanding of historical problems. Knowledge of the law of uneven and combined development is just as essential in the study of comparative history today as is knowledge of the periodic law of the elements in chemical research.

The Problem of
Transitional Formations

The problem of transitional formations has immense methodological significance in both the natural and social sciences. It has special theoretical and political importance for contemporary Marxists, because the twentieth century is preeminently an age of transition from one socioeconomic formation to another.

Each epoch in the progress of humanity has its dominant form of economy, politics and culture. In the eighteenth and nineteenth centuries this was the capitalist system in its stages of expansion. The distinctive general form of the twentieth century is its *transitional* character. This is a period of rapid and convulsive motion from the dominion of world capitalism as the ultimate form of class society to the establishment of postcapitalist states oriented toward socialism, which will eradicate all vestiges of class differentiations.

"The Old surviving in the New confronts us in life at every step in nature as well as in society," Lenin observed in *State and Revolution*. He wrote this during the First World War and the Russian Revolution—the two cataclysmic events that ushered in the new epoch of history. Although that epoch is already fifty years old, it is far from maturity, and its progeny suffer from many congenital maladies of infancy.

The fundamentally transitional character of this period and the prevalence of conspicuously contradictory traits necessitate research into the essential nature of this phenomenon. The presence of transitional formations, types, and periods has been empirically noted, and their concrete characteristics analyzed in the writings of many Marxists, and not by them alone. But the topic has seldom been treated along systematic lines. This theoretical deficiency is regrettable because a host of perplexing sociological and political problems could be illuminated through a correct understanding of the peculiarities of this widespread aspect of things.

In the unceasing cosmic process of becoming and being, all things pass from one state to another. This means that transitional states and forms are everywhere to be found in the physical world, in society, in intellectual development.

The antithesis to a transitional formation is a fixed and stable one with clear-cut characteristics that compose a definitive pattern. The distinction between the two is relative, since even the most enduring entity is subject to change and transformation into something else over a long enough stretch of time.

The dynamic polarity of physical forms is exemplified by a liquid. This is a more or less stable state of matter on earth—intermediate between a solid and a gas, being partly like one and partly like the other, yet essentially different from both. A liquid has more cohesion than a gas and more mobility than a solid. It resembles a solid by having a definite volume but differs from it and resembles a gas by the absence of any definite shape.

The qualitative transformations of H_2O and other chemical compounds result from changes in molecular constitution. A solid consists of rigidly locked molecules. When these are disaggregated by changes of temperature and pressure, they pass over into a more fluid condition in which the molecules maintain a certain proximity to one another while acquiring more mobility than in a solid. Once the molecules move farther away from one another and are fully loosened from their mutual bonds, they become gaseous. Gaseousness is the state of matter most unlike the solid in respect to the interlock of its molecular constituents.

Thus a liquid is *negatively* defined by its relations to the solid state on one of its boundaries and the gaseous state on the other. It is *positively* determined by its special intermixture of cohesiveness and mobility. If the capacity of a liquid to turn into its opposite at either end exhibits its intermediate character, its combination of contrary properties brings out the intrinsic duality of its being.

But when a liquid boils, these polarities of definite volume and variable shape are sharpened to the extreme of contradiction. At one and the same time, within the system as a whole, there is both definite and indefinite volume, as well as indefinite shape. This difference is distributed over parts of the system, over different molecules. Thus, water and steam coexist; some molecules are in a gaseous state, others in a liquid state. But for the system as a whole, we can say neither that it is exclusively gas nor exclusively liquid; it is in fact both gas and liquid: it is boiling. This is the transitional stage between liquid and gas.

All things have a dual nature, as an example taken from geography rather than chemistry will illustrate. A beach is defined both by water and by land. Each of these opposing physical entities are essential components of its makeup. Take away one or the other and the beach no longer exists.

But transitional formations are distinguished from ordinary things by the *heightened* character of their dual constitution. They belong to a special kind of processes, events and forms in nature, society, and individual experience that have exceptionally pronounced, almost outrageously, contradictory traits. They carry the coexistence of opposites in a single whole to the most extreme and anomalous lengths.

These phenomena are so self-contradictory that they can embody the passage from one stage or form of existence to another. Since the major features of transitional formations belong to consecutive but qualitatively different stages of development, they must represent a combination of the old and the new.

In the life process, the first products of development are necessarily inadequately realized on their own terms. What is new makes its first appearance in and through underdeveloped forms and asserts its emerging existence within the shell of the old. The new becoming is struggling to go beyond its previous mode of existence. It is passing over from one stage to the next but is not yet mature, powerful or predominant enough to destroy and throw off the afterbirth of its natal state and stand fully and firmly on its own feet. Like a fetus, it is still dependent on the conditions of its birth or like an infant, dependent on its parents.

In a full and normal development, transitional formations go through three phases: 1) A prenatal or embryonic stage, when the functions, structures and features of the nascent entity are growing and stirring within the framework of the already established form. 2) The qualitative breakthrough of its birth period, when the aggregate of the novel powers and features succeeds in shattering the old form and stepping forth on its own account. At this point the fresh creation continues to retain many residues belonging to its preceding state. 3) The period of maturation, when the vestigial characteristics unsuited to its proper mode of existence are largely sloughed off and the new entity is unmistakably, firmly, strongly developing on its distinctive foundations.

It takes time for the unique features and functions of something novel to manifest their potential, engender the most appropriate type of expression, and become stabilized in normal or perfected shape. At the beginning of their career they are trammeled, often even disfigured, by the heritage of the past.

These borderline phenomena are so significant—and puzzling—because they form the bridge between successive stages of evolution. Their hybrid nature, embodying characteristics belonging to antithetical phases of growth, casts light upon both the old and the new, the past and the future. Through them it is possible to see how and where the carapace of the old is being broken through by antagonistic forces striving to establish the groundwork, the basic conditions, for higher forms of existence.

Each turning point in the evolution of life has produced species with contradictory features belonging to different sequential forms. These betoken their status as links between two separate and successive species.

*   *   *

The most momentus turning point in organic evolution was the changeover from the ape to man. Here scientists have found fossils with opposite characteristics. Structurally, the South African *Australopithecus* was not altogether an ape nor altogether a man; it was something in between. He habitually stood and walked erect as ably as man, and his brain volume came close to that of man. The fact that these beings used tools, and thereby engaged in labor activity to get their means of existence, proves that they had crossed the boundary separating the ape from man and had embarked on a new mode of existence, despite the heavy vestiges of the primate past they bore with them.

Precisely because of their highly self-contradictory and unfinished traits, transitional forms present exceedingly vexing problems of precise definition and classification to scientists and scholars. They are the most enigmatic of phenomena. It is often difficult, and sometimes impossible, to tell on which side of a frontier they definitely belong.

The task is to discriminate the genuinely new from what is rooted in the preceding conditions of existence and then to assay the relative weights of the conflicting traits and tendencies of development incorporated in the specimen. Taxonomists among biologists, botanists, and physical anthropologists have engaged in prolonged, bitter and sometimes inconclusive controversies over whether a given specimen properly belongs to one category or another.

What settles the locus of classification? The mere possession of one or another trait of a higher or lower type is not considered conclusive evidence. The question is decided one way or the other by the totality of characteristics in relation to what went before and what came out of it.

For example, the fossil remains of *Archaeopteryx* show many characteristics now found only in reptiles or in bird embryos: reptilian tail, jaws with teeth, and clawed wings. Yet it is a true bird. This superior classification is warranted by the presence of feathers and the structure of the legs and wings that fitted it for flight. *Archaeopteryx* had broken through the confines of the reptile state to become the first incarnation of a higher form of living creature.

The difficulties of classification arising from the contradictory characteristics of transitional phenomena are well illustrated by a controversy among authorities on early man over the fossil finds at Olduvai Gorge in Tanganyika. (See *Current Anthropology*, October 1965.) This famous site has yielded evidences of tool-using and tool-making hominoids at levels that are dated as far back as 1,750,000 years ago.

The problem posed by these finds concerns a group of fossil remains named *Homo habilis*. The *International Code of Zoological Nomenclature* (1961) insisted on dividing the *Hominidae* into two genera: *Australopithecus* and *Homo*. It did not permit any intergeneric or ambigeneric groups.

However, *Homo habilis* did not fit into either one of these counterposed categories. It diverged from *Australopithecus* in its more humanized morphological pattern (biological traits), but even more significantly because it had taken the decisive step of making stone tools according to a regular and evolving pattern. While *Australopithecus* used and modified tools and may even have improvised them for immediate purposes, he did not fabricate implements according to a set pattern. On the other hand, the biological and cultural traits of *Homo habilis* fell short of the status of *Homo*.

The dilemma facing the classifiers was formulated as follows by Phillip V. Tobias, professor of anatomy at the University of Witwatersrand: " . . . the *habilis* group was in so many respects intermediate between *Australopithecus* and *Homo*. Were we to regard it as the most advanced species of *Australopithecus* or the most primitive species of *Homo?*" Neither of these solutions was satisfactory. "We had come face to face with a fundamental weakness in classical taxonomic procedure: Our systems of classification make inadequate allowance for intermediate or transitional forms."

How was the issue resolved? Tobias and Louis S.B. Leakey concluded that, on the basis of the evidence regarding these hominid remains, it was necessary to recognize a new species of early man, which they designated as *Homo habilis*. This species of hominid was older and more advanced than *Australopithecus* yet younger and less matured than *Homo*.

The great significance of *Homo habilis* as a bridge between *Australopithecus* and *Homo* is that it closes the last remaining gap in the sequence of Pleistocene hominid phylogeny. The lineage of human evolution now comprises three distinct stages: partially humanized (*Australopithecus*); markedly humanized (*Homo habilis*); and fully humanized (*Homo*).

Professor Tobias concludes:

> There will always be arguments about the names to be given
> to transitional forms (like *Homo habilis*); but the recognition of
> their crucial intermediate status is of more importance than the
> name given to the taxon. It seems that our nomenclatural
> procedure is not equal to the naming of "missing links" when
> the gaps have narrowed to such fine gradations as now exist in
> the hominid sequence of the Pleistocene.

As Tobias remarks in answer to objections from his critics,
"Intermediate forms ('missing links') always cause taxonomic
headaches, although they make good phylogenetic sense." Once
it had been established that *Homo habilis* did not properly
belong to either group, it had to be accorded a separate status.
What that should be was determined by its specific place in the
evolutionary ascent of man.

It was not an *Australopithecus* because it had attained the
capacity to make tools with the aid of other tools. Yet it had not
progressed sufficiently along the road of humanization to justify
inclusion with *Homo*. There was no alternative except to recognize it as a new and distinct species of the genus *Homo*.

Tobias suggests that the new group of hominids might have
been designated *Australopithecus-Homo habilis*. The compromise
of making it a subcategory would have brought out its emergent
position but not its distinctive nature or subsequent destiny. It
evidently has enough important attributes of its own to deserve
independent status.

Like all transitional formations, the qualitative difference of
Homo habilis consisted in its peculiar combination of features,
one set resembling its predecessor, the other anticipating its
successor. The relative weight of these contradictory features
changed in the course of its development. It moved away from
and beyond the antecedent genus as it more closely approached
the earliest members of the next higher stage.

Hegel supplied a key to comprehending transitional formations
by the concepts of determinate being and limit analyzed in the
first section of *The Logic*. Anything is what it is by virtue of the
negations that set its qualitative limits. Both what it comes out of
and what it passes into are essential elements of its being. This
being is a perpetual process of becoming, of continual determination and redetermination through the interaction of the conflicting
forces within itself. These drive it forward to becoming something
other than it has been or is.

Thus *Homo habilis* is to be designated as a determinate being, that is, a qualitatively distinct grouping bounded on one side by *Australopithecus* and on the other side by *Homo*. This transitional species is delimited through its organic connections with both the anterior and posterior stages of human evolution. Its special standing depends on its qualitative differences from these opposing determinants. To the extent that these differences are effaced it passes over into and merges with one or the other.

*   *   *

The major transitions within the development of society manifest contradictory features in as striking a manner as the transition from ape to man. Further modifications in man's physical equipment recede in importance with the appearance of *Homo sapiens*. From that point on, the laws of social and historical development, which originate in labor activity and are based on the growth of the forces of production, have taken full command of the evolution of our species.

It would be possible to go through the whole course of social history, so far as it is known, and pick out for study a diversity of transitional forms in which the new is mingled with the old and struggling to replace it with more or less success. We can give only a few salient examples to clarify in broad terms the inwardly divided nature of transitional processes.

Let us start with the substructure of the first chapter of human existence, the Stone Age, which lasted for hundreds of thousands of years. Throughout that time no fundamental changes occurred in economic activities. Primitive humans acquired the means of subsistence exclusively through different means of food gathering: hunting, fishing (which is hunting in water), and foraging for roots, nuts, fruits, insects and small game.

This primeval state of savagery ends, and the next higher grade of social existence, barbarism, begins with the replacement of food gathering by food production. This new stage in the creation of material wealth was brought about from ten to twelve thousand years ago by the domestication of animals and the introduction of cereal crops.

Since the close of the Second World War, archaeologists, teamed with other scientific specialists, have been extending their investigations in both the Old World and the New to find out how, why, and, more precisely, when and where this epoch-making changeover took place. They have unearthed many more traces of the origins of agriculture and stock raising than were known before, so that a distinct outline of the steps in the great food-producing revolution is beginning to take shape.

Agriculture may have originated independently in several places on our planet. It emerged almost simultaneously at opposite ends of the earth—in the Middle East and in Mexico—roughly around 7,000 B. C. More is known about the origin and spread of farming from the archaeological sites in the Middle East than as yet in Middle America.

In the former it appears that animal domestication preceded plant cultivation. At the Zarvi Chemi Shanidan, not far north of Jarmo in the hills of northern Iraq, archaeologists from Columbia University found indications that, in shifting from cave living to open-air encampments around 9,000 B. C., the inhabitants, who had formerly hunted many wild goats and occasionally wild sheep, had tamed sheep.

The type of tools at similar open sites in northern Palestine and in Iraq and Iran showed that the people who lived in these camps, while hunting and collecting most of their food, possessed sickles and mortars. Taken together with the many bones of animals capable of domestication, this suggested that they may have already become regular food producers.

The oldest site yet excavated of a community on the boundary line between the Old and the New Stone Age is at Jericho in Palestine. Nine thousand years ago the inhabitants of this oasis in the desert grew cereals and bred sheep and goats, in addition to hunting and collecting. However, they did not yet make pottery or use ground stone axes.

It is therefore difficult to ascertain whether the villagers of Jericho I, the most ancient settlement, simply supplemented their diet through food production, or whether they had gone so far as to make food production the foundation of their economy. In that case they would have passed beyond the borders of savagery and entered barbarism.

The situation is clearer, though not yet unmistakable, in the case of the next oldest village, Jarmo in Kurdistan, a settlement of about thirty houses, which was rebuilt fifteen times after its founding. Its deepest layers date back to about 6,750 B. C. The inhabitants had domesticated goats and sheep. They not only raised grains as cultivated plants, which implies a considerable previous history, but they possessed most of the equipment used by later neolithic farmers to make grain into bread. They had flint sickle blades, mortars or querns to crack the grain, ovens to parch it, and stone bowls out of which to eat their porridge. In the upper levels pottery had begun to replace some of the stone vessels.

All this implies that Jarmo's residents had left food gathering behind and subsisted on what they themselves produced. They had become full-fledged food producers, genuine villagers and farmers.

An interesting sidelight on the botanical aspect of this process of transformation has been provided by the data accumulated by the archaeological botanist Hans Helbaek of the Danish National Museum. The successive changes in the details of carbonized grain and of the imprints of plant parts can tell a sharp-eyed botanist just as much as successive changes in tools and artifacts can tell an archaeologist. Domesticated plants and animals are living artifacts, products of man's modifications and manipulations.

The Danish botanist concluded that the Jarmo wheat and barley were early cultivated varieties that had been grown for a number of generations. Their growers were several steps removed from the first farmers, who would have taken the seeds from plants in their wild state. Who, then, were these pioneers? Diggers have recently come across caches of wild cereal grain in villages of hunters and seed collectors. They may possibly have started to reap wild grain before purposively planting the first wheat and barley.

Thus a hunters' village of about two hundred small stone houses excavated at Mureybat in northern Syria contained bones of wild animals at all seventeen levels. Seeds of wild barley and wheat showed up at the fifth level from the bottom, along with sickle baldes, mortars, flat stone slabs, and small raised fire pits filled with big pebbles and ashes. Mauritz Van Loon of the Oriental Institute of Chicago believes the pebbles were heated and used to crack the wild seeds.

It took about 2,500 years to make the changeover from hunting to farming and arrive at the earliest farming villages. According to present indications, the sequence of steps in this food-producing revolution began with animal domestication about 10,000 B. C., proceeded through hamlets of seed collectors, and culminated with the emergence of farming communities by 7,500 B. C.

This record shows that, before they could shake off dependence upon food gathering, the first domesticators of plants and animals had to pass through intermediate steps in which the primitive mode of procuring the means of subsistence was combined with either food or stock raising, or even both. In the first phase, food production remained subordinate and supplementary to hunting and foraging pursuits until the new techniques and forces of production gained predominance. Just before this crucial turning point, a period must have come when the total activities and output of communal labor were about equally divided between the two, and it would have been difficult to tell whether the group belonged to one category or the other.

This internal contradiction would be resolved by the further development of the more dynamic new productive forces. This, when food and stock raising were introduced into the less advanced Old Stone Age culture of Europe some thousands of years later, the Starcevo folk who lived in the Balkan peninsula learned to practice a system of rotating crops and pasture that made hunting and fishing less and less vital to their economy.

The insuperable ambiguities of the boundary separating food gatherers from food producers have been underscored in an account of the rise of Mesopotamian civilization by George Roux in *Ancient Iraq:*

> We cannot with the material at our disposal pinpoint the crucial passage from a food-gathering to a food-producing economy. It can be argued that hoes could be used for uprooting as well as for tilling, sickles for reaping naturally growing or cultivated wheat, querns and mortars for grinding and pounding wild seeds or even mineral pigments; and it is not always easy to decide whether bones of sheep or cattle belonged to wild or to domesticated animals. All considered, our best criterion is perhaps the presence on a site of permanent habitations, for agriculture ties man to the land. But here again, it is sometimes difficult to draw a firm line between the stone huts of hunters, for whom agriculture was an occasional activity, and the farms of fully settled peasants.

Agriculture is the basis for the permanent human settlements that have supplied the main motive forces for progress since savagery. The village, town and city are the three kinds of communities that line the road from barbarism to civilization. The evolution of the village to the city highlights the transitional and contradictory character of the town, the second link in the sequence of human habitations.

Agriculture consolidated and proliferated, if it did not actually create, the village. This type of enduring settlement is the cell, the basic unit, of all social structures rooted in agriculture. These comprise forms of society extending all the way from the birth of barbarism up to industrial capitalism.

The problem of transitional formations is most sharply posed after the emergence of the farming community by the development of the village into the city at the beginnings of civilization. Based on farming or mixed farming with family handicrafts, the village is common to both barbarism and civilization. It is small in numbers, self-subsistent, with a rudimentary division of social labor.

The town is an enlarged village growing out of the expansion of the forces of production. It is an agglomeration of permanent residents situated between the village and the city and transitional between them. It is difficult to draw a clear-cut line between a village and a town, but there is a definite point at which the town grows over into a city.

The city is not only quantitatively but also qualitatively different from either a village or a town, because it has a different economic foundation. It is the outgrowth of a far more advanced division of labor between the rural and urban inhabitants. The kings, priests, officials, soldiers, artisans and merchants in the cities do not produce their own food. They subsist on the surplus food coming from the output of the direct producers, farmers or fishermen, who may in some cases dwell within the city precincts but for the most part reside in village communities outside its walls or borders.

The city is the organized expression, the visible embodiment, of a highly stratified society based on the division between cultivators of the soil who provide the sustenance, and those layers of consumers who produce other goods, and the administrators of various kinds who serve higher social functions. The city comes to dominate the country and is the force that civilizes the barbarians.

The town is an overgrown village at one end of its growth and an embryonic city at the other. It displays characteristics common to both types of settlement without being either. Unlike the village, it is not completely rural but is larger and more complex. At the same time it is smaller, less diversified, less developed, less centralized and less powerful than the city.

Neither rural nor urban, the town has an indeterminate character and an imprecise and fluctuating connotation. It is not easy to single out the ensemble of positive features that distinguish the town from the village it has come out of or from the city status it may be heading toward. This ambiguity is built into its constitution as an intermediate form of permanent settlement.

Thus the town exemplifies the congenital fluidity of a transitional form. Its structure is amorphous; its boundaries are blurred. This indefiniteness, which is inherent in its very nature, is reflected in the concept "town," which is likewise clouded with an insurmountable fuzziness.

The transition from food gathering to food production, from the village to the city, and from communal to private property are major instances of fundamental changes in the life of mankind on the way to class society. As class society climbed from slavery to capitalism, many highly anomalous formations arose from the supersession of one basic mode of production by another. One case that has provoked considerable controversy both among academic historians and Marxist scholars concerns the nature of the social organization in the West that issued from the downfall of the Roman Empire.

West European society from the fourth to the ninth centuries A. D. was situated between the ruin of the Roman slave state and the birth of feudalism. This intermediate formation resulted from the blending of elements derived from decadent Roman civilization and disintegrating Germanic barbarism—two societies at very different levels of development—into a variegated configuration that did not conform either to the antecedent slave mode of production or the feudal form which came out of it.

The historical movement from slaveholding antiquity to European feudalism followed a more complex and circuitous path than the changeover from feudalism to capitalism. The feudal organization did not emerge directly and immediately from its predecessor in the sequence of class societies.

The Roman Empire contained no forward moving social force that was capable of replacing the obsolescent exploitative order with a more productive economy. The slave population revolted on various occasions but did not have access to the economic and social prerequisites for establishing a new order. The slave system foundered in a blind alley, which provided no way out through a progressive social and political revolution.

From the fourth century on, Roman civilization slid downhill. The imperial government went bankrupt; the cities decayed; commerce shrank to petty proportions; the estate owners and agrarian masses vegetated in rural isolation. The general disorder and decline in the productive forces ushered in the Dark Ages.

These conditions of decomposition endured for almost five centuries. During this time, however, a slow revitalization of economic life began to stir beneath the surface stagnation.

Agriculture was the center of the regenerative processes. To form the groundwork for a superior form of social production, two classes had to be reconstituted. One was the laboring force of the cultivators of the soil; the other was the class of landed proprietors.

The original nucleus of the subject peasantry came from the small farmers, or *coloni*, though not as they were under Roman rule. The *coloni* passed from their marginal status as semiserfs under Roman rule to the status of free farmers organized in dispersed communities until, fleeing from hunger, distress and danger, they fell in considerable numbers under the protection and therewith the domination of the landed gentry.

Their masters were also of a new breed. They were made up of the newly created nobility, military caste and church hierarchy that grew into a distinct and powerful agrarian aristocracy from 500 to 1,000 A. D.

The main seat of Western feudalism was not in Italy but in France and Germany. The transformation of the Germanic conquerors of Rome from barbarism to feudalism was more determinative of the future than their concomitant conversion to Christianity because of the indispensable contributions they made to the postimperial social organization.

The dissolution of tribal and clan ties led to pronounced social differentiations among the Franks and other peoples. From more or less equalized members of tribal groupings, the mass of the agricultural population changed first into free peasants and thereafter into serfs as they became impoverished and passed into hereditary submission to their liege lord. Serfdom seems to have become widely established beginning with the ninth century.

Although feudalism depended upon large landholdings as a property form, it was not rooted in large-scale production. Cultivation of the soil was carried on by petty producers. However extensive the landlord's manor or domain, it was tilled by a cluster of serf or peasant households. The economic transition from slavery to feudalism therefore consisted in the replacement of the slave *latifundia* of the Roman proprietors and the individual households of the Germanic communities by a more productive type of small farming.

The invaders provided important ingredients for raising the technical and social level of the nascent feudal regime. They introduced such new crops as rye, oats, spelt, and hops, along with soap and butter. The heavy-wheeled plow permitted the development of the three-field system of tillage on which the medieval manor depended. Thanks to the horse collar, the tandem harness and the iron shoe, horses could be used in place of oxen for pulling the plow; they had four times the tractive power of earlier draft animals.

Another key innovation was the water wheel, which was known to antiquity but utilized only in the simplest form. The medieval water mills were large and costly installations that belonged to the feudal lords, but to which their dependents could bring their grain for grinding. The creation of a more efficient agricultural technology during the Dark Ages paved the way for increasing agricultural productivity in northern Europe from the ninth century on. As Professor Lynn White points out in *Technology and Invention in the Middle Ages*: "In technology, at least, the Dark Ages mark a steady and uninterrupted advance over the Roman Empire."

Certain features carried over from tribal collectivism were equally consequential in preparing the advent of the new order. When the lands conquered by the Germans were allotted to individual households and the hierarchy of subordinates and superiors arose, woods and pastures were reserved for common use, and many other customs of collective activity were retained. These vestiges of common possession incorporated into the agrarian economy strengthened communal solidarity, made the serfs and villeins less dependent upon their masters, and gave the mass of rural toilers some measure of control over their means of livelihood, which mitigated their servitude and enhanced their margin of freedom.

The society that stretched from the Roman to the Carolingian empires was a conglomerate of elements encompassing slavery, barbarism, peasant farming and incipient feudal relations. The feudal structure eventually crystallized out of this variegated plasma as both the Roman dependents and the Germanic settlers forfeited their positions as free peasants and entered serfdom.

The contradictory course of development that marked the prolonged period of transition from Roman slavery to the feudal age invalidates any rigid scheme of historical evolution predicated on an undeviating line of succession from one form of production to the next. The native population of the Romano-Germanic world sank to a lower level of production and culture before it went on to assemble the conditions for a higher mode of existence. This discontinuity in economic growth illustrates the dialectical nature of the concrete processes of social evolution. Far from following prescribed paths in a mechanical manner, the peoples of the past have often fallen backward before taking the next step in historical progress.

Capitalism did directly supplant feudalism in Western Europe and, in the course of doing so, brought forth an assortment of transitional economic phenomena. Among these was manufacture, which, as the bridge between medieval and modern industry, was one of the pivotal developments in the emergence of bourgeois society.

In the urban craft guilds the master handicraftsman possessed all the means of production, from the raw materials to the shop, which usually housed both his family and work force of apprentices and journeymen. He sold the finished product in a local and regulated market and pocketed the proceeds. This simple small-scale commodity production was extremely restricted, dispersed, routinized, static and monopolistic.

The manufacturing system bypassed, broke up and replaced the guild associations, going beyond this kind of industry in important respects. Unlike the guild master, who was a petty personal producer, the manufacturer brought together under one roof many propertyless workers, purchased their labor power for wages and subjected them to the control of capital. Labor thus became social instead of individual. Every element of the entrepreneur's operations was on a larger scale: He needed more money, greater amounts of raw materials, extensive workshops, better tools, a detailed subdivision of labor, intense supervision, more careful calculation and longer-range planning.

This quantitative growth generated many qualitative improvements in industry. Capitalist manufacture was far more productive, innovative and progressive than the guild system. Yet its artisans, craftsmen and foremen used essentially the same technical methods as their medieval predecessors. They had little or no mechanical power at their disposal and relied exclusively on hand labor, using simple tools. In this rudimentary form of a capitalist economy, advanced relations of production were yoked to an ancient technology dating back to the dawn of civilization.

The inner contradiction of this transitional type of capitalist activity was broken through and overcome with the introduction of steam-driven machinery into industry and transportation. Mechanical industry fashioned the modern proletariat; it enabled the capitalists to exploit wage labor to maximum advantage by reducing the value of commodities and thereby increasing the surplus value that the workers produced and the capitalists appropriated. On this technical basis the capitalist mode of production stood squarely on its own feet for the first time and went forward to conquer the globe. But it could not have embarked on that career unless manufacture had left the guild system behind and prepared the advent of that technology best adapted to the needs of capital accumulation.

*   *   *

Let us skip from the beginnings of capitalism to its concluding stage and focus upon the principal problems presented by the transformation of society in the twentieth century, which is witnessing both the death agony of capitalism and the birth pangs of socialism.

The contemporary revolutionary process aims at undermining and abolishing the power and property of the capitalist owners and whatever archaic privileged classes cling like parasites to their domination. The political mechanism of this social revolution consists in the transfer of state power from these possessing classes to the primary producers of wealth, the proletariat and its allies.

Twentieth-century revolutionists must operate in three main types of transitional situations. Let us consider these in the order of progression toward the ultimate objectives of the socialist revolution.

The first extends over the period of preparation for the overturn of the old regime. The working masses are moving from a nonrevolutionary condition, where the social and political foundations of the established order are stable and strong, into a prerevolutionary period or, beyond that, toward a direct showdown with the possessors of power. At this stage, although the ruling class is losing its grip, the forces destined to dislodge and replace it are not yet ready or able to challenge its supremacy.

The advance from a less to a more revolutionary situation calls for a special strategy employing a set of demands that, on the one hand, are adapted to the conditions and consciousness of the masses and, on the other, will lead them forward to the goal of the conquest of power. The recognition of the special characteristics of this interim period in the development of the class struggle—which is neither wholly nonrevolutionary nor fully revolutionary but heading in that direction—is the objective basis for the transitional demands incorporated in the program of the Fourth International adopted at its foundation in 1938.

The avowed purpose of that program is to promote and facilitate the shift of the proletariat from concern with its immediate needs to a grasp of the necessity for directing its struggle ever more consciously and energetically against the bases of the bourgeois regime. In this way a prerevolutionary state can be transformed into a revolutionary one, as the masses pass over from defensive positions to offensive action. Such a leap was taken, for example, during the French general strike of May-June 1968.

The revolutionary process of our time has a permanent character. And so, once engaged in direct revolutionary action on a large scale, the masses enter upon a second and higher kind of transitional period. The ascending class that is destined to exercise sovereignty in place of the old rulers cannot concentrate all power in its hands overnight. Even less can it effect a thorough reconstruction of social relations in its own country in a few decades. Thus, after the preceding alignment of class forces has been radically upset, there usually ensues a more or less protracted interval when the capitalist or colonialist regime has been shattered but a stable new governmental power, squarely resting on the revolutionary class forces, has yet to be securely established.

During this transitional period, when the supreme power is being transferred from the old rulers to the working masses, forms of government may arise which are extremely contradictory, inwardly divided, unstable and short-lived. The first example of such an interregnum had a classical character. It was the Provisional Government which tried vainly to rule Russia from the February to the October revolutions in 1917.

The partisans of this crippled regime sought to impose upon a nation in the flood tide of revolution a political setup which would be intermediate between tsarism and Bolshevism, between the obsolete domination of the monarchy and the landlords and the rule of the workers and peasants, between feudalized capitalism and socialism. It was a hopeless, ill-fated experiment, because, under the given circumstances of the world war and the severity of the class conflicts, no such hybrid government could solve the urgent problems of peace, bread and land. The real choice lay between a counterrevolutionary military dictatorship and the dictatorship of the workers supported by the peasantry.

The Provisional Government and the soviets constituted a dual power in which the contending class camps offset each other. In order to break the deadlock, one or the other of these opponents had to be smashed and eliminated. In the ensuing test of strength, the soviets emerged victorious, thanks to the kind of leadership provided by the Bolsheviks.

Since 1917 analogous situations of dual power have appeared in numerous revolutions with varying results. Cuba and Algeria have provided the most recent and dramatic instances in the colonial countries. In Cuba, by virtue of the exceptional qualifications of Castro and the July 26 leaders, the transitional period of dual power, from 1959 to 1961, eventuated in the ousting of the procapitalist conciliators, the consolidation of the revolutionary regime, and the expropriation of the native and foreign property owners.

In Algeria, on the other hand, the revolutionary process has yet to culminate in so happy a conclusion. After the winning of national independence, the drive toward socialism was interrupted by the coup d'etat against Ben Bella and has been sliding backward under Boumedienne. Algeria is the prime example of an uncompleted revolution halted midway in its progress from colonialism and capitalism to a workers' state.

This brings us to the third and highest category of the transitional periods in our epoch. Once the question of class power has been decisively settled with the victory of the workers and peasants, and the socioeconomic bases of the new order have been laid down by the dispossession of the capitalists and landlords, a new social formation begins to take shape. The workers' state necessarily has a transitional character. While it has cut loose from the exploiters of labor and taken the road to socialism, it has still to develop the productive forces and create the human relations proper to the new system.

The historical task of the proletarian power is to bring the preconditions for socialism into existence on the basis of the new relations of production. This would be an arduous and prolonged job under the best conditions. Unfortunately, the world historical setting during the first fifty years of the present transitional period from capitalism toward socialism has turned out to be far more unfavorable than the founders of Marxism anticipated, because the first victorious anticapitalist revolutions took place in countries least prepared for the new methods of production and politics.

All the peoples from Russia to Cuba who drove out the possessing classes and established a revolutionary state power of a socialist type had not previously experienced any renovation of their social and political structures along bourgeois-democratic lines. They were therefore obliged to undertake such presocialist tasks as the abolition of feudalism, agrarian reform, national independence and unification, and the democratization of their political life along with the overthrow of imperialist domination and capitalist relations. They were overloaded with the colossal combination of presocialist and socialist tasks at one and the same time. Their construction of a new social order has been rendered still more complicated and difficult by the encircling pressures and interference of imperialism and by their inherited economic and cultural backwardness.

As a result, these transitional regimes have been subjected to varying degrees of degeneration or deformation. They exhibit bizarre blends of progressive and regressive features, the first belonging to the new society in the making, the second stemming from past conditions and imperialist pressures.

For example, the Soviet Union abounds in contradictions on all levels of its life. In this workers' state the workers have no political power, and freedom of expression is severely restricted. In transportation, huge jet passenger planes speed over the trackless wilderness and the dirt roads where peasant carts creak along in well-worn ruts as they have for centuries. A country in the front rank of technology, science and industry is weak in the very social sciences—political economy, sociology, history and philosophy—where its Marxist heritage should make it the strongest. The Soviet public had no access to any reliable history of its revolutionary origins on the fiftieth anniversary of October. Such anomalies are the hallmarks of the Soviet social structure shaped and misshaped during the first phase of the epoch of transition from capitalism to socialism. However, contradictions are not only stigmas and stumbling blocks but motive forces of contention and progress. The workers' states are not stagnant but highly mobile. In the last analysis, they must either go backward to capitalism or forward to socialism. So far, none of the peoples that have abolished capitalism have restored it. In this respect twentieth-century history to date has been a one-way street. This fact testifies to the immense power and vitality of the new institutions as well as to the debility and disintegration of world capitalism.

The governments of the workers' states are equally in flux. They can either relapse into bureaucratic despotism or move ahead to greater democracy. The three stages in the political history of the Soviet Union since 1917 demonstrate this dialectic. After the seething democracy of the early revolutionary years, the country was plunged into the dreadful darkness of Stalin's tyranny for three decades. Since then, too slowly but surely, there is developing a turn toward democratization that must culminate in a showdown between the bureaucrats and the workers.

In Cuba, from the first, despite resistance and brief detours along the way, the main trend has been toward increased decision-making by the masses. Czechoslovakia's break from authoritarianism and its drive toward democratization in 1968 was halted and reversed by Moscow's military intervention.

The program of the Fourth International likewise contains a series of transitional proposals for the struggle against bureaucratism within the degenerated and deformed workers' states. These demands are designed to accelerate and consummate the movement toward workers' democracy in the postcapitalist countries and the adoption of revolutionary socialist policies and perspectives that can lessen the birth pangs of the new society and shorten the interval between the abolition of capitalist power and private property and the creation of harmonious and equal relations for all mankind.

Although postcapitalist economic relations and their superstructures have existed for half a century, they are only in the elementary stage of their historical process of formation and remain subject to all the infirmities of infancy. Furthermore, they have yet to be installed in the habitat most propitious for their growth.

When bourgeois society came forth from feudal Western Europe, capitalist relations did not all at once take possession of the whole of social life. They first preempted the field of commerce, where monetary wealth was accumulated. Meanwhile, the production of material wealth either continued in the old ways or else, as with industry, passed over into manufacture, which retained the old handicraft techniques. The new laws of capitalist development did not break through all limitations, take full command of economic and social life, and unfold their immense potency until the industrial revolution of the early nineteenth century, based on the steam engine, large-scale industry and the factory system, thoroughly transformed the methods of production.

A comparable incompleteness has characterized, and even disfigured, the first period of the transition from capitalism to socialism. Since 1917 the laws of socioeconomic development bound up with the new system of production have had to function under the least favorable and most restrictive conditions. Whereas they required the most advanced productive forces for effective operation, they were confined to the poorest and most backward countries, where they had to contend with incompetent and bureaucratized regimes at home and imperialist encirclement and hostility on a world scale.

Even under such adverse historical circumstances the new mode of production based on nationalized property and the planning principle disclosed its effectiveness and registered colossal achievements.

*   *   *

Despite these successes, the methods of socialist development have not yet been given the chance to manifest their real potential. Implanted in poor soil, they have not had the right nutriment or atmosphere for their flowering. As Marx long ago pointed out, socialism needs a preponderant and highly cultivated working class, a powerful industry, a well-rounded economy and an international basis. None of these prerequisites for socialism prevailed in the first half-century of the international anticapitalist revolution. They have had to be created largely from scratch under forced draft and with intolerably heavy sacrifices by the working masses.

Consequently, the laws of the transition from capitalism to socialism have thus far received a mutilated and inadequate expression. Fortunately, the configuration of historical conditions responsible for this deviation does not have a permanent but a temporary character. The distortions of the workers' states are the malign product of the confinement of proletarian power to the less developed countries and the grip of capitalism upon the most industrialized economies. These handicaps can—and will—be weakened and removed once the workers overthrow capitalist rule in one or more of the imperialist powers. This breakthrough will enable the new laws of social development to find a far more appropriate arena and broader scope for their expansion and fulfillment.

The present historical conjuncture has this paradoxical character. The transitional period from capitalism to socialism has itself been obliged, because of the uneven progress of the world revolution, to pass through an agonizing transitional situation in which the forces of the nascent social system have been penned up in an area least suited to their capacities. These abnormal and episodic restraints upon their growth can be eliminated provided the socialist revolution is extended to Western Europe, Japan, and, above all, to North America. Once the new tendencies of socialist development can operate freely and fully in a favorable environment, emancipated mankind will be astonished by the results.

Notes to Hybrid Formations and the
Permanent Revolution in Latin America

1. See Url Lanham, *Origins of Modern Biology* (New York, Columbia University Press, 1968), pp. 213-15, for a critical examination of Haeckel's theory of recapitulation that during embryonic development an organism repeats its evolutionary history. "In no instance is an embryo a replica of the mature form of any ancestor," writes the author.

2. Cited in Eugene Genovese, *The World the Slaveholders Made* (New York, Pantheon, 1969), p. 51. His chapter "The Slave Systems and their European Antecedents" also contains an interesting criticism of Andre Gunder Frank's ideas.

3. See my essay "The Problem of Transitional Formations," reprinted in *Key Problems of the Transition from Capitalism to Socialism,* three articles by Pierre Frank, George Novack, and Ernest Mandel (New York, Pathfinder Press, 1970).

4. It is instructive to observe that for the past decade or so a comparable controversy has been going on in the United States about the nature of the Southern slave civilization among scholars specializing in this subject.

One school argues that the slave society must be regarded as predominately capitalist, despite all its other peculiar features, because of the commodity relations that surrounded and permeated it. The contrary tendency asserts that, despite its commercial characteristics, the plantation-based society had an independent foundation and the planters constituted a pure slaveholding class with a clearly distinctive way of life.

Both views are one-sided, failing to take into account the totality and duality of the Southern slave system. As I have written elsewhere in an extended analysis of the dynamics of its development in the nineteenth century: "The slave economy of the South had a peculiarly *combined* character. It was fundamentally an archaic precapitalist mode of production which had become impregnated with the substance and spirit of bourgeois civilization by its subordination to the system of industrial capitalism." *The Rise and Fall of the Cotton Kingdom:* "The Ultimate Stage of Chattel Slavery in the South." In *Studies in Afro-American History* (New York, National Education Department of the Socialist Workers Party, 1968).

5. A good account of how the Russian Marxists wrestled with this question and came to divergent political positions that in some instances led to individual disaster and in others to leadership of a successful revolution is to be found in Samuel H. Baron, *Plekhanov: The Father of Russian Marxism* (Stanford, California, Stanford University Press, 1966). Baron, it should be noted, does not himself share a Leninist or Trotskyist position.

Notes to Law of Uneven
and Combined Development in Latin America

1. Rosa Luxemburg, *The Accumulation of Capital* (New York, Monthly Review Press, 1964), p. 358.

2. Karen Spalding, "Hacienda-Village Relations In Andean Society to 1830," *Latin American Perspectives*, Spring 1975, pp. 107-21.

3. Kyle Steenland, "Notes on Feudalism and Capitalism in Chile and Latin America," *Latin American Perspectives*, Spring 1975, pp. 49-58.

4. *Ibid.*, p. 52.

5. Karl Marx, *Capital*, Vol. I (New York, International Publishers, 1967), part VIII.

Notes to The "Second Serfdom"
in Central and Eastern Europe

1. *Capital,* Vol. 1, International Publishers, New York, 1967, p. 236.

2. It can be obtained through *Les Éditions de la Nouvelle Critique,* 29, rue du 4-Septembre, Paris 2.

3. *A History of Europe from the Invasions to the XVI Century,* New York, 1939, p. 534. (Quoted from *The Transition from Feudalism to Capitalism,* a symposium, by Paul Sweezy, Maurice Dobb, H. K. Takahashi, Rodney Hilton, Christopher IIill. Science & Society, New York, 1967.)

4. *History of the Russian Revolution,* p. 8.

5. *Feudal Society,* University of Chicago Press, 1964, p. 445.

6. *Collected Works,* Vol. 3, Moscow, 1960, pp. 194-95.

7. *Ibid.*, p. 32.

8. See "Hybrid Formations and the Permanent Revolution in Latin America," in which the implications of this fact are considered.

Index

Also from Pathfinder

An Introduction to the Logic of Marxism
by George Novack, $11.95

The Origins of Materialism
by George Novack, $18.95

Woman's Evolution
From Matriarchal Clan to Patriarchal Family
by Evelyn Reed, $21.95

How Far We Slaves Have Come!
South Africa and Cuba in Today's World
by Nelson Mandela and Fidel Castro, $7.95

Che Guevara and the Cuban Revolution
Writings and Speeches of Ernesto Che Guevara, $20.95

Malcolm X Talks to Young People
by Malcolm X, $9.95

The Revolution Betrayed
What Is the Soviet Union and Where Is It Going?
by Leon Trotsky, $18.95

Cosmetics, Fashions, and the Exploitation of Women
by Joseph Hansen and Evelyn Reed, $11.95

FBI on Trial
*The Victory in the Socialist Workers Party Suit
against Government Spying*
edited by Margaret Jayko, $16.95

The Changing Face of U.S. Politics
The Proletarian Party and the Trade Unions
by Jack Barnes, $18.95

Revolutionary Continuity
Marxist Leadership in the U.S.
by Farrell Dobbs, 2 vols., $15.95 each

Socialism on Trial
by James P. Cannon, $14.95

Many Pathfinder titles are available in Spanish and French. Write for a free catalog.

New International

A MAGAZINE OF MARXIST POLITICS AND THEORY

IN ISSUE 7

Opening Guns of World War III: Washington's Assault on Iraq

BY JACK BARNES

Also includes: "1945: When U.S. Troops Said 'No!'" by Mary-Alice Waters ■ "Lessons from the Iran-Iraq War" by Samad Sharif ■ $12.00

IN ISSUE 8

Che Guevara, Cuba, and the Road to Socialism

Articles by Che Guevara, Carlos Rafael Rodríguez, Carlos Tablada, Jack Barnes, Steve Clark, and Mary-Alice Waters ■ $10.00

IN ISSUE 5

The Coming Revolution in South Africa

BY JACK BARNES

Also includes: "The Future Belongs to the Majority" by Oliver Tambo ■ "Why Cuban Volunteers Are in Angola"—3 speeches by Fidel Castro ■ $9.00

IN ISSUE 6

The Second Assassination of Maurice Bishop

BY STEVE CLARK

Also includes: "Cuba's Rectification Process"—2 speeches by Fidel Castro ■ "Washington's Fifty-Year Domestic Contra Operation" by Larry Seigle ■ $10.00

Further reading

The Communist Manifesto
by Karl Marx and Frederick Engels

"The history of all hitherto existing society is the history of class struggles," explains this founding document of the modern working-class movement. 47 pp., $2.50

The Origin of the Family, Private Property, and the State
by Frederick Engels

INTRODUCTION BY EVELYN REED
This classic work traces how the oppression of women and the structure of the family have their origin in changes in the social relations of production and ownership. 191 pp., $13.95

The History of the Russian Revolution
by Leon Trotsky

"Trotsky's masterpiece, the single greatest work of history in the Marxist vein" — Irving Howe, *Trotsky*. Unabridged edition, 1,369 pp., $35.00

America's Revolutionary Heritage
edited by George Novack

Explanatory essays on Native Americans, the first American revolution, the Civil War, the rise of industrial capitalism, and the first wave of the fight for women's rights. 414 pp., $20.95

Available from Pathfinder. See front of book for addresses.